edgy...
daring...
hilarious...

You've never seen words like these being used to describe a book on real estate investing before. And yet, these are exactly the things people across the country are saying about *Full Frontal Real Estate Investing*. Why? It's simple:

There's never been a book quite like it before. Ever.

After all, what other real estate book exposes you to the wealth secret that's hidden inside of a Steven Wright joke? And where else can you go to find out what wave surfers, Ferris Bueller, and a CSI crime scene all have to do with your odds of achieving wealth? Or learn how to leverage the tactics of selling $4 caramel lattes so that you can more easily close profitable deals with unreasonable sellers?

Full Frontal Real Estate Investing pulls no punches as it takes you where no other real estate investing book has gone before; and not just because you need it to, but mostly because no one else had the guts to do it until Nick came along.

Bottom line: it's the most fun you'll ever have getting educated. Guaranteed.

Here is what people are saying about it:

"*Full Frontal Real Estate Investing* is exactly what I would have expected from Nick, because it's not like anything else out there—just like Nick. I've known him for nearly two decades, and he's an outside-of-the-box kind of guy with a bit of a goofy side who's never been afraid to try something new. I can't think of anyone who'd have been better qualified to write a book like this with so much information and insight, and yet still be this much fun to read. This is one book that's an absolute *must* for every real estate investor's library."

- Ron LeGrand
Real Estate Guru & Millionaire Maker: Jacksonville, Florida

"Nick literally 'bares it all' with this book! There is no fluff or puff... It takes you down to the bare bones of what you truly need in order to be a successful real estate investor. It is a must read for anyone who is interested or already involved in real estate investing."

- Wendy Patton
Author, Speaker, Real Estate Broker: Detroit, Michigan

"I love this book. It's very personable, catchy, and informative, plus it also reflects many real life strategies that go beyond just real estate investing. It's a fun and worthwhile read for entrepreneurs in any field."

– Izabella Vaz
Real Estate Investor and Entrepreneur: Miami, Florida

"It's about time I found a book that reads like a conversation between friends. I love to read, but I'm usually bored beyond belief after only a few chapters. This book has kept my attention since the first page... I literally can't put it down."

– Jeff Hornbeck
Real Estate Investor: Burlington, Kentucky

"This book is excellent! I wish I'd had it when I first got involved in real estate. I would have saved a lot of money on my real estate education, and unnecessary mistakes too."

– Bryan Scott
Real Estate Entrepreneur: Chicago, Illinois

"**Full Frontal Real Estate Investing** is full of contrarian ideas, which I can tell you from personal experience can be extremely profitable. I'll continue to use the strategies in this book while all the other 'guru' courses on my bookshelf continue to collect dust."

– Shirley Wise
Real Estate Broker and Entrepreneur: Ft. Lauderdale, Florida

"I have gained many excellent business ideas from this book and also find Nick's writing style relaxing, funny, informative and enjoyable! It's hard to stop reading a good book that makes you laugh and feeds you with good ideas!"

– John Nuzzolese
Founder/Owner Landlord Protection Agency: East Meadow, New York

"Engaging. Brilliant. Interesting. Creative....Witty and edgy content.... Real tips for investors and Nick is in the trenches practicing what he teaches in this book."

– Leslie Briskman
Real Estate Broker Associate: Palm Desert, California

"I love this book! It's funny... and the familiar pop culture references make it entertaining and easy to relate to. Nick uses real world examples and everyday language to explain things simply, but without making you feel like he thinks you're an idiot."

– Jena Crouch
Mortgage IT Business Analyst
Denver, Colorado

FULL FRONTAL

REAL ESTATE INVESTING

How to **crush it** in virtually any economy without ending up broke, burned, or butt-naked.

For information, address:
Publication Sales and Marketing
Premier Resource Group, Inc.
P.O. Box 54613
Cincinnati, Ohio 45254
Email: sales@FullFrontalRealEstate.com

Cover design © 2016 Nicholas Modarelli
Printed in the United States of America.

Library of Congress Cataloging-In-Publication Data

Modarelli, Nicholas, 1959 —

   Full frontal real estate investing:
   how to crush it in virtually any economy
   without ending up broke, burned, or butt-naked

   ISBN-13 978-0-9844757-4-2
   ISBN-10 0-9844757-4-5

   This publication was previously released with
   a separate cover under the following ISBN's:
   ISBN-13 978-0-9844757-3-5
   ISBN-10 0-9844757-3-7

The Fine Print:
(Magnifying glass not included)

General Disclaimer: This material was assembled to provide general information regarding the subject matter covered. Although the information herein is believed to be accurate, it cannot and should not in any way be construed as an endorsement or inducement to engage in any particular real estate practice or technique; nor should it be considered a substitute for legal, accounting, or other professional advice. For all such professional advice, the experienced counsel of qualified, licensed experts in your area should be sought in advance. Remember, it's a lot easier to prevent a disaster than it is to clean one up.

Legality Disclaimer: Due to some poor choices made by a small handful of unconscionable investors over the past few years, some states have begun to impose new legislation designed to restrict or even prohibit the use of some of the techniques mentioned in this book under certain conditions. Since this publication was created for general distribution (including worldwide on-demand electronic downloading), it is impossible for the author to adjust the content to reflect the laws and practices of every area—including yours *(Hello... I'm talking to you!)*. Therefore, it is imperative to reinforce again that the information appearing in this book is not to be viewed as advice or encouragement to engage in any particular real estate investing technique, especially if any such technique happens to be prohibited or subject to restrictions in your area.

Liability Disclaimer: In case you haven't been "disclosured" to death yet, there is just one more thing we need to get straight between us before we go any further. This is something you should already be big enough to understand, but if not, please go get your mommy and have her explain this to you very slowly... and in smaller words, if necessary:

It is now, and always will be, your sole responsibility to be aware of all real estate laws and prevailing practices in your area. By continuing beyond this page, you are agreeing in advance to accept full responsibility for your own actions from this point forward, and you are furthermore waiving any liability of the author to you for any reason whatsoever regarding your use, abuse, or misuse of any of the techniques found in this book. If you do not agree with this statement, you may return this book unread for a full refund within 5 business days of purchase (if it takes you any longer than that to ask for a refund, it means you've read the book and you're just too much of a tightwad to pay for it).

Otherwise, you are hereby affirming your full agreement and understanding that it is your burden to secure the counsel of local licensed professionals before using any real estate investing technique of any kind... found in any book... for any reason... anywhere... anytime... ever.   Amen.

PETA Disclaimer: None of the techniques in this book were tested on animals.

contents

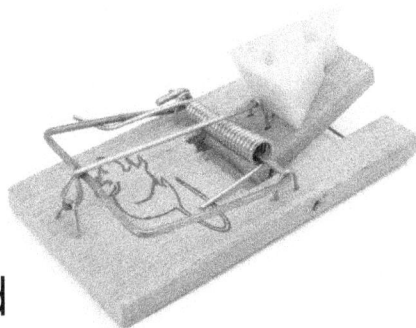

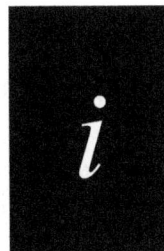

the second
mouse gets the cheese

J ack Welch, in all of his Six Sigma glory days as Chairman and CEO of GE, couldn't have said it better. Neither could have Bill Gates, Donald Trump, Sir Richard Branson, or any of the other famous and wildly successful captains of industry that we've all come to know and love (or *hate* as the case may be).

No. Believe it or not, this brilliant and deeply philosophical business proverb came from—of all places—a short YouTube clip featuring the monotone ramblings of deadpan comedian Steven Wright:

"The early bird gets the worm… the second mouse gets the cheese."

That's funny, but it's more than just a joke. If you're an entrepreneur, it's actually an indispensable pearl of wisdom. Don't see it? Then you haven't had enough *merde* kicked out of you by the real world yet (pardon my French). But don't panic, because I'm about to spare you the painful learning curve.

"The early bird gets the worm…"

The first half of this quip implies that the abundance of rewards (worms for birds, cash for you) are reaped at the leading edge of an opportunity. This is simple logic that you could've grasped while you were still flashing a full rack of baby teeth. But have you ever paused, even as an adult, to consider the sub-text of that remark? It suggests that if you *don't* operate at the leading edge of opportunity, you may not get anything at all; and if you do, it'll be the shriveled, picked-over remnants that your industry's early birds left behind (read: sloppy seconds).

"…the second mouse gets the cheese."

This a lot more than just a good punch line; it's actually a warning. That's because one of the riskiest aspects of habitual "early-birding" is the possibility of being the first one to arrive at the leading edge of a new opportunity. This can be very dangerous, because pioneering into any uncharted territory without the hindsight of mistakes made by other people essentially puts the entire burden—and cost—of the learning curve squarely on you. Being the first mouse to enter the maze of a new marketplace niche literally puts *your* neck on the line, as you're forced to sniff your way through by trial and error; cautiously figuring out how to collect your "cheese" without tripping the spring-loaded booby trap of real life.

Trust me, when it comes to navigating a new real estate niche, there's a lot to figure out, such as: *What are the best buying and selling methods for this new niche? What protection language should my contracts contain? What marketing approach would be the most cost-effective? What kind of consumer objections will there be? How do I avoid risk?* And finally, the most obvious question of all: *How the hell am I supposed to figure all of this out without losing my butt in the process?*

Sounds like a great big conundrum, doesn't it? First, you're told to race to the leading edge... and then you're warned to make sure that you're not the first one who actually *gets* there. What's up with that? So is there a way to effectively move yourself towards the leading edge of opportunity, and yet be assured that you won't be the first one to arrive? Sure! Just read this book. It was literally built around reconciling the apparent paradox of the early bird and the first mouse.

Sound crazy? Well, maybe. But there's no doubt that Mr. Wright's sardonic wit provided me with the perfect framing for the contents of a book that's been sitting half-written on my computer's hard drive since 2004. In simple terms, this is the core insight I've been trying to find the right words to express:

You need to leverage the experiences of people who've already *been* to the leading edge of past marketplace changes, so that you can safely position yourself at the leading edge of every *new* marketplace change—even before they occur.

This one strategy alone is enough to keep you perpetually cruising along and picking up the big chunks of cheese that are lying around all of the real world mousetraps that were sprung on someone else's neck—perhaps even mine.

A couple more thoughts before we get started...

As you read through this book, you will probably notice—even if you're not paying attention—that there are a few concepts being repeated throughout; each time illustrated in a slightly different manner. There is a reason for this, and it's not because I kept running out of things to say (yeah, like *that* could ever happen).

These concepts kept popping up because they're literally more important than the creative real estate techniques themselves. Mentioning them just once would have only exposed you to them, and that wouldn't have been enough to do you any good. But I brought them up over and over, each time in a different context, so that they could eventually become real for you. This was the only way to make them an integral part of your subconscious belief system, so that you'd be able to automatically act upon them as needed. And by the way, they *will* be needed.

The last thought I want to share is for you to carefully consider to whom you're listening as you pursue a real estate education. If you're looking to buy single family homes and small investment properties, it might be a good idea to seek out speakers and gurus who have not only done this successfully many times in the past, but who are also still doing it right now on a regular basis. They are the only ones who can tell you what's really working in today's world; which, by the way, is markedly different than yesterday's world—in case nobody's told you.

And unless you plan on building skyscrapers, casinos, and glitzy resorts, it's probably not the best use of your time or money to study what the titans of real estate are doing. After all, I like watching Donald Trump fire somebody on TV as much as anyone, and even occasionally reading one of his *Get Off Your Lazy Ass Already and Go Make Something Happen!* books. But let's face it… the last time he bought a split-level handyman rehab special in a working class neighborhood, if ever, was probably while he was still in diapers—which would have been pretty funny to watch if you think about it.

Just imagine being a fly on the wall of some Queens, New York nursery back in the late 1940's. In that nursery is a ten month-old baby boy sitting quietly in his crib, not making a sound except for the occasional gentle rustling of fabric as he reaches up in fascination to touch his first little comb-over*. After a few moments, the door opens, and in walks a disheveled French au pair carrying a stack of paper and a box of crayons. The next sound you would've heard would have been the soft "Pop" of the binky coming out of the child's mouth.

And then…

> *"What's this? Hmmmmm. You know, I may not get out of this playpen much, but I certainly know when a counter-offer stinks to high heaven. And guess what? This one smells worse than what I've got percolating in my diaper right now. So take this back to that goofy seller and tell 'em I'm not willing to pay one dime more for that suburban dump."*

Before the nanny/*slash*/lackey could have even processed a reaction, *The Drooler* (who, upon learning to control his salivary glands, would later go on to be known as *The Donald*) would have abruptly dismissed her with:

> *"Well, don't just stand there—GO already! And on your way out, track down my mommy and get her in here pronto. All this stress is giving me a headache, and I'm gonna need some nummy-nummers to chill me out."*

Kids… they just say the darndest things. Don't they?

---

* Well… there you have it. Regardless of whatever else you may have heard, it's his real hair. Honest.

the "catch-22"
nobody told you about

You probably wouldn't be real surprised if I told you that the best way to significantly improve your odds of success in real estate investing is to get a good education on real estate investing. That's pretty obvious.

But what you may be shocked to learn is that today's system of real estate education may actually be doing more to *hinder* your pursuit of success than *enhance* it. And if you think that's disturbing, you're really going to be screwed up when I tell you who's been orchestrating the conspiracy to suppress your wealth all along—especially since it's not who you think it is.

So in the spirit of David Letterman, here is a countdown of the Top Five Reasons (sorry, not enough time or room to do a Top Ten) of why today's current system of real estate education may actually be hazardous to your bank account.

Reason #5: *Some real estate gurus are simply out of touch with reality.*

This is not a universal indictment of all real estate gurus (after all, some of my best friends are gurus), but there are two particular species you need to be wary of in your educational pursuits: the *Gurusaurus* and the *Guru-noob*.

The Gurusaurus—and its larger cousin, the Gurusaurus *Rex*—are both fairly easy to spot. They're typically older and sluggish moving, and they tend to use overhead projectors with faded gels rather than fancy new technology like PowerPoint. Although they usually don't bite, their courses have been known to suck pretty hard. Apparently, being on the talk circuit so long has rendered most of them clueless as to what's actually working in today's marketplace.

Unfortunately, decades of successful snake oil salesmanship has refined their closing pitches to the point where they're capable of convincing intelligent people like yourself to fork over $695 or more for antiquated courses that feature techniques which haven't worked since the first Reagan administration.

As for Guru-noobs, they're a different creature altogether. They're much more difficult to recognize, because they blend in so well among us. After all, they used to be investors just like you and I. But after turning a couple of quick and profitable deals, they got seduced by the dark side into believing they were instant experts worthy of full guru status—when the truth is they were probably just more lucky than anything else. And that's what makes them so dangerous.

These deadly weekend, part-time, wet-behind-the-ears, wannabee gurus can show you some techniques that actually work in today's environment, which means there's a good chance you'll get some offers accepted. But since these guru newbies don't have enough first-hand experience to know what can—and inevitably *will*—go wrong when their fairy tale course collides with the hardened streets of real life, they're unable to warn you about the potentially severe consequences. Therefore, since they haven't truly paved the path through the deadly learning curve yet, that dangerous distinction will fall to you—just like the first mouse in our introduction. Sadly for many, this is a tale that all too-often ends in catastrophe.

Reason #4: *Speakers, gurus, and group leaders are trained to sell—not educate.*

When it comes to speakers and gurus, you have to understand that anyone addressing you from the front of the room will have an agenda that is different from yours. You want to buy real estate. They want to sell courses.

This is not necessarily a bad thing, and it's certainly not wrong. In fact, when someone takes the time to put their lives on hold and fly to your town to share their extensive knowledge with you, they have an obligation to themselves, their families, and their craft to get paid well for doing so. The problem comes when the compensation they receive far exceeds the value they deliver, which is unfortunately happening more often than not these days.

This isn't surprising when you consider that most speakers and gurus invest a lot of money on courses that teach them how to sell more courses. I refer to these types of courses collectively as "Guru U", and in general, they are designed for one purpose only: to extract as much money from you, the consumer, as possible. Many of these programs feature honest marketing and merchandising tips, designed to legitimately enhance sales—and that's just fine. But some will also encourage the use of underhanded tactics, such as spinning the truth about the quality, quantity, and profitability of past deals. One program I attended a few years back actually featured some of the industry's biggest Hall of Fame Gurusauruses, who walked us step-by-step through the process of how to make up fascinating "true stories" that never really happened. They taught us that outright lying is a normal and acceptable practice, so long as the intent is to make the presentation more interesting and relevant. I can't tell you how discouraging it was to hear people whom I'd admired for so many years say things like that.

As for tactical lessons, here's one of the first I ever learned at Guru U. I'll let you decide whether it's a deviant ploy, or a legitimate means of boosting profits.

Sell "home study courses"... not "books".

Why? Well, consider this: books sell for about $15 to $30 (just look at the cover). Given that limitation, it's much more profitable to take that same information, thin it out, enlarge the font size, print it onto a stack of 3-hole punch paper (one side only for extra bulk), and snap it into a $3 OfficeMax binder. That way, you can call it a "home study course" and sell it for $200 to $1,000 or more instead.

But wait... that's not all. Delivering your information in a course manual, as opposed to a book, creates a completely different context that not only carries a much higher perceived value (as we've just seen), but also sets the stage for much easier up-selling into increasingly expensive information products and events, such as $2,000 bootcamps and $10,000 personal mentoring programs.

So am I bashing the process? Absolutely not! Progressing customers into more advanced, personalized, and expensive forms of education is a perfectly legitimate strategy, so long as there actually *is* some educating taking place. My only reason for exposing you to this practice is to help you make intelligent future buying decisions with your eyes wide open, so you can avoid being naively manipulated inwardly through the concentric circles of a guru's revenue funnel.

But speakers and gurus are not the only ones who share a stake in how much you spend on educational materials. Investment groups usually get to keep about half of the total sales generated at their sponsored meetings (minus a small travel allowance for the speaker). Because of this, you cannot automatically let your guard down with respect to group leaders. Just like gurus, they educate themselves by spending lots of money on expensive workshops, so that they can learn how to sell more expensive workshops. And they're pretty damn good at it.

Again, there is nothing conceptually wrong with this, because groups incur hefty operating costs, and are justifiably entitled to generate profits. However, some groups have become obsessed with only one thing: how much revenue a speaker can generate for them. Too often these days, groups will plan their bookings based on which speaker is producing the highest sales figures at the moment, rather than concerning themselves with whether or not the speaker's materials will actually provide any real value to their members.

I remember one incident from the late 90's when I was contacted by a group leader who wanted me to come to his town and speak, but only if I doubled the price of my course, which was $197 at the time. I responded by saying that I wanted to leave my price point alone so that it would be affordable for as many of his group members as possible. Immediately after I said that, there was an awkward silence; and if it hadn't been for the faint sound of chirping crickets coming over the line, I would have been absolutely convinced he'd just hung up on me.

Turned out... he just didn't know quite how to respond. So, after a brief pause to collect his thoughts, he said that pricing my course so low was problematic for two reasons. Not only would it risk generating low sales (half of which would be his group's cut), but it would also make some of the other courses his group had recently sold look ridiculously over-priced—especially since most of them were far less comprehensive than mine. So you tell me, who was he looking out for?

Again, remember there's nothing wrong with someone—be it a speaker, guru or group leader—trying to maximize every opportunity they get. That is the very essence of capitalism. But it does become an issue when separating you from as much of your money as possible becomes their one and only objective. When that line gets crossed, someone's going to get the short straw. And trust me, it's not going to be the speaker, the guru, or the group leader.

So whenever you attend a conference or an investment group presentation—especially if it's free or extremely cheap—go into it with the full awareness of what it really is: a live infomercial. Don't be duped into believing that you're going to get something of any real value for nothing, because you won't—and quite frankly, you don't deserve to. Please also understand that by simply attending a free meeting or low-priced workshop, you are making yourself fair game as a highly targeted, pre-qualified, up-selling prospect. Unfortunately, in too many cases, that's absolutely all you are anymore.

Caveat emptor.

Reason # 3: *You're being taught to look for success in the wrong place.*

Far too many books and courses are built upon the flawed premise that true wealth and lasting success can be found in whatever real estate technique happens to be the subject matter of that particular publication. This is a woefully inadequate and incomplete strategy.

For starters, suggesting that you can achieve wealth and success as an investor merely through the mastery of a single real estate technique is like claiming that mastering one gourmet dish, such as *Feuilletés de Saumon aux Asperges* (puff pastry with salmon and asparagus in a lemon butter sauce), qualifies you to open an upscale French restaurant. This is, of course, utter nonsense.

Michael Gerber has thoroughly debunked the delusional *"If you build it, they will come"* ideology time and again in his business classic *The E-Myth*, and the successive *E-Myth* sequels. And yet, despite all evidence to the contrary (most of which people never notice until it's too late) entrepreneur wannabees continue to launch business ventures built solely upon a single passion or talent, only to lose everything they have—and sometimes more—when it fails miserably.

Of course the euphemistic lesson I'm trying to hammer home is that being able to bake great pies is not by itself enough to ensure a successful bakery. So it should really be no surprise when I tell you that it will take much more than just a single "hot" technique to give you a lasting, successful real estate investing career.

Let's look at a few reasons why this is true:

One of the first challenges in attempting to generate long-lasting success from a single creative technique is that the earning power of *any* method—no matter how hot it may be at the moment—is always confined to a limited life cycle of effectiveness. This life cycle is driven primarily by external factors over which you have little or no control, such as rapidly increasing competition, legislative forces, and other local and national economic trends. These factors do more than just influence the marketplace. They actually define the exact parameters and earning power of each technique's life cycle.

An objective look at the life cycle of every past hot technique bears this out, and a simple graph of their earning potential reveals a distinct pattern, with all the elements of a typical ocean wave: a point of origin, an upsurge, an apex, a rapid decline, and a crash—which is often spectacular (as we'll explore later). In other words, there has never been a single creative technique that has demonstrated the ability to exist in a perpetual state of static or increasing profitability—and there never will be. So if every creative technique has a limited life span of effectiveness, and is, in fact, declining for roughly half of that life cycle, then should any single technique ever be heralded as a valid tool for creating lasting wealth and success? Obviously, no. Unfortunately, too many real estate investing courses suggest otherwise, even if that suggestion is only implied.

Another big problem with being led to look for success within a technique is that your attention is directed away from dealing with the most critical income inhibitor of all... you. That's because the full earning power of any technique—no matter how powerful it is—will always be limited by your internal ability to accept and deserve the success it can provide.

You'll learn a little more about this later, but just understand that you essentially have an internal income thermostat, the programming of which will always have more of an impact on your financial status than all of the creative techniques in the world. Of course, a few real estate courses out there take a cursory stab at this issue by teaching you to create some daily "Rah! Rah!" affirmations as a means of improving your income. But without a deeper understanding of the underlying forces behind these affirmations, all of the positive post-it notes in the world aren't going to amount to anything more than just a waste of bathroom mirror space.

So clearly, as we've just seen, there are several external influences that can— and eventually will—trump the earning power of *any* creative technique, no matter how "sizzling" it may be right now. And since most courses steer you only towards mastering the technique itself, largely ignoring these highly relevant outside influences, they're basically teaching you to look for wealth and success in the wrong place.

Reason # 2: *You're been conditioned to look for success at the wrong time.*

Another critical defect of today's real estate educational system is something called "lag time"; and although it is often overlooked, it is nonetheless one of the most severely restricting constraints to your quest for success. That's because unlike some of the misdirection challenges we just talked about, which can be cured by augmenting program content, lag time is actually a default feature that has been hard-wired right into the educational system in such a way that it simply cannot be overcome.

So what is lag time? It's a phenomenon that represents the time it takes for an idea, product, or service to cross the gap from one geographic or demographic area to another. It exists in every industry, but the extremely time-sensitive nature of creative real estate investing means that even brief lag time delays can have devastating consequences.

In our business, lag time influences can permanently keep you out of the leading edge of every real estate market cycle, denying you access to that fleeting, coveted window of maximum earning power. That is something you simply cannot allow, and in fact, should no longer tolerate.

Here's how lag time works against you:

Whenever there is a significant change to any aspect of your local real estate market, new niches of consumer needs are created on the leading edge of that change. These niches bring with them brand new opportunities for earning money that either didn't exist before, or were previously much less lucrative. At first, you're probably not going to be sure how the changes will impact your area, if you're aware of them at all; nor are you likely to recognize where new profit opportunities can be found. Even if you suspect that you *do* know where these new opportunities are, chances are good you're not prepared to do anything about it. So you continue to muddle along working your current niche, while keeping an ear to the ground for more details on how these new developments might affect the real estate market in your area.

Several months go by, and you begin to notice an increasing amount of interest regarding a particular creative strategy at your local real estate club meetings. In fact, the buzz seems to indicate that it's "the hottest technique today". You're really interested, but still skeptical about shelling out $995 for a slick-looking new course, or investing $10,000 for a personal coaching program. Even though the speaker is showing you overhead slides featuring photocopies of really big checks, you decide to hold off for awhile.

Fast-forward another six to eight months later, and someone less flashy shows up at your group meeting with a down-to-earth presentation and a much more reasonably-priced course about this same technique. Now you're sold. You buy the course, read it, study it, listen to the CD's, copy the forms, and eventually you're ready to start looking for some deals. Right about that time is when the Feds decide to drastically change interest rates... or FHA revamps its lending guidelines... or the largest employer in your community begins massive layoffs... or... *whatever*.

Something unforeseen always happens, invariably changing the direction of your local real estate market. Suddenly, all of that super-cool new stuff you've just learned becomes virtually useless in the real world; reduced to little more than a fresh network of synaptic brain tissue inside your head. How do I know all this? Because it happened to me, once. But just once.

I vividly remember exhaustively deliberating over whether or not to fork over $495 to a TV guru for a creative course about how to take over freely assumable FHA and VA mortgages. When another guru came along a few months later with a similar course for only $395, I convinced myself it was time to take the plunge. I bought it in December of 1987, and devoured the information voraciously.

By mid February, 1988 I had developed enough confidence to begin calling sellers—backed by the firm conviction I'd found an awesome strategy that would be my ticket to financial wealth and independence. But just two weeks later, on March 1, 1988, VA began inserting a "due on sale clause" in all of its mortgages, rendering every future VA loan as non-assumable unless the buyer met the lender's requirements—which I knew I wouldn't.

At first I was quite disturbed by this new development, but I remained optimistic, buoyed by the knowledge that FHA, not VA, had underwritten the majority of the freely assumable loans in my area. Alas, what little hope I had left was soon dashed when FHA followed VA's lead and began inserting its own due on sale clause in all HUD mortgages closed after December 14, 1989. As a result, my real estate assumption dynasty ended just a few months after it began, and ultimately consisted of just one duplex in a bad part of town that was full of street-smart tenants who routinely ate my lunch.

What's more is that I'd wasted the $395 I'd paid for the course, because I had actually bought that lone duplex on a loan assumption about a year before I'd ever even heard about the course. The truth of the matter was that I had luckily stumbled into that first deal by accident, not by design, so my real reason for buying that exciting new course (other than to satiate my desire for an exciting new course) was to have someone show me a system for buying properties with assumable financing more frequently, and with greater profitability.

In the end, that course ultimately did teach me a very valuable lesson, but it was very different from the one I was expecting. I thought I was buying a course on real estate *investing*, but what I got was a seminar on real estate *education*.

Fortunately, I was paying attention, and managed to discover very early on that there was a tiny, but critical flaw in the burgeoning real estate educational system that many people didn't notice—and perhaps never will.

You see, there is a natural and unavoidable progression of events that precedes the release of virtually every new course on creative real estate (the details of which you'll see in a moment). Why is that an issue? Because it means that nearly every new course, no matter how fresh and exciting it may appear to be, won't even be available for you to buy until after the greatest window of opportunity to profit from the technique has already passed. And in fact, many of these new courses aren't even written until the featured technique is at, or near, the very end of its effective life cycle.

When I figured this out over twenty years ago, I immediately shifted the pursuit of my real estate education into a different direction. This clearly paid off, because it wasn't too long before I was being viewed as somewhat of a real estate investing expert myself. Soon after, I was hesitantly persuaded (at the insistence of others) to begin writing and selling courses—oftentimes feeling a bit like a modern day version of Don Knotts in *The Reluctant Astronaut*.

Unfortunately, what brief training I *had* received (with regard to becoming an author/speaker) caused me to play right into the same pattern as everyone else—writing courses one at a time about each "hot" new technique as they became relevant. Therefore, I had essentially gone from being an innocent *victim* of an inefficient educational machine, to an unwitting *perpetuator* of it.

Take a look at the following chart, and see if you can detect the pattern (or progression of events) I'm talking about. Once you see it, the futility of chasing a real estate education one technique at a time as they become popular—which is today's standard operating procedure—should be instantly apparent to you.

Of course, pursuing an education this way is not a total loss by any means. It's still quite possible to make some money in the process. But the chart clearly illustrates how this strategy will perpetually keep the majority of investors well behind the lucrative power wave at the leading edge of every change.

And by the way, even though this chart is a generic point-to-point illustration of a fictitious cycle, it has been drawn from nearly twenty-five years of firsthand experience, gained from watching the belated effects of a gradual real-time education.

So go ahead... look at the next page, and find out for yourself in two minutes what took me nearly two decades to fully comprehend.

Typical Lag Time Scenario

Point	Lag Time	Progression of Events
A	0 months	A confluence of various market and economic conditions converge to create one or more hot new market niche opportunities.
B	0 – 2 months	A few properly positioned investors spot the new opportunities, and begin the process of experimenting with some techniques to profit from them.
C	2 – 6 months	The early adopter investors spend the next several months maximizing profitability by refining every aspect of the most lucrative technique(s).
D	6 – 18 months	The ensuing chaos of milking their new cash cow keeps these investors busy. To avoid competition, they fly under the radar as best they can.
E	18 – 24 months	A few colleagues notice the rapid success their investor friends are having, and after a little investigating, decide to jump in and compete for the deals.
F	24 – 30 months	Rapidly increasing competition and some local market or economic changes start noticeably impacting the profit curve of the early investors.
G	30 – 34 months	A few early investors decide it's time to augment their waning profits by writing a course about their incredible experience, and selling it to other investors.
H	34 – 36 months	The course is finished and a presentation is created to pitch it. Now, the investor switches careers from "entrepreneur" to "infopreneur".
I	36 – 38 months	The investor-turned-speaker begins to contact investment group leaders to pitch his or her new course. Bookings are made.
J	38 – 42 months	The speaker appears at your local group and tells their compelling story. You end up buying the course today for $995. Others decide to wait awhile.
K	42 – 48 months	You attend follow-up workshops and begin the learning curve just as the marketplace borders on critical mass participation from competitors.
L	48 – 60 months	You finally try the technique, but your results suck compared to those of the speaker, who had operated earlier during a far better window of opportunity.
M	60 – 65 months	You try refining tactics to boost profits, but the already saturated market suddenly gets swarmed by a locust horde of "me too" investors, trained by dozens of weekend gurus who are popping up at everybody's group meetings.
N	65 – 72 months	By now, your ability to make money with the technique is fading fast or completely gone, because the 5 or 6 year-old opportunity isn't really so "hot" anymore. So you decide to pay $5,000 more for a mentorship program with the same guru who sold you the $995 course that didn't work.
O	72 + months or more	You hear about another new technique that's really "hot", so you head to next Thursday's group meeting to start the cycle all over again.

In case you've ever wondered why you never seem to be able to get a bunch of really big checks like the ones many speakers tend to show at high-energy presentations, maybe now you get it. So stop beating yourself up about being unable to replicate the results of someone who was operating with little or no competition during a much better window of opportunity (Points A thru F). After all, the technique's effective life cycle had probably progressed to Point J before you had even heard about it, and had probably surpassed Point K (critical mass) well before you were ever ready to actually *do* something with it!

Now that you understand how lag time can be an effective obstruction to reaching the profitable leading edge, it's time for you to use that knowledge. And if you're not sure exactly how, here's a hint for you: Lag time works both ways.

How lag time can work **for** you:

Every dark cloud has its silver lining, and lag time is no exception. Check out the chart again. Do you see anything interesting? If not, then you probably have a tendency to automatically (and subconsciously) view yourself as one of the general population investors.

So look again, but this time imagine that you are one of the few properly positioned early investors; the ones who saw the opportunity first, were prepared for it when it got there, and had all that time to run with it before everyone else caught on. Now the benefit of lag time should be obvious to you. As one of the first ones in, you stand to collect the largest checks and enjoy the longest span of revenue growth from each new opportunity. Lag time essentially becomes a gauntlet that prevents the majority of other investors from reaching the leading edge with you too quickly; which would prolong the profitability of that coveted marketplace position for yourself, and the handful of other prepared individuals.

This is called *advance positioning*, and whether you are positioned in advance of an opportunity by accident or design makes little difference to the outcome. Either way, you'll have a distinct advantage over everyone else in your marketplace, because as you make your move to tap into the incredible earning power of the approaching new power wave, the lack of any direct competition will geometrically increase your odds of wealth and success.

To give you an everyday metaphor of this, try to imagine how many games a professional football team could win if they could just be allowed to play the entire first quarter of every game without an opponent. Most teams could probably score 150 or 200 points in fifteen unopposed minutes, slowed only by their exhaustion of running the full length of the field on every play (unless you're from Cincinnati, in which case your pro football team might have to settle for a couple of field goals after going three and out on the first four drives, fumbling twice, and having three wide receivers arrested for drug possession).

Of course, once the other team is finally allowed onto the field in the second quarter, they may very well score some points also—maybe even a lot of points. But by then, the fate of each game should have already been sealed (even in Cincinnati), with the advantage going to the team that was positioned on the field alone and unopposed in the first quarter. The two-fold moral of this illustration is:

1. You need to position yourself *in advance* of new opportunities,

    and...

2. You need to do it *by design*, so you can repeat the process at will.

You see, being lucky is a lot of fun. But skill beats luck in the long run every time, because you just can't depend on luck alone. And although being skillful is still no guarantee of wealth or success, it sure stacks the odds in your favor.

So now that you've been exposed to lag time, and its full range of negative and positive effects, the choice as to whether it will be a hindrance or a help to you from this point on is fully yours to make. That's liberating. That's exciting. And that's also something your favorite guru has probably never told you.

And now... *(insert drum roll here)*
The # 1 reason today's real estate education may be killing you:
You want the sizzle more than you want the steak.

Surprised? Well... don't be. Smarmy gurus, greedy group leaders, and shifty event organizers are not necessarily the primary engineers of the crappy education you've been getting so far. In all likelihood, *you* are.

As a consumer of educational products, you vote for the courses you want with your credit card—and up until now, you've been perfectly clear about what you want. And just in case you're not exactly sure what you've been asking for, here's what your Visa statement reveals: You want excitement. You want sizzle. And you want the granddaddy of them all: buzz—especially if that buzz is packaged in a system of just four brainlessly easy steps that can be done while sitting on a beach in a Hawaiian shirt, with a Mai Tai in each hand and flip-flops on your feet.

As for reality... well, let's just say that history has shown time and again when books and courses come along that can teach you what you really *need* to know (instead of the gimmicky things you think you *want* to know) you generally run the other way—and fast. But you're not alone. People rarely invest in highly useful courses anymore. And when they do, it's not until the speaker slashes his price to the bone, and then agrees to throw in five free special reports, free bonus software, a two-year subscription to his newsletter, the course audio, the course video, fifty free hours of one-on-one mentoring, and a naked picture of his trophy wife or hunky pool boy (depending on the buyer's orientation). And even then, many fickle course buyers still want to go home and sleep on it first.

So is it any wonder that gurus have had to resort to ever-escalating pie-in-the-sky bullcrap to sell you books and courses? Is it really a shock that they have to promise you a changed life and wealth beyond imagination, created by a proven magical system that automatically generates $250,000 per year in profits while you sleep, and requires only 3 to 5 hours per month of your time for maintenance?

Today's real estate educational propaganda is a grab-bag blend of art imitating life and vice-versa. Some of the over-the-top hype is merely a response to your own unrealistic expectations, while the rest is a cacophony of noise from speakers and authors who have to shout ever louder and longer in an attempt to overcome your increasing skepticism—which was ironically caused by the failure of so many past books and courses to live up to all the hype it took to get you to buy *them*.

Look, I knew you were going to be freaked out to discover that the biggest contributor to the problems of today's real estate education were the students themselves, and not some underground conspiracy of greedy gurus. But somebody had to have the guts to tell you this; otherwise you would've never recognized the downward-spiraling vortex for what it is, nor figured out that you should probably consider trying to escape from it. Remember: speakers and gurus—even the really good ones—are just basically following your lead. After all, if there wasn't a need for hype, they wouldn't bother creating any. So... let's eliminate the need.

JSYK (if you're over 40, that's text talk for *just so you know*), I understand there will be at least three types of people who may disagree with some or all of my observations in this countdown. They are most likely to be:

- People who already ignore all of the hype and buzz, and have been actually buying the books and courses they really need. If that's you, then my sincerest apologies for lumping you in with the masses.

- People who simply have a totally different and fully objective point of view, which they can reasonably defend. And while I can respect their opinions, I'll probably continue to disagree with them.

  and finally...
- People who are just plain 'ol pain-in-the-ass-know-it-alls.

BTW (text talk again), if you suspect that you might be a pain-in-the-ass-know-it-all (which is unlikely, since most of them don't realize they are), then you might want to just convert this book to a doorstop right now. This will, of course, save you from exposure to any more of my nonsensical musings. But don't come crying to me if the next real estate cycle crushes you or leaves you behind, sending you back to selling life insurance policies or stocking plumbing supplies in an orange vest. Oh, yeah...that's some *smack* right there.

2

the LEAP
real estate strategy

Conventional wisdom is almost always bad advice—especially when you consider that it represents the aggregate opinion of a society whose members are 95% likely to find themselves fully dependent upon the financial support of others by their 75th birthday. Perhaps that's a clue.

Now of course, not all conventional wisdom is wrong. Certainly, it's still a good idea to look both ways before crossing the street—so long as those two ways are not up and down. But when it comes to investing in real estate, there are some principles to which many people still subscribe that are either no longer practical, or are profitable only under conditions that are infrequent, unreliable, and beyond one's ability to control.

In today's world, general marketplace cycles that used to last eight to ten years or longer (depending on the industry) can now see radical transformations in as little as eight to ten *months*, thanks largely to exponential advances in technology. Real estate is no different. Shrinking market phases are creating more frequent demands for shifts in basic strategies, and even bigger challenges are coming from the increasing number of local and national micro-cycles, which are fueling rapid bursts of value fluctuations in both directions; throwing wrenches into everyone's cogs. As a participant in this new era of real estate, you'll need to approach investing differently than it's been taught in the past—even as recently as 3 to 5 years ago.

That's what the LEAP Strategy is all about. It not only exposes you to new ways of looking at real estate cycles, it also teaches you how to think for yourself. This will empower you to adapt quickly in the face of current changes, as well as enable you to extrapolate new solutions when future changes come along. Because of all this, you might be better off—perhaps for the first time in your life—to literally LEAP before you look… at least for real estate deals, that is.

WHAT IS THE LEAP STRATEGY?

LEAP stands for <u>L</u>eading <u>E</u>dge <u>A</u>dvance <u>P</u>ositioning. It is the art and skill of positioning yourself so that you can instantly capitalize on the new and highly lucrative niche opportunities that are found only at the leading edge of market changes. However, successful investing is not entirely about LEAP to the exclusion of everything else. There are other critically important, but admittedly less sexy elements you'll also need to incorporate, such as risk reduction tactics, effective marketing, and business systemization—all of which we'll cover later. But for now, we'll just be discussing what makes LEAP unique.

The LEAP Strategy is a direct contrast to today's piece-meal education, in that rather than chasing after an education in a gradual and aimlessly reactive style, it is instead an intentional and proactive pursuit of a specific education in advance of the need. In other words, while the conventional system encourages you to learn one technique at a time as they become "hot" (or more accurately, after they've *been* hot for awhile), the LEAP philosophy advocates mastering several complementary techniques up front and all at once before they're needed.

To begin exploring the LEAP concept more thoroughly, let's take a closer look at the meaning of the key operative word in that last sentence: *complementary*. When it is spelled with an "i" (as in compl<u>i</u>mentary), the word means *"a favorable comment or the giving of something free of charge"*. But when it's spelled with an "e" instead (as in compl<u>e</u>mentary) the root meaning changes to *"complete"*, giving the word an entirely new definition of *"fulfilling or supplying each other's lack"*.

To see this concept in action, fast-forward your DVD to the end of the 1996 classic *Jerry McGuire*, where Tom Cruise's character is trying to win back the affection of his estranged wife, Dorothy, played by Renée Zellweger. When he tearfully stammers, "You...*complete*...me...", not only is he capturing the very essence of the word complementary (with an "e"), he's also setting up the second most memorable line from the film (behind *"Show me the money"*), when Renée whispers back, "You had me at *'Hello'*." That one still gets me every time.

Anyway, the point here is that just as Jerry McGuire (fictional nature aside) is not a whole person without Dorothy, neither are you—as a real investor in the real world—whole without the complete range of capabilities afforded to you by possessing the right mix of complementary real estate techniques. With them, you can instantly create profitable transactions in the midst of—and even in spite of—virtually any market shift. Without them, you're like a leaf on the winds of change, which means it would only be a matter of time before you'll find yourself at the mercy of some negative marketplace dynamic that's too powerful for you to defeat, too widespread for you to get around, or too long-lasting for you to financially endure.

Hopefully, now you understand how ineffective a real estate educational system can be when it teaches adaptability in the *wake* of change, rather than in *anticipation* of it—as this book recommends. Maybe it also makes a little more sense to you why the current educational approach has resulted in greater than a 95% failure rate among its graduates.

Regardless, there is a significant difference between pursuing individual techniques one at a time, and pursuing an individual strategy (built upon several techniques) all at once. If you can just grasp that difference long enough to make a marginal shift towards the latter, it can yield tremendous results for you in both the short-term and in the long run.

SHIFT Happens...

Change is an inescapable fact of life that is rarely appreciated for the blessing that it is. People get so caught up in the turmoil it creates that they can often view it as an obstacle to their quest for success—when, in fact, the real threat to success is the *lack* of change in the marketplace, as you'll soon see.

Despite all of the negative connotations associated with change, it does have at least one positive attribute that makes it worthwhile—even welcomed by the few who understand it. Change always transforms the marketplace, which inevitably gives rise to a power wave of new and highly profitable niche opportunities.

The Power Wave

At the leading edge of every real estate market change, there is an initial power wave of earning potential. The fuel for this wave is created by the low ratio of properly positioned investors, relative to the high volume of profitable deals that have been made available by the newly emerging consumer niches. Another way to say it is that every market change brings with it rich new veins of gold, but only a very small handful of people are sharp enough—or lucky enough—to already own a pick and shovel when it arrives.

The power wave is so named because when you graph the revenue potential of each new opportunity that comes along in the marketplace, the line resembles an ocean wave. And what's really interesting is that, believe it or not, the effect that a new power wave will have on an individual investor can be reliably predicted in advance, by simply looking at where the investor has positioned himself or herself along the power curve prior to the appearance of the surge. As you will see in a moment, this advance positioning will determine if the impact of the power wave on an individual will be minimal, highly positive, or devastatingly negative.

The easiest way to illustrate this concept is to use a simple (and yes, humorously crude) diagram that draws upon the analogy of surfers on an ocean wave; where the surfers represent real estate investors with various mindsets and levels of preparedness, and the ocean wave represents the power surge of marketplace momentum. Placing a few of these "surfers" at a variety of points along the wave line creates a compelling visual depiction of the physical effects that marketplace momentum can have on each type of investor.

As you look at the following diagram, you may even notice that the quantity of each type of surfer has significance, in that it loosely approximates the proportions of these types of investors that make-up of virtually any random real estate investment club. But truly, the most important point of this entire illustration is for you to take a moment to consider the educational strategy you're subscribing to at the moment, and then honestly answer this simple question:

Which one of the ten surfers on the next page is you?

Then... if you really want to give yourself something to think about (especially if you're one of those people who thinks that the short sale and foreclosure bonanza will last forever), ask yourself the far more provocative question:

Which one of them will you be five years from now?

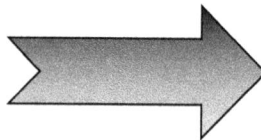

Diagram of Power Wave Effects
a.k.a. = *The 10 Little Surfers*

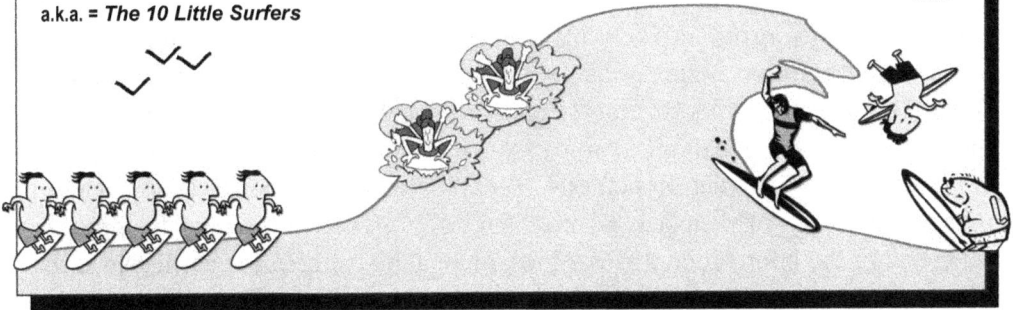

Ocean Wave = Illustrates the potential revenue curve of a "hot" technique's life cycle.

= **Clueless Dudes:** These are the five surfers who got left behind because they were blissfully unaware of the huge wave surge that had passed right underneath them. Although well versed in the latest surfing jargon (thanks to time spent at surfer clubs), most of them have never actually *surfed*. Today, they're waiting patiently for a surfing opportunity to come along, but unfortunately their eyes (and their rented surfboards) are aimed in the wrong direction.

= **Cathy Catch-ups:** These two surfers saw the surge coming, but waited until it passed by so they could purchase a surfing course and be told what to do. After studying the program, they frantically paddled their surfboards up the steep backside of the wave, but never made it to the top because they were traveling sideways most of the time. Today, convinced that the $895 they paid for the surfing guru's course was a total waste of money, they decide to get "really serious about surfing" by charging $10,000 more on their MasterCard to buy a two-day bootcamp and one year mentoring program from that very same guru.

= **Kelly Slater:** As 9-time ASP World Surfing Champion, this lone surfer was not only intentionally positioned at the leading edge of the coming surge, he was also prepared in advance to handle the ride, both professionally and psychologically. All he had to do was hang ten and make some minor course corrections, while the natural hydraulic power of the wave did everything else. Today finds him debt-free and driving his convertible Ferrari to his 8 a.m. tee time at Pukalani Country Club in Maui.

= **Wally Wipeout:** This sad surfer was also positioned at the leading edge of the new wave, but since it was by accident, and not design, he was unprepared for the wave's raw power. Fortunately, his spectacular wipeout was captured on a tourist's iPhone, after which it was uploaded to YouTube where it quickly went viral and received more views than *David after Dentist*. Today finds him bussing tables in a plastic pirate hat at Long John Silver's.

= **Tsunami Sam:** This unfortunate surfer enjoyed a thrilling ride on the last wave, but was totally dumbfounded when the wave eventually died out and his surfboard just stopped moving. He remained fixated in such a state of confusion that he didn't even notice he was only moments away from being pile-driven six feet into the ocean floor by a huge incoming new wave and a wildly careening Wally Wipeout. Today, his near-fatal injuries prevent him from ever being able to surf again. But on the upside… he found Jimmy Hoffa.

EFFICIENT MARKET THEORIES

The double-edged nature of every marketplace (including real estate) is that even while changes are creating profitable new niche opportunities, there is another force that immediately kicks in to start destroying the profitability of those new niches. It's a hypothetical force known as the Efficient Market.

The Efficient Market Hypothesis (EMH) is a hotly debated theory which asserts that every marketplace is informationally efficient, meaning that prices reflect all of the information that is known among the marketplace participants. It is further theorized that this common knowledge makes it unlikely that any one marketplace investor will consistently and disproportionately out-perform all of the other participants—except through sheer luck, or by the use of illegitimate tactics such as fraud, deception or illegally obtained inside information.

For example, real estate values reflect the "known" prices of recently closed sales, and since all buyers and sellers have easy access to this data, it can be difficult (but not impossible) for any one real estate investor to routinely and consistently generate huge profits without somehow compromising *somebody* in the process.

Of course, the reason the Efficient Market Hypothesis is still just that—a *hypothesis*—is that there are those who would dispute its validity. For instance, some behavioral economists argue that the EMH is a fatally flawed concept, which is hysterical when you consider that their proof usually has very little to do with real life experience, but instead relies heavily upon extremely complex paper analyses, such as vector autoregression models (Google it) and other such virtual bullshit.

These studies are often conducted by cubicle-dwelling pseudo-intellectuals, many of whom are pale, hairless virgin geeks who don't see enough daylight. These so called "experts" reach skewed findings by applying conjectural behavior to theoretical econometric presumptions. In other words, they take a guess at what might happen if an imaginary trend were to work its way through one of their virtual worlds. This, of course, means that their "quantifiable" conclusions regarding the EMH are about as firmly rooted in reality as Spiderman or the Tooth Fairy—who, as it turns out, was actually just my dad in fairy drag. Bummer.

Other "experts" who disagree about the existence of the EMH forgo all the number crunching and just point fingers at people like Warren Buffet, proclaiming that they are smoking gun evidence that the EMH is a hoax. After all, Mr. Buffet and a few others like him have clearly defied the EMH for years, making untold millions of dollars in profits with powerful investment portfolios that have consistently and disproportionately outperformed most everyone else on Wall Street. But referring to Mr. Buffet and his ilk as proof that the EMH doesn't exist is even more absurd than the claims made by the goofy geek economists. After all, most people understand that there is no such thing as a rule without at least a few exceptions. You know, like 'i' comes before 'e', *except* after 'c'. Right?

Never-before-seen images shot during a clandestine "Black-Ops" summit of radical fringe behavioral economists...

Hey guys, watch this! If you tweak variable "A" and switch vectors, something *REALLY AWESOME* happens!!

What is it?? The missing link that finally **PROVES** the EMH is a *hoax?!*

NO! You end up with a graph that looks like a BOOB!

How would YOU know? Have you ever even *SEEN* a naked woman?

NO!

»Sigh«

In fact, when it comes to debating the EMH, it is the very presence of a handful of exceptions which actually *proves* the rule—not the other way around. You see, every marketplace has a few participants who are simply better and faster than everyone else at interpreting how the "known" information will impact the game. But it is precisely their small numbers which confirms the existence of the EMH, as this is a demonstration of its power to suppress opportunities for the majority.

Look, as someone who has had to slay this dragon personally several times in the past, I can tell you for a *fact* that the real estate industry has a very real efficient market force. And I can tell you something else, too: it's a bitch. In mixed company, this force is sometimes called the *Efficient Real Estate Market*, but we'll refer to it as EREM for short (although when nobody's around, I just call it *WTF?*). In real estate, this force controls more than price alone; it is also the self-appointed Robin Hood equalizer of both opportunity and income disparities.

Here's what I mean: When changes in the real estate market create profitable new niches, the positioned investors at the leading edge (a.k.a. the early birds) benefit from an initially disproportionate share of both opportunity and income potential—but not for long. The Efficient Real Estate Market force soon restores balance to the marketplace by drawing other investors into participating as well, in numbers that are commensurate with the opportunity's profit potential, i.e., the more money that can be made in the niche, the more people who will be drawn to it.

This leads to progressively *increasing* income potential for the new investors, and proportionately *decreasing* income potential for the early adopters. The redistribution of opportunity will continue until eventually all of the participants have the exact same mediocre income potential—at which point the EREM will have again done its job of destroying yet another once-lucrative endeavor.

A real example of the EREM in action:

In the late 1980's, the U.S. economy was entering a soft economic recession. Home sales began to fall nationally, and by the early 1990's, both the economy and the real estate market had still failed to fully recover. Most national sales figures remained relatively flat, as buyers were becoming more cautious and slow to act. At the same time, the number of people needing to sell their properties continued to increase disproportionately, which resulted in a steadily rising inventory of real estate for sale.

That marketplace shift effectively created two brand new niches of consumers: highly motivated sellers, and cautiously interested buyers—both of which were large in numbers and relatively untapped. Fortunately, since these two niches were complementary to one another, a single shift in investment strategy was able to provide a powerful solution for both of them simultaneously—and that single shift was to move towards using term methods to buy and sell real estate.

Term transactions come in three basic flavors; lease-purchase (or lease-option), land contract, and *subject to*'s. All three of these utilities have been around for many years, and even though they vary from one another in both form and function, that wasn't what mattered at the time. What *did* matter was that in practice, all of these utilities provided an alternative method for buying and selling properties via monthly installments, as opposed to conventional purchases and sales funded through typical bank financing.

Savvy real estate entrepreneurs who specialized in these methods found it extremely easy to get properties under contract from the glut of sellers who were willing to sell on monthly installments, because they were so anxious to get some relief from their monthly mortgage payments. At the same time, these heads-up investors found it was just as easy to sell their new inventory of properties. Many retail buyers were quite willing to pay above-market prices in exchange for getting good terms, especially since it allowed them to defer commitments to borrow large sums of money from banks during uncertain economic times.

It was a match made in heaven.

As usual, some investors were slow to give up their regular routine of buying and selling the only way they knew how—via conventional methods with bank financing. They didn't want to be bothered with learning how to do something new. As a result, many of them didn't survive in the face of this wide-sweeping market change; and the ones who *did* survive had to work a lot harder than necessary to make a whole lot less money than they otherwise could have.

As time went on, the Efficient Real Estate Market lured more and more investors into using term methods. This quickly created lots of competition, which reduced profits and opportunities for the initial investors who began using terms before everyone else. Pretty soon, the marketplace was flooded with properties available on terms; so much so that the ability to purchase properties on monthly payments (versus conventional methods) was no longer perceived by consumers as a unique opportunity, worthy of fast action and above-market pricing.

By the mid to late 1990's, interest rates plummeted to record lows, and lenders also began aggressively offering mortgages that were incredibly easy to qualify for. This re-established a hot market for selling properties conventionally, which quickly put an end to the once-profitable (but now over-crowded) term deal bonanza.

Some inflexible investors remained in denial of the facts, and were routinely forced out of business as they continued pushing their stagnant lease-option deals onto an increasingly shrinking and disinterested marketplace well into the 2000's. In the meantime, properly positioned smarter investors had already moved on to service the growing niche of conventional wholesale and retail buyers.

...And the cycle continues, even to this day.

DEFEATING THE EREM PHENOMENON

Clearly, the effects of an efficient market are problematic for anyone seeking to establish career-long real estate income. But there is a way to stay one step ahead of it, and that is to stop being *re*-active to the market and become *pro*-active instead.

Reactive vs. Proactive

Most people make adjustments to their investment methods in response to market conditions. This is being re-active, and although it seems like a reasonable strategy, it's just another example of conventional wisdom gone wrong. Reacting to the consequences of the EREM *after* they've manifested keeps you perpetually stranded at a point in the power curve where the influence of critical mass participation has already diluted the opportunity's full potential, as we explored in our earlier discussion on lag time.

If you were to choose instead to adopt a pro-active approach, and prepare yourself to capitalize on new niches before they even appear, you would be positioned to begin exploiting every new opportunity in advance of everyone else—at a time when profitability is high and competition is low. In other words, you'll get to surf the power wave just as if you were the Kelly Slater of real estate (although perhaps maybe just a little less tan and buff).

And by the way, another very interesting point we haven't even discussed is that when it comes to staying ahead of the Efficient Real Estate Market, you don't necessarily have to wait for a market change to create brand new niches for you. If you're proficient enough in your real estate training, you can spot—or even create—ancillary niches within the *current* hot trend.

For example: as of this writing, short sales have been a red-hot technique for many years. But competition has been increasing exponentially, record fore-closure rates have been causing backlogged lenders to take much longer to process offers, and large inventories of available properties have been driving property values down—which essentially means that short sale deals are getting harder to find, taking longer to close, and generating increasingly smaller profits on average.

So some heads-up investors decided to change course a little and capitalize with a different strategy in the exact same marketplace. Rather than continuing to buy properties on short sales (like everyone else was doing), they opted instead to start purchasing the defaulted loans directly from the lenders at huge discounts. This lateral move not only put these investors into a largely untapped niche with very little competition, it also allowed them to get their deals done with far less effort, with much less paperwork, with very little seller participation (if any), with much shorter approval times (days or hours versus weeks or months), and with much higher profits than if they had bought those very same properties from the owners and negotiated short payoffs.

EMBRACING CHANGE

Here is a quick summary of the characteristics of change, and why utilizing LEAP's advance positioning philosophy to become proactive instead of remaining reactive can make a lot of sense in today's ever-changing marketplace.

Market changes are inevitable.

They're coming anyway... so you might as well get the jump on them.

Market changes create niche vacuums.

We've probably beaten this horse to death, but only because it's so vitally important for you to grasp this concept. When changes occur in the marketplace, many people are pushed (often beyond their control) into circumstances they did not anticipate, creating vacuous new niches of immediate consumer needs for which very little, if any, help exists. It's your job to have solutions ready and waiting for these emerging niche consumers to latch onto right away. The sooner you can meet their needs, the sooner the checks will start rolling in... and the bigger they'll be.

Market changes are Kryptonite to the EREM

Market change suppresses the diluting effects of the Efficient Real Estate Market, because each change requires the EREM to start all over again from scratch. This provides you with brief, recurring windows of opportunity to grow as fast as you want, and profit as much as you can. But in the same way that a small dose of Kryptonite is only temporarily crippling to Superman, the disabling effects of change will eventually be overcome by the sheer strength of the Efficient Real Estate Market—so you'd better be able to act fast.

Market changes clear out competition

Unlike you, very few people in real estate—or any business for that matter—are willing to prepare and position themselves for change in advance of the need. And since real estate opportunities will always cycle, your competition will be regularly cleared out again and again, as the majority of obtuse investors who refuse to change tactics or take too long to react are driven back to punching a time clock.

Change can occur without brand new market conditions.

You do not necessarily have to wait for new changes to create brand new marketplace niches. Change can also refer to lateral moves within the same marketplace in order to service untapped ancillary niches that everyone else may be overlooking—as in our earlier example of investors switching from short selling houses to short selling mortgages.

LEAP WORKS FOR EVERYTHING

As we close out this chapter on the LEAP strategy, it's important to point out that the LEAP formula is not just limited to real estate. It can be adapted to work in virtually any market, and in virtually any industry. So if you ever decide to chuck the real estate business someday, remember what you've learned here—because LEAP can help you dominate no matter where you go next.

psych

What does psychology have to do with real estate? Actually, nothing... unless attics or crawlspaces happen to trigger some deeply repressed Freudian mommy issues for you. But psychology does have absolutely *everything* to do with how high you'll climb—or fall—as a real estate entrepreneur.

To begin with, psychology matters because everything around you in the real world is a manifestation of the virtual world inside your head; the fruits of your seeds of thought, to say it another way. That means if you want apples in your life, don't plant orange seeds... because you simply cannot get apples from an orange tree no matter how badly you want them. This is true even if you try really, really hard, work 16 hour days, or invest $25,000 in a one-on-one mentoring program with Johnny Appleseed's grandson. You simply cannot defy the laws of physics.

Unfortunately, that's where most gurus have a major disconnect. They focus on showing you how to mimic what they've done, without considering if your particular mental wiring will even allow you to be *capable* of replicating their actions. In other words, they're teaching you how to harvest apples by the bushel full, without first making sure you even *have* an apple tree to work with. This is an exercise in futility, which leads to frustration and failure for most students. That's why I'm going to lay a couple of basic psychological concepts on you before we go anywhere near the real estate techniques themselves. After all, the best weapons in the world are useless if you're not prepared to wield them.

But your own mental underpinnings are only part of the equation. You also need to understand how to speak to the psyche of the consumer mind, because it is their fluid beliefs that will drive the size and frequency of your paychecks. The first issue we'll explore in this chapter is the *Law of Income*, which proves that consumer perception—and not reality—sets the value of your efforts. Later, we'll take a look at how consumers listen, because what you say isn't nearly as important as what gets *heard*. In between, we'll sandwich a brief chat on accepting success, where you'll learn some basic ideas on how to switch the nature of your subconscious mind over from saboteur to ally in your quest for wealth.

THE LAW OF INCOME

Did you know there is a universal law that actually determines what your income will be, literally to the dollar? It's called the *Law of Income*, and it applies to everyone on the planet whether they're aware of it or not.

It simply states:

> **You are paid in direct proportion to the quantity of your value that is delivered to a marketplace, according to the perception of the consumers.**

Sure, it's a mouthful—but what exactly does it mean? The best way to explain it is to take a look at the three key words: *value, delivered* and *perception*.

Value

First, let's explore the word *value*. In commerce, value is the term that represents any product or service which meets a marketplace need or fulfills a marketplace desire. So, what would be your "value" as a creative real estate entrepreneur? Well, that will depend upon with whom you are speaking at any given moment. For example:

- If you're talking to a seller who needs relief from their monthly mortgage, and you have a buying program that provides monthly payments, your value would be in the payments that you can arrange for the seller to receive—and not in the fact that you'll need an extended time to purchase their property on installments.

- If you're talking to a seller who needs cash now, and you can close quickly with all cash, your value resides in the speed with which you can get them their cash—and not in the really low price you'll have to pay.

- If you're talking to a buyer who needs to purchase a property on monthly installments, and you have a property you can sell on extended terms, your value is in the terms you can offer—and not in your above-market selling price.

Delivered

Quantity is not a key word in the Law of Income, because your income isn't affected by how much of your value is possessed or produced—only how much of your value gets *delivered*.

Here's why: People just don't willingly hand over their money unless something of equal or greater value is being delivered in exchange for it. This is true everywhere—even in places where the rules of fair commerce don't typically apply, like in dark allies at gunpoint. After all, anyone who's caught staring into the open end of a .38 would be willing to actively engage in the exchange of cash and jewelry for something of far greater value—their life.

But doesn't the fact that we have to be constantly exchanging our value for cash (sans the illegal use of weaponry, of course) suggest that we must always be on the *selling* side of every negotiation? Yes, it does. But if that's true, then how do we adopt a selling posture when we're actually trying to *buy* a property?

It's simple: As professional buyers, we have to sell property owners on the idea of allowing us to buy their property either at a wholesale price, or on wholesale terms. In other words, we have to convince sellers to agree to a price that will net them less than their full equity, or else get them to accept paper (monthly payments) in lieu of cash for their equity. Surprisingly, these concepts are not difficult to sell if you're able to show property owners how they can likely benefit more by working with you than by *not* working with you.

Perception

Finally, we'll look at *perception*. The psychological concept of perception is pretty self-explanatory; it's simply how someone interprets what they've seen or heard. Consumer perception plays a critical role in your business, because it sets the price tag of your value, i.e., the market price of your value is equal to the benefits that consumers *believe* they'll receive from you—not necessarily the benefits they'll *actually* receive from you. In fact, their perception of your value trumps even the *reality* of your value, which is why you need to understand how people think.

By the way, did you happen to notice the absence of any reference to reality in the Law of Income? That was not an oversight. It is absent by design. Reality is not a fixed concept, but rather a subjective one. That is because everybody's perception *is* their own personal reality. This makes reality not only interpretive, but fluid as well—which is good because that means it can be altered through the introduction of new information. Here is a brief story demonstrating fluid reality:

> You're walking down the street, when up ahead you see a man deliberately kick a very small dog. You immediately perceive that the man must be a total jackass to abuse such a defenseless animal. Then, someone coming from the opposite direction tells you the man kicked the dog because the dog had viciously bitten the man's ankle.
>
> Now you've switched over to the belief that the dog had it coming, and man was justified in kicking it. Then another witness mentions to you that the dog bit the man because the man had stepped on the dog's tail with his full weight.
>
> Again, you're back to thinking the man is a jerk, but only for a moment. That's when you notice his cane and sunglasses, and switch back to mentally exonerating the man once again, because you realize that he's blind and had stepped on the dog's tail accidentally.

I could continue to add detail after detail to switch your "reality" back and forth forever, but I won't. The point of the story was to help you see how quickly and easily your own perceptions and subsequent conclusions can be manipulated.

This is how it is in the real world. Reality is never anything more than a series of perceptions, which means that absolutely *everyone's* reality is subject to change. Simply being aware of reality's fluid nature will position you miles ahead of everyone else in your marketplace; and learning how to harness it can be an asset that can change the course of your entire career. Why? Because once you fully understand the concept, you'll be able to gently shift the perspective of any prospect you meet by merely exposing them—as necessary—to tidbits of new information that you've hand-selected just for the occasion.

Your Report Card

There is something equivalent to a report card that reflects how well you understand the Law of Income. It's called your bank account. Your bank account is the most sincere, yet brutally honest critic of your internal philosophies on income. It turns a deaf ear to any of your excuses or rationalizations, but on the plus side, you can rely on the fact that any testimony it provides will always be real and unbiased. Your bank account is never condescending or judgmental, however it also doesn't sugar-coat the truth in consideration of your feelings, either. It's nothing more—or less—than an unemotional record of your true take on the LOI.

So if you look at your bank balance and don't like what you see, it simply means that there is some aspect of the Law of Income you don't know, don't understand, or just haven't implemented yet. This is most likely due to some aspect of your income psychology being out of whack, as we'll explore in the next discussion regarding accepting success. Regardless of whatever issues you're wrestling with, fortunately, there are only two possible things that can negatively impact your income:

1. **The marketplace perception of your value is too low;** *or*

2. **Enough of your value is not getting delivered to the marketplace.**

These are the only two factors that can *possibly* affect your income—or anyone's income, for that matter. Your particular problem could be with one or both of these two challenges; but it can't be anything else, because there just *isn't* anything else.

Therefore, your first homework assignment over the next few weeks will be to utilize the information in this book to either raise the marketplace perception of the value you have now, or to create a brand new value for yourself.

Your second homework assignment, which should be conducted over the rest of your natural career, will be to use the marketing, systemization and duplication strategies in this book to position yourself for the *delivery* of your value to ever-increasing numbers of marketplace consumers.

The Law of Income can be easily summarized like this:

> ❖ **If you want to get paid, your value must get delivered to the marketplace.**

> ❖ **If you want to get rich, a <u>massive</u> <u>amount</u> of your value must get delivered to the marketplace.**

One final thought on the Law of Income before we move on: The law clearly says that your value has to get delivered to the marketplace, but it doesn't say that *you* have to be the one who delivers it. So as you go through this book, ask yourself repeatedly if what you've just learned could be systemized and duplicated to allow you to leverage such tools as the Internet, or the resources of other people (time, money, talent, etc.), so that more of your value can get delivered to as many people as possible without your direct involvement. And just so you know, true wealth can never be achieved without some form of leverage.

ACCEPTING SUCCESS

Psychology doesn't only apply to buyers and sellers—it applies to you too. In fact, your mental profile will directly determine your level of success, because you simply cannot achieve and retain success beyond the limit of your psychological ability to accept it.

This might sound contradictory to the last section, which claimed that the Law of Income is what determines your paycheck. But it actually doesn't conflict at all. You see, your ability to properly engage the principles of the Law of Income is directly proportional to your psychological attitudes about the effects that the resulting success might have on your life. In other words, if you have any fears or concerns about how success may change your life, you will literally *invent* ways to sabotage the delivery of your value, whether you're conscious of this or not.

Even your goal-setting efforts will be flawed. For instance, you might be inclined to set a goal to become wealthy through real estate investing. This may sound like a worthy objective, but in fact, setting such a goal would actually be an obstacle to attaining wealth for a couple of reasons.

For starters, "becoming wealthy" is an abstract concept that's far too vague and subjective to be an effective goal. Without a tangible definition of what wealth actually means to you, there's no way to design a path to move towards it—or to know when you've finally achieved it. Even more daunting is that by consistently affirming your desire to *achieve* wealth, you're further reinforcing your own subconscious identity as someone who is *lacking* wealth right now. After all, why would you need to pursue something you already have?*

---

*This same goal-setting dichotomy applies to any type of desired outcome. For instance, you can't reconcile the need to set a weight loss goal without first subconsciously labeling yourself as someone who's overweight right now, etc.

Unfortunately, your subconscious mind operates only in the present tense. So, no matter how wealthy you may want to become someday, it is obligated to protect your current identity—which is that of someone who's *not* wealthy right now. More than that, your subconscious mind is also responsible for figuring out *why* you're not wealthy today, and linear reasoning will cause it to eventually arrive at one or more of the following conclusions, which it will then vigorously defend:

> **You don't have wealth today because you haven't earned it,**

> > **You don't have wealth today because you don't deserve it, *or***

> > > **You don't have wealth today because you don't really want it.**

Regardless of any preconceived notions your subconscious mind may have regarding wealth, its foremost function is to defend whoever or whatever you are right now. So if you truly believe that you're a non-wealthy individual today, it will keep you that way by leading you to say and do the things that are consistent with someone who hasn't *earned* wealth, doesn't *deserve* wealth, or doesn't *want* wealth— depending on which perception applies to you. The end result is that wealth will continue to elude you as it has your whole life; however not because of bad luck or random circumstances as you've always assumed, but rather by your own design.

Income Thermostat

This identity protection phenomenon is sometimes referred to as your *income thermostat*. It is the manifestation of your subconscious perception regarding your worth in monetary terms. Your particular thermostatic settings have been shaped by the influence of certain people and situations that you've been exposed to during your lifetime thus far, often in ways you probably weren't consciously aware of at the time. But despite how, why, or where your thermostat is set, you will—within reason—continue to accept and pursue your target income level, regardless of what your income *potential* might be at any given moment.

In other words, if you were to suddenly experience a rapid decline in your income, you would likely discover untapped levels of resourcefulness that would help you create ways to boost your income back up to your minimum acceptable level (although the same cannot be said about gradual declines, because they tend to lower your bottom-end acceptable income threshold too slowly for you to notice).

Conversely, if you were to find yourself suddenly positioned for a quantum leap towards massive income growth, you would probably end up sabotaging your prospect for wealth by procrastinating critical tasks, becoming over-analytical, or engaging in activities that could compromise or eliminate the opportunity altogether.

If you've ever experienced something like this, you were just responding to your subconscious need to stay as close as possible to your income thermostat setting.

Lottery Train Wrecks

The following true stories illustrate what can happen when people encounter sudden wealth far in excess of their income thermostat. Unfortunately, stories like these do not represent the minority when it comes to windfall gains landing on the psychologically unprepared. It's a fact that many lottery winners end up far worse off—both financially and mentally—than before they'd won.

05/22/99: Billie Bob Harrell, Jr. commits suicide. In June 1997, Harrell won $31 million in the Texas state lottery.

12/19/01: British lottery millionaire Phil Kitchen is found dead on his couch. Kitchen had apparently drunk himself to death with whiskey.

07/11/02: British lottery winner Dennis Elwell dies at work, shortly after telling a coworker that he had drunk cyanide.

06/09/03: Lottery millionaire Jody Lee Taylor is arrested in Collinsville, Virginia for attempting to run over a sheriff's deputy. The night of his arrest, Taylor was driving naked down the wrong side of U.S. Route 58 with his headlights off.

08/05/03: After lottery millionaire Jack Whittaker passes out in a West Virginia strip bar, a burglar steals his briefcase containing $545,000 in negotiable bonds out of his unlocked truck, which was left running in the parking lot.

09/13/03: The *London Telegraph* reports that 16-year-old British lottery millionaire Callie Rogers lost her boyfriend, fought with her father, got mugged, and was accused of stealing someone's man. "Some days I don't even want to leave my house... Two months ago I thought I was the luckiest teenager in Britain. But today I can say I've never felt so miserable."

09/15/03: In his Egg Harbor Township, New Jersey home, lottery millionaire Oscar Cordoba repeatedly stabs his wife and her mother, eventually killing his mother-in-law.

11/18/03: An English court issues a bench warrant for lottery millionaire Satish Patel, charging government fraud for three years' worth of unemployment claims.

01/06/04:   After getting banned from Billy Sundays Bar and Grill in St Albans, West Virginia, lottery winner Jack Whittaker reportedly threatens to have the manager and his family killed. A few weeks later, he reports that someone had broken into his SUV and stole a bag containing $100,000 cash. Not quite finished with his busy January, he is arrested just a few days later for driving drunk; blowing an impressive .190 on the breathalyzer.

04/2004:   A judge rules that broke Virginia lottery millionaire Suzanne Mullins owes $154,146.50 to the People's Lottery Foundation, a lending institution that specializes in loans to lottery winners.

06/26/04:   At his Longmont, Colorado home, state lottery millionaire Kevin Lee Sutton allegedly shoots Cristobal Lopez in the head. Lopez survives and Sutton is charged with attempted murder.

09/2004:   Minnesota lottery millionaire Victoria A. Zell is arrested for having allegedly violated the terms of her bail and possessing 0.7 grams of methamphetamine. Zell had also reportedly wired $500,000 to a Canadian bank in an apparent tax evasion scheme.

10/10/04:   Seattle police officers shoot California lottery millionaire Rick Camat to death in a parking lot near Qwest Field. Officers claim that Camat refused to drop his pistol, but Camat's brother claims the cops give him no instructions to do so.

10/02/05:   Having spent his $10 million prize in just seven years, Winnipeg lottery winner Gerald Muswagon hangs himself. Notable events in his monied spree include a high-speed chase in 2000 and a sexual assault arrest in 2002.

10/02/05:   Bankrupt ex-lottery millionaire William "Bud" Post III dies of respiratory failure. Post had won $16.2 million in the Pennsylvania lottery. A former girlfriend successfully sued him for a share of his winnings. His brother was arrested for hiring a hit man, hoping to inherit the winnings. Other siblings coaxed him into investing in two failed ventures. Post even spent time in jail for firing a gun over the head of a bill collector. Within a year of winning, he was $1 million in debt. At the time of his death, he was living quietly on $450 a month and food stamps.

Resetting Your Thermostat

Resetting your own income thermostat is a simple process, but not necessarily an easy one. In order to accomplish it, you'll need to rewire some—if not all—of your most basic thinking patterns. Please understand that this is not something that can generally be done overnight, because it didn't happen to you overnight. In fact, for many people it will be a journey that will last the rest of their lives.

Despite the enormous range of past and present variables that are too numerous to discuss here, there are, however, at least two basic things you can do which can go a long way towards reformatting your mindset towards a more healthy perception of your income possibilities.

1. Visualize an end goal, and develop a plan to reach it.

This is one of the first things almost every success trainer teaches, and that's good because it works on *two* levels; not just one as many people believe. The most obvious benefit of developing a specific plan is that it provides you with a series of simple steps that can move you consistently towards a desired goal—that much everybody gets. But what fewer people recognize is that the greater reason this exercise is so effective is because it engages your subconscious.

Here's why: The very act of writing a goal down requires you to identify and clarify your specific objective, because you can't write down an abstract thought. And since we think and dream in pictures, the more clearly you describe your goal, the more clearly your subconscious mind will "see" it as an *actual* reality that exists today—even though it is still only a *virtual* reality in your head.

Overwhelming evidence suggests that the subconscious mind perceives as reality whatever it sees—because it is literally unable to make a distinction between tangible images observed with your physical eyes, and crystal clear virtual images generated within your mind's eye. That means if you can visualize a new reality clearly and often enough, your subconscious mind will eventually assume that you must have a corresponding identity—which it will be forced to protect (that's it's only job, after all) by adjusting your income thermostat accordingly.

From that point on, instead of silently undermining your efforts to succeed as it did before, your subconscious mind will now become your ally; actively engaging in the defense of your new reality by giving you all the permission and support you need to materialize it as quickly as possible.

2. Separate your "accounts".

Everyone is born with two metaphorical "accounts"; each one a cumulative score card consisting of a series of credits and debits. One of them is your financial bank account, the other is your self-esteem account.

Your financial bank account is a figurative representation of your total net worth in the physical world, rather than a reference to any one bank account. As the sum total of all your cash, checking and savings account balances, paychecks, personal belongings and equity assets, your financial bank account is the market value, in dollars, of everything you own. This account balance is evolving minute-by-minute, as deposits and withdrawals are constantly being made. And since this account exists in the physical realm, it is often subject to the influence of outside forces that are beyond your control.

Your self-esteem account, on the other hand, is purely intangible and psychological. It represents the quantity and quality of your self-worth. Just like your financial bank account, it is also evolving minute-by-minute. But this account is different, because your balance rises and falls with your perception of every bit of new information and feedback you receive. And since your perceptions can be managed, the power to control the balance of your self-esteem account always resides with you—and never with any external forces.

The challenge for most people is that they aren't aware that they even *have* a psychological bank account, so they tend to base their entire value as a person on whatever their financial bank account balance happens to be at any given moment. This is tragic, because you simply cannot tie your worth as a human being to something as temporary and volatile as your financial status. When compared to things that really matter, such as compassion, health, dignity, honor, courage, sacrifice and other characteristics with broad-sweeping and sometimes eternal consequences, financial net worth is meaningless (remember Mother Teresa?). The truth is that your value as a person is incalculable.

Too many people fall victim to a cycle of *"validation by income"*, because they often misinterpret external market feedback as evidence of their personal value. For example, when money flows abundantly towards someone, it can often be misconstrued as personal approval, when in fact it is only marketplace confirmation of the value of their *professional* goods or services. Likewise, when money seems scarce, people can feel as though they're being rejected personally, when it's really just negative marketplace feedback to their professional offering.

It's no wonder so many people take business rejection so hard. They are often incapable of distinguishing between their value as a person, and the commercial value of their product or service. And, since the prospect of pursuing financial growth carries with it the high probability of encountering even more rejection, many people are content to forgo the pursuit altogether; opting instead to accept mediocrity. Can you relate to any of this?

If so, then you need to go to work in your own life to recognize and properly separate these two accounts, so that you can begin to eliminate the deeply subconscious concerns and fears which may be inhibiting your ability to move forward both professionally and financially.

COME AGAIN??

Everyone's done it. At one time or another, we've all said something that didn't come out quite right. Usually, when something gets interpreted in an entirely different way than what was meant, the results are nothing more serious than a few harmless laughs—as in the case of the innocent little comment on this sign that was merely intended to encourage some spontaneous family fun:

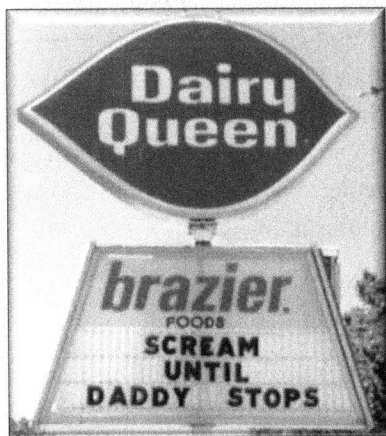

Ooops...

Of course, "funny" may be okay in everyday life, but when it comes to real estate investing—which often involves large figures containing several digits and at least one comma—a misinterpreted phrase may not be quite so humorous. In fact, it can sometimes have financially disastrous consequences.

Now, I'm not suggesting that you shouldn't have a sense of humor—far from it, as this book frequently demonstrates. This is more about your ability to properly convey your message while marketing to, and negotiating with, potential customers. Because it's not so much what you *say* that matters, it's what people actually *hear* that counts. And there can be a huge difference between the two.

This is where psychology comes in to play once again. You have to be completely aware at all times of how the messages you're sending out are being received by your prospective customers.

How You Say It

When it comes to negotiating, *what* you say can sometimes be less important than *how* you say it. There are intangible aspects of communication which can broadcast messages on a subliminal level that can easily overpower your voice, no matter how much volume or conviction your words may appear to carry. The three main components of your negotiation that will ultimately support or destroy your vocal communications are:

1. The framing of your discussion;
2. Your negotiating posture; and
3. Your physical appearance.

I WAS FRAMED...

Your customer is smart enough to know you need to make a profit, so don't offend them by lying about it or trying to conceal the obvious. Instead, base your negotiating platform on showing people how they can benefit *while* you're profiting—and they'll not only be fine with it, they'll actually want to help you.

After all, every time you walk into a store, you know you're going to pay more for everything you buy than they paid for it. Why doesn't this upset you? Because having everything you need brought together into one convenient location saves you lots of time and effort. In fact, the more stuff they have that you like, the more often you shop there... and the more money they make. Right?

In the same way, if your prospective buyers and sellers believe that their lives or circumstances can somehow be made a little better as a result of dealing with you, then your need to generate a profit will be a non-issue for them.

Focus on benefits

There's a very good chance that you are routinely telling potential customers everything in the world, except the one and only thing they need to know, which is "What's in this deal for me?" For the most part, nobody cares how long you've been in business, or how "good" you are at what you do. That means before you start talking, you should figure out how to frame every aspect of the proposed transaction in such a way that your customer will feel as if they're getting some kind of value in exchange for working with you (remember the Law of Income?).

This is doubly important to understand in real estate investing, because unlike conventional businesses, we are sandwiched by customers on *both sides* of our retail cycle. Now, if you're a foodie like me, you need to calm down a moment while I explain what I mean by sandwiched; because in this context, the term has nothing to do with deli meats and cheeses on wickedly soft white bread. The sandwich I'm talking about refers to the unique *dual* consumer dynamics of creative real estate. To fully grasp the unusual nature of this double-sided customer concept, let's first look at how the conventional retail cycle works:

> **Inventory Supplier (A)** sells some inventory at wholesale prices to their customer, **Middleman Storeowner (B)**, who then resells that same inventory at retail prices to their customer, **End Consumer (C)**.

So as you can see, the conventional business world has a selling burden that is linear, beginning at Point A, and then moving from left-to-right in a straight line (A→B→C) until it reaches the end. In this scenario, the middleman Storeowner (B) is the customer in the first step, which means he only has one customer that he needs to sell to, and that is the End Consumer (C).

This is not the case in creative real estate. Even though the creative real estate investor is still the middleman between the inventory supplier (the property owner) and the end consumer (the property buyer), they have the unique obligation of having to sell themselves to the people on both sides. That means instead of the typical A→B→C pattern of conventional commerce, the selling burden starts in the center and moves outward in both directions, like this: A← B→C. Here's why:

> The middleman, **Investor (B)**, must first sell their initial customer, **Property Owner (A)**, on the concept of trading their property at a wholesale price or on wholesale terms. Then they must pivot and sell their second customer, **Property Buyer (C)**, on the idea of purchasing that same property at a retail price or on retail terms.

Do you see how the selling chain in our industry differs from virtually every other type of business in the world? We have to sell to both sides. Both our sellers *and* our buyers are essentially our customers.

Certainly, this dual customer arrangement is a bit more challenging (and bizarre) than, say, selling dog collars or tacos. But the upside is that since we are effectively the seller in both scenarios, we are positioned as the initiators of every transaction. This gives us some negotiating leverage, because it means that we get to set the rules of engagement; which is actually advantageous for us as you'll see in the next segment on negotiating posture.

But before we discuss posturing, let me share with you a basic idea of how framing your presentation with the liberal use of benefits can improve the receptiveness of your message. I'll take a hypothetical situation and juxtapose two radically different ways of delivering it.

Example:

Let's assume that you're preparing to negotiate with a fairly motivated seller to buy their vacant property on terms, rather than purchasing it conventionally using cash or bank financing. Let's also say that the deal you're looking to create will involve making monthly payments for a period of up to five to seven years (you'll learn more about the specifics of when and why you'd want to strike a deal like this in a later chapter, but for now, let's just assume that this is what you're trying to accomplish).

First, we'll look at what *needs* to be said to the seller to get the deal structured properly, then we'll look at how it probably *should* be said to the seller so that your deal will have a reasonable chance of getting accepted. You'll soon see that there is more than one way to essentially say the same thing, and the choice as to which way you choose to say it can make all of the difference in the world to your potential customer... and by extension, to your wallet.

First, here's the message that needs to be conveyed:

"Mr. Seller, you can't afford the payments on your vacant home anymore, so I'll need to use a Land Contract to take over complete control of your home for the next five to seven years. My price will have to be for less than market value, because I have to make a profit—otherwise I have no reason to get involved with you or your property.

"Also, this is an offer to buy your home on monthly payments, which means there's no guarantee I will ever actually cash you out. So you need to be prepared for the possibility of getting your property back someday, and possibly even going into foreclosure. And since your situation was your own doing, I can't justify risking my own cash or credit to bail you out.

"Oh... and I can only afford to give you a $10 downpayment because I don't actually have any money.

"Please sign here."

Now, here's a better way to convey it:

"Mr. Seller, since your house is vacant, you could probably use a little help making your monthly payments. I'll tell you what; our company has a special program where we can buy your house at a fair price, while making your mortgage payments for you until we can get to a closing table to cash you out at some point in the future.

"Now, I'm not sure exactly how long it will actually *take* us to get you cashed out, but we're prepared to make the payments for as long as it takes—even if that means 3 to 5 years or more.

"And when I say "fair price", what I'm saying is that we're usually capable of netting you about the same amount of cash as a Realtor would, if you were to list and sell it conventionally.

"Of course, like anything in life, there is no solution that can always be 100% successful, I'm sure you understand that, right? However, this would certainly tip the odds of success heavily in your favor, and that sure beats the certain foreclosure you said you were facing before we met, don't you agree?

"Okay, then let's get this paperwork approved. I just need you to initial here, and put your John Henry there, and that'll do. Oh, and by the way, in order for this to be valid, some money has to change hands. We need to show you getting at least $1, but is it okay if I give you $10 instead so you can at least pick up some milk, eggs and bread on the way home? I'd love to give you more, but the circumstances just don't support it—especially with the upcoming investment of my time and money to help make this fly for you."

Both of these discussions convey the exact same message, but the words that are used to do it are quite different in each one. Obviously, the second approach is going to be far more successful, because every aspect of the dialogue was carefully spun in such as way as to highlight some sort of real or perceived benefit for the seller. If you get good enough at doing this, you can actually make your sellers want the deal to happen more than you do.

Notice that the second message doesn't even mention that the agreement being pitched is called a land contract. The reason for this is because homeowners don't care what a transaction is *called*, they only care about what it *does*.

Also, in case you didn't catch it, there was a subtle context change in the second message, referring to the seller's property as a *house* instead of as a *home*. This helps the seller begin the detachment process so that they can view it for what it really is; a dwelling for sale. Transitioning them away from emotional ties and into a more objective point of view allows them to focus less on the property and more on the benefits of your proposed transaction. It's much easier to get someone to part with a house than a home, because a home is more than just a structure— it's a psychological concept, full of complex feelings and nostalgic emotions.

YOUR NEGOTIATING POSTURE

Another one of the three most important aspects of negotiation is the posture that you maintain throughout the process. In this case, posture is not a reference to body language and mechanics—although they're important too—but rather to the relationship hierarchy between you and the other person. It's really all about who is holding the upper hand; and in every negotiation, it should be you.

The way you accomplish this is by gently placing the psychological burden (not the actual burden) of selling the deal onto the other person, regardless of whether they're the buyer or seller. As long as the person on the other side of the table feels as though they need the deal to close more than you do, they will be forced to adopt and maintain a "pseudo-selling" posture. When that happens, the unspoken upper hand shifts to you. And do you know what it does to me when I feel the momentum of one of my negotiations make a noticeable shift like that?

SCHWING!!
(if you have to Google this... please don't)

You see, the business of creative real estate is not so much about selling real estate—even though real estate may appear to be the commodity being negotiated. The true product we're selling is the transaction itself.

Here's what I mean: When you are the buyer, in order to make a profit you have to sell the property owner on the concept of taking a discounted price or accepting a note instead of cash for their equity. However, if you can sell the property owner on either of these concepts by presenting enough benefits (such as: they will get their cash quickly without hassles by discounting the price, or they will get a fair price and debt relief from mortgage payments by taking a note for their equity), the property owner can easily become very motivated to want the deal. When they reach that point, you control of the negotiations.

When you're the seller, you will be marketing your inventory of properties for sale either at very attractive prices (if you're wholesaling properties), or on very attractive terms with built-in monthly payment financing. Since both types of deals provide very enticing benefits for potential buyers, there will always be a market demand for them. And since your buyer will want these terrific benefits, they will often feel the need to sell you on the idea of letting *them* have the deal before someone else gets it. When they reach that point, the upper hand is yours.

Essentially, negotiating posture is really all about positioning. And in order to position yourself so that people will always feel the need to "sell" you on the deal, you'll need to quickly establish the perception that you have the solution they need. It's that simple.

The best time to begin laying the groundwork for positioning is before you even meet your prospects; ideally in your marketing materials (letters, postcards, flyers, yard signs, etc.). That way, once you actually meet them, it'll be so much easier for you to get the pendulum of advantage to swing in your direction first. This initial momentum is critical, because if negotiations begin while the other person holds the upper hand, you will be forced to go on the defensive—and that is a very weak and ineffective negotiating posture.

YOUR APPEARANCE

Your appearance also plays a vital role in how your message is received by potential customers. Even though it's completely non-verbal, your appearance can convey silent messages that can totally undermine your spoken communication.

The four major components of your appearance are: your clothing, your grooming, your transportation, and your posture (and this time, it *does* mean body language).

1. Your Clothing: Dressing for success is about knowing who your customers are and dressing accordingly; not necessarily wearing $2,000 Armani suits all the time—which can actually back-fire if you're meeting with lower- or middle-class property owners who despise intimidation. Emulating your customer's attire means that ironically, in some cases, faded blue jeans and Birkenstocks could actually qualify as acceptable garb when meeting with the owners of a Beverly Hills mansion; assuming the owners happen to be a real life equivalent to Jed Clampett (cement pond and all), or perhaps a remaining member of the Grateful Dead.

In general, a good rule of thumb is to aim for being just slightly better dressed than your potential customer. Doing so gives you a slight negotiating advantage without running the risk of intimidating or offending them. Specifically, you should avoid dressing in a manner that is overtly sexual, which means no more visible whale tails or bras worn on *top* of shirts (this includes men), and steer clear of clothing that display controversial politics or sophomoric humor. In other words, keep your T-shirts with *Hillary '12: Because Bitch is the new Black*, or *I'm an amnesiac, do I come here often?* in your closet until the next weekend barbeque. Also, avoid clothing that spews inflammatory comments about contentious issues, like wearing fur or global warming. Remember, activism is dangerous stuff, and should be left to the people best qualified to handle it—Hollywood actors.

Oh, and specifically for men, although jackets and ties are not required, sleeves are usually a pretty good idea... especially if the shirt had them at one time.

2. Your Grooming: How well you're groomed for an appointment tells your customer a story about you and how much you respect and appreciate the opportunity they've given you to pitch your value. You should always be neatly groomed and, without fail, always cleanly shaven—particularly if you're a woman.

3. Your Transportation: If you're trying to convince a seller you can pay cash for his $250,000 property just minutes after he's watched you step off the city bus that brought you to the appointment, you're going to have a pretty big credibility challenge to overcome. Likewise, if you expect a seller to let you take control of their property for the next 5 years, when the interior of your filthy Mercedes is overflowing with garbage, empty beer cans, and pieces of debris that may or may not have once been McDonald's french fries, you might be in for a rough negotiation.

Essentially, the car you drive is far less important than how well you care for it. You really don't need flashy wheels; just clean ones. It's a fact that the majority of real millionaires in this country (as opposed to the pretentious pseudo-millionaires who are leveraged to their eyeballs in debt while *Livin' La Vida Loca*) drive clean *used* cars, typically 3 to 5 years old, or older. Generally speaking, it's a good idea to drive the newest and cleanest vehicle you own to your appointments (unless it's a Lamborghini) so that your cash offers won't be treated with skepticism, and also so that your term offers won't be shot down because the seller is afraid you'll trash their property like you've trashed your car.

4. Your Physical Posture: Of course, this time the term posture means exactly what you usually think it does: the mechanics of how you sit and stand while negotiating. A good rule of thumb when it comes to body language is to basically mirror your customer's movements and mannerisms in a subtle way, being careful not to be too obvious or condescending, lest you offend.

don't end up as real estate road kill

Back in simpler days, when Aunt Bee was still terrorizing the citizens of Mayberry with her kerosene cucumbers, and our moms were busily preparing meals in Technicolor dresses with matching heels and faux pearls (no less), there was a general belief that, *"What you don't know can't hurt you."*

Unfortunately, this was just a Pollyanna sentiment that reflected the innocence of those earlier generations; because as anyone with mesothelioma can tell you, it simply wasn't true. And if it wasn't true then, it's even *less* so now. In fact, subscribing to that philosophy in today's litigious society is more than naïve; it's a recipe for disaster that can leave you looking like a possum carcass on I-75 in July.

Life is just more complex than it used to be. Competition is fierce, corporate scandals abound, lawsuits are routine, job security is non-existent, and the stock market is more volatile than a can of hair spray in a bonfire. Our increasingly narcissistic culture has all but abandoned the concepts of right and wrong, casually tossing them aside in an unending pursuit of entertainment and self-preservation.

Sadly, today's attitude of entitlement has many people believing that contractual obligations are merely suggestions, rather than binding commitments; which is why they feel that walking away from a contract is acceptable behavior— except, of course, when it's "the other guy" who's walking away. This mind-set has become so pervasive, in fact, that I once overheard someone at a small-group Bible study claim that God had revealed to her she should back out of a contract and leave her builder holding the bag on a $350,000 house he'd just finished for her. Now... it's one thing to lack the decency to honor a contract, but it's another thing altogether to ram a giant screw into someone's backside, and then dodge responsibility for it by claiming that it was *God's* idea. That's just twisted.

Of course, the explosion of this skewed mentality doesn't mean you can't be both successful and profitable in real estate. But it does mean you'll have to structure your negotiations and agreements with the advance understanding that your odds of experiencing default will be escalated by today's situational ethics; rising from an occasional *possibility* to a likely *probability*.

That's why this chapter is so critical for you. It explains dangerous aspects of this business you might otherwise be unaware of, and exposes you to street-smart ways of eliminating preventable risks that can sometimes be caused by bad advice from the very professionals you're supposed to be able to rely upon for guidance; such as gurus, real estate agents, and (believe it or not) even some attorneys.

This chapter alone is worth a hundred times whatever you paid for this book.

NOTHING DOWN:
Why it doesn't fully eliminate risk.

People everywhere are still being preached one of the most dangerous myths in the business of real estate investing, and that is:

"If you don't have any money in the deal, you've got nothing to lose."

If you've been to at least two real estate seminars in your entire life, you've probably heard this before—maybe even more than once. On the surface it sounds pretty reasonable; and to an extent, it is a critical first step towards minimizing risk. But as a stand-alone premise, as it is often pitched, it is a deadly assumption that has destroyed many promising and otherwise spectacular careers.

The truth is that risk is not fully defined by how much cash you put into a deal, especially when it comes to creative nothing down transactions that don't involve using any of your own money. The real risk in little or no money down deals will actually come from three less conspicuous sources, and they are:

1. The promises you make to others;

2. The remedies against you for breaking those promises; and

3. The entity you were operating in while making the promises.

Everything about risk management revolves around minimizing or removing the impact of these three core issues, so let's look at each one separately.

YOUR PROMISES

First, we'll explore the promises you make. In contracts, they're often referred to as covenants. They consist of every performance issue that you've agreed to be responsible for, such as making monthly payments, keeping a property insured, closing a purchase on or before a specific date, delivering clear title, taking care of maintenance and repairs, etc.

In order to make promises less dangerous, the obvious first step is to limit the actual promises you make, both in quantity and scope. So as you create your own contracts, or examine contracts that have been drafted by others, take a close look at what you're being asked to do, and then decide if you feel reasonably confident that you can fulfill each and every promise. If there are any that make you uneasy or uncomfortable, you need to address them properly before signing the contract, or be fully prepared to walk away—like a true professional should.

As an example: Let's say that you're making an offer to buy a property, and the seller has told you that the only way he will consider your really low offer is if you agree to pay the entire purchase price in cash, and close within 14 days. Assuming the price is right, and that you're educated enough to be confident you can close, then it would be okay for you to sign, because you can easily limit your liability (as we'll see in a moment) in the event of any unforeseen problems.

However, if you're *not* reasonably certain you can close with him for whatever reason, I'd rather see you be a professional and walk away without making an offer, as opposed to recklessly moving forward just because you know how to limit your liabilities to near zero. Extinguishing liability should be used only as a means for protecting yourself on legitimate deals, and never as a license to run around tying up every property you can with hasty, half-wit offers—as some gurus suggest.

So does this example mean I'm condemning the process of making lots of offers, or bashing the gurus who teach that real estate is a numbers game? Absolutely not. Real estate *is* a numbers game, and you need to make lots of offers to be successful. I'm just saying you should do it responsibly. Make sure you have the resources available (or at least identified) to close any of your offers that get accepted.

Remember, just because you can legally get away with something doesn't make it okay. The world is not your playground. It's not only unprofessional to experiment for fun and profit at the expense of other people's lives, but if you're not careful, the most important asset you have in this business—your reputation—can easily get trashed beyond repair if you leave too many people hanging.

Personal Guarantees

When it comes to real estate transactions, without question one of the most dangerous promises you can make is to personally guarantee the repayment of a debt—especially when it's a mortgage loan.

Most loans involving real estate consist of two separate instruments: a note, which is sometimes called a *promissory* note; and a mortgage or a deed of trust, depending on which state you're in. The mortgage or deed of trust is the document you give to the lender that pledges the property as collateral to secure the loan.

Even though this security instrument is what gives the lender authority to foreclose if you default on payments, this document is not your primary concern. Simply having your mortgage or deed of trust foreclosed upon does not, in itself, create any civil or financial liabilities for you. The note is where the danger lies.

The note constitutes a written promise to pay—hence the common term *promissory note*—and is therefore the instrument with the potential to do you the greatest harm. The note identifies how much is being borrowed, the interest rate, the monthly payment, and other details involving the funding and repayment of the loan. It also contains the recourse language that defines exactly which (if any) actions the lender can take against you personally to recover the money you borrowed, as well as all the interest and legal fees that accrue while collecting it.

What many people fail to realize is that if your note contains a personal guarantee of repayment—and most of them do—your lender could decide to simply forgo the foreclosure route, and just come after you personally for all the money that's due. You see, just because a lender has the *right* to foreclose on you, it doesn't mean they will. If you have enough cash or other easily liquidated assets on hand, they could legally choose to skip the foreclosure route altogether and simply get a judgment that attaches your assets. And even if they do choose to foreclose—which they nearly always will—you're not necessarily out of the woods, because your liability may not be fully extinguished at the auction sale.

You see, most foreclosure auctions do not provide the lender with sufficient net proceeds to satisfy the entire debt, which technically includes all of the accrued back interest plus costs and legal fees. This shortage is called a *deficiency*, and your personal guarantee gives them the right to hold you responsible for the deficiency amount. In fact, if a lender gets a deficiency judgment against you, they can attach it to anything you own personally, such as your car, boat, bank account, other real estate, etc. This would allow them to take possession of your assets and force the sale of as many of them as necessary until they've been paid in full.

Another choice your lender would have in a deficiency situation would be to "forgive" or "cancel" the shortage. Although this sounds like they're doing you a favor, in fact, they're not. Whenever they choose to write off a loss, they're obligated to file a Form 1099-C with the IRS for that same amount. This process effectively converts the forgiven debt into taxable income for you. In other words, if a lender forgives you for a $30,000 deficiency, the 1099-C form will turn that cancelled debt into $30,000 worth of income for you, upon which you now owe taxes—unless you qualify for protection under a state or federal program, such as the temporary Mortgage Forgiveness Debt Relief Act passed in December of 2007.

Loans that contain guarantees are referred to as recourse financing, because the lender has been granted the right to exercise collection remedies against you. Non-recourse financing, on the other hand, does not permit the lender to look to you for any satisfaction of the debt. In the case of a non-recourse mortgage loan, the lender would still be permitted to take legal action, but it would be limited only to foreclosing on the note, and forcing the sale of the security asset (the property).

But beware: recourse dangers are not just found in mortgage loans. Recourse is a risk concern in any type of contract, because contracts, by definition, are written promises made by two or more parties to one another. Wherever there are promises, there exists the potential for promise breaking. And wherever there is the possibility of a broken promise, recourse language can—and really always should—be found.

Recourse language is actually the only element of any agreement with the capacity for causing you any harm. Therefore, in order to reduce or eliminate your risks in any contract, you must take pre-emptive steps to control the remedies available against you—which brings us to our next topic: managing remedies.

MANAGING REMEDIES

Recourse language identifies the legal remedies that parties have against one another to either enforce performance or to collect damages. You need to be in complete control of this language whenever possible, which is why you should do whatever you can to avoid using agreements drafted by "the other side". As you'll soon see, removing the danger of recourse against you is a pretty simple thing to do, but surprisingly, it's not done the way you might think.

Some gurus teach that the best way to extinguish the threat of recourse is to draft your agreements in such a way as to completely eliminate all remedies against you, while leaving remedies against the other party in place for your benefit. This seems like a pretty obvious approach, but it's actually not a very good idea. In fact, it can literally backfire and create greater liabilities for you than if you were to allow the other party to retain some recourse against you.

So, how can having a contract with no recourse against you possibly be problematic? It's simple: Whenever you remove every remedy against you in a contract while allowing yourself a disproportionate amount of recourse against the other party, you're effectively creating something known as a *contract of adhesion.*

A contract of adhesion is one that grants an unreasonable degree of control and recourse to one party, while simultaneously restricting or eliminating all of those same benefits for the other party. This creates a situation where one party has effectively been denied any practical negotiating latitude or bargaining power, and is required to either accept the entire contract as a whole, or walk away.

In some industries, such as insurance or institutional lending, contracts of adhesion are so common that they have become standard practice. But in many other applications, they can generally be viewed as unfair and sometimes even unconscionable—especially when the majority of the bargaining power, control, and recourse favor the drafter (author) of the contract; which in your case would (or at least *should*) always be you.

If your agreement fits the profile of a contract of adhesion, it won't really be an issue, except for the one time when it can hurt you most—if litigation should arise. Your opponent's attorney or the judge himself would have legal grounds (with settled case precedent reaching to the U.S. Supreme Court level) for voiding your contract. Without the protection of your contract, you would then be completely exposed to risk, with the judge holding sole discretion as to not only *if* you have liability for damages, but also *how much*. And believe it or not, there's often very little you can do, from a practical standpoint, to reverse the carte balance damage a judge can inflict while making mincemeat of both your reputation and your bank account.

Of course, even in litigation this isn't a likely concern, unless your opponent stumbles onto an attorney sharp enough to even consider crafting such an argument, or unless your case rolls to a rogue judge who happens to be bent on sending a message to capitalist America. But all the same, you have to eliminate any possibility of this happening, regardless of how remote the odds may be. Because unlike legendary creatures such as Bigfoot or the Loch Ness monster, there is hard evidence suggesting that brilliant attorneys and maverick judges actually exist—even if they are as scarce as documented UFO abductions.

Ironically, that means the most effective first step to eliminating recourse risk would be to actually leave some recourse language in your agreements, and allow the other party to have a few remedies against you in the event of default. The key, however, is to maintain complete control of that recourse language so that you can make sure that it not only identifies the limit of the remedies against you, but also provides for the full liquidation (satisfaction) of those remedies in a manner that is easily manageable for you.

For example: When you're a buyer, you could put a clause in your contract that says something like: *"In the event Buyer should fail to close, Buyer's entire liability to Seller shall be limited to the forfeiture of Buyer's earnest money"*. This would mean you'd have to forfeit your earnest money for defaulting, but you'd never owe any more than that. If you're a seller, you could include a clause like: *"If Seller is unable to deliver clear title, Seller's entire liability to Buyer shall never exceed the refund of Buyer's earnest money"*. This means you would have to refund the Buyer's earnest money, but that's okay because you'd get to avoid shelling out potentially huge performance liability damages.

These types of clauses provide the other party with some recourse, which removes any chance of your agreement being labeled as a contract of adhesion. But to your benefit, they also identify—in advance—the *limits* of the recourse against you, as well as *how* the remedy is to be satisfied (liquidated). That way, no aspect of the recourse or remedy would remain open to subjective—or worse, *judicial*—interpretation.

Just like the old adage that says, "Sometimes the best place to hide is in plain sight," so too, it's true that, "Sometimes the best way to eliminate the danger of recourse against you, is to allow some recourse against you."

YOUR ENTITY

Even though you can greatly manage and reduce risk by controlling your contractual promises and the subsequent recourse language, there is still another very important factor that remains to be discussed: your entity.

Your entity is defined by how you sign your agreements. If you sign personally, you are personally responsible for fulfilling all of the covenants and absorbing all of the remedies. If you sign as an officer or employee of an artificial entity, such as a corporation or limited liability company (LLC), then that corporation or LLC is the responsible entity—so long as you are not using the corporation as a shield to engage in fraudulent, illegal or unconscionable acts, in which case the corporate veil can be pierced, and you can be held responsible.

Each type of entity has its place, its benefits, and its particular drawbacks. We will only be discussing these on a very superficial level, because your entity of choice not only has liability concerns, it also has tax implications. This means you would be wise to get the majority of your entity structure advice from a team of experts, consisting of both a competent real estate attorney and a well-informed accountant or other tax professional.

An artificial entity can be a very effective component of your overall risk management strategy, because you absolutely cannot rely solely on the tactics in the two previous discussions to remove *all* liabilities from your investment business. As effective as they are, some residual or incidental liabilities can still rear their ugly heads, and so it's important to put at least one more layer of protection between you and a dangerously cold and litigious world. Your entity represents your last line of defense. Use it wisely.

Here is a very basic look at some of the most commonly used entities in real estate:

Sole Proprietor: In a sole proprietorship, you are the entire entity. You sign everything personally, and you own everything personally. There is no legal distinction made between yourself and your company activity or assets. This entity is the easiest and least expensive route to take—at least initially. Signing personally means there are no government artificial entity application forms to fill out, no fees to pay and no extra tax returns to file. But if you end up in court, everything you own is at risk. And if you lose, that can cost you much more than if you had invested some time and money in establishing an artificial entity.

Corporation: This is an artificial entity that comes in two varieties: a "C" corporation and a subchapter "S" corporation. A "C" corporation is a separate stand-alone taxpaying entity that you create by filing the appropriate paperwork with the Secretary of State where you are intending to operate. An "S" corp. is formed the same way (it actually begins life as a "C" corp., which you've elected to give a Subchapter "S" status to by simply checking a box on the application paperwork), and is also a stand-alone entity with its own unique taxpayer identity number. However the "S" corporation is different from a "C" corporation, in that even though a separate tax return is required, all profits and losses pass through directly to the shareholders who must then report these profits or losses on their own personal tax returns.

Either type of corporation can be formed for anywhere from $250 to $1,000 (or more, depending on who's preparing the paperwork) so they can be relatively inexpensive to create and register. Once activated, you can begin signing agreements as an officer of the corporation, which means that the corporation is liable for any default issues—not you personally. This is good, but not bulletproof, as your corporation's assets would be at risk in the event of litigation. Also, as a corporation you can no longer take advantage of filing cases yourself in small claims court, because in most jurisdictions, corporations must be represented by an attorney in any court proceedings.

Corporations must follow very strict state and federal guidelines, such as holding annual meetings of shareholders, keeping accurate minute records, submitting an annual statement of corporate officers to the Secretary of State, keeping all corporate revenues separate from all personal revenues (to avoid what is referred to as the *co-mingling of funds*), creating corporate resolutions and specific resolutions to officially grant general and specific powers respectively to corporate officers, and so on.

With "C" corporations, there also exists the possibility of double taxation, which can negatively impact your true bottom-line. "S" corporation status does away with most double taxation issues, but both types of corporations require a competent individual to prepare complex IRS tax returns every year. And unless you have the time to stay on top of the huge and ever-changing U.S. tax code, that's a job best left to a properly trained professional.

Another challenge to being incorporated is that failure to observe every single state and federal securities law regarding the operation and conduct of a corporation can lead to revocation, or to an official declaration of the corporation as nothing more than an alter-ego of one or more of the officers. Either of these scenarios would place all of the company officers at personal risk of liability and loss for all of the corporate obligations and guarantees. Once the protection of the corporate veil is dissolved or pierced, you become a virtually defenseless target in the cross hairs of a dangerously litigious society.

LLC: Probably the most popular entity of all, the LLC, which stands for Limited Liability Company, provides insulation from personal liability similar to a corporation, but without all of the requirements of annual shareholder meetings, copious minute-taking, and other headaches mandated by state and federal securities law. LLC's are also very easy to organize. In most states, you simply check with your Secretary of State (on their website is the easiest) to see if the name you want is available, fill out just a few of the blanks on the LLC application form supplied by your Secretary of State (generally, not all blanks are required to be completed), identify a statutory agent (someone of legal age who resides in your state upon whom legal process can be served), and then send in a check for a couple hundred dollars or so. That's usually about it.

Another benefit is that in some states, if the LLC is a single-member organization (having only one member, such as yourself), the LLC is ignored for the purposes of taxation, and all of the profits are reported as pass-through income for the individual member on an attachment (Schedule C, E, or F) to his or her personal Form 1040. This can save tax prep fees every year, as all corporations require a completely separate tax return, even if it is an "S" corporation, where the profits are also treated as pass-through income for the shareholders.

LLC membership is also very flexible, and can include an unlimited number of individuals, corporations, foreign entities, and even other LLC's as members. However, if the LLC's sole member is a corporation, the LLC's income and expenses are reported on the corporation's return, usually Form 1120 or Form 1120S, instead of your own. Be sure to consult a local attorney and tax professional for all of the legal and tax consequences of an LLC before deciding if it's the best entity for you.

Partnerships: There are three basic forms of partnerships: general partnerships, limited partnerships (LP's), and limited liability partnerships (LLP's). With all of them, the partners share directly in the profits and losses of the partnerships, which can have some positive tax advantages over corporations. The major differences between each of these various partnership entities are found in the liability and management aspects.

In general partnerships, each partner has the right to incur debt and other obligations on behalf of the partnership, as well as manage the day-to-day operations. Under a general partnership, all partners have liability for the repayment of debt, the fulfillment of all contractual responsibilities, and exposure to consequences of the actions of each partner, and the partnership as a whole.

In limited partnerships, there are two types of partners: general partners, who usually handle the daily operations (including the incurring of debt and other obligations), and limited partners, who typically provide the capital resources. Limited partners may not incur obligations on behalf of the partnership, but they are excluded from liability on any obligations incurred by the general partner.

Limited liability partnerships are a complex blend of the first two partnerships, in that all partners have a right to incur obligations on behalf of the entity, but each partner has little or no liability for the actions of the other partners, or the partnership as a whole.

Operating Under the Radar

Just like Harry Potter had a cloak of invisibility that allowed him to move about Hogwarts unnoticed, so too, do you have cloaking devices behind which you can hide from public view while running your real estate empire.

These shrouds are called trusts. There are many different kinds, and they vary greatly depending upon the need. But regardless of their different names and specific uses, they share a common function; they are all agreements by which one person or entity (the trustee) has agreed to be responsible for holding and/or managing some particular asset (including real estate) on behalf of another person or entity (the beneficiary). There are several benefits for using trusts to hold assets as opposed to owning them in your own name, or in the name of your corporation or LLC. Among them are privacy, asset protection, estate planning, and convenience, just to name a few. And even though there are quite a number of trusts, the only two we'll be covering here are land trusts and paper trusts.

Land Trusts

The one and only thing you can use a land trust for is to hold title to land (funny how that works). And though they may be a new concept to you, they've been around since the days of the Roman Empire. Literally.

Land trusts are permitted in most states, and are usually very easy to create. The first step is to deed the property to the trustee of your land trust, instead of into your own name or company's name. You can have the seller do this if you're buying the property, or you can do it yourself if you already happen to own the property. The trustee can be anyone or any entity you want, such as a good friend or relative (preferably with a different last name than yours) or a company you own. However, you must remember to include "Trustee" or "as Trustee" after the trustee's name. For example: **Bob Jones, Trustee** or **Bob Jones, as Trustee**. If you forget to do this, your buddy Bob Jones will own your property instead of you, which would be a disaster with no upside—except for maybe the cool Christmas card and fruitcake that a very grateful Bob would send you every year.

In some states, deeding the property to your trustee is all you have to do to create land trust ownership. But I would never stop there. It's also highly recommended to fill out a trust document for your own records, even if your state doesn't require one—and even if you are likely to be the only person who ever sees it. The land trust document identifies some very important things, such as the trustee's powers and duties, and who the beneficiary or beneficiaries will be. This is critical, because the beneficiary (you or your entity) is the one who will have full authority over the trust. This includes the right to enjoy all of the property's use and ownership privileges, the right to receive any and all rental or sale proceeds, and the power to dismiss and replace the trustee at will.

When it comes to tax consequences, there is no need to apply for a special EIN or tax ID number when it comes to land trusts. Land trusts, unlike many other trusts, are not taxable entities—which means as far as the IRS is concerned, the beneficiary has the same tax consequences as if they were holding title in their own name.

What are some of the specific reasons to consider using land trusts? Privacy and asset protection are two big ones. If you take title in land trusts, no one knows when you are buying, selling, or holding real estate. This allows you to operate under the radar of public scrutiny, which is important for everyone, and even more so for high-profile individuals, like sports stars and celebrities.

Asset protection from land trusts can come in two ways. One is by preventing your name from coming up on public records in the event of litigation. This lack of recorded assets to attach can help curb an aggressive attorney's desire to sue you, because attorneys don't get paid when they win, they get paid when they collect. So if they don't see anything of significance to attach, they can lose a great deal of enthusiasm to sue—especially if they're working on a contingency basis. And even if they do get a judgment against you, it won't attach to your trust properties unless the attorney knows how to dig more deeply—and most don't.

The second way trusts can help you with asset protection is by creating small entities in which to hold each property, thereby compartmentalizing your real estate assets. This is good, because if an unfortunate accident were to occur at one of your properties (i.e., if someone were to slip and fall and wanted to sue the owner), the owner would be the trust—not you—and the trust would only have one asset: that particular property. This can help keep disasters occurring at one property from becoming a financial liability to all of your other holdings.

Another big benefit to owning properties in land trusts is that it can help avoid probate. That's because people die, but trusts don't. Land trusts have beneficial interests that are treated as personal property, not real property. So if the language is handled right, the beneficial interest can transfer from the deceased to any other beneficiary without going through probate—even in the absence of a will.

Paper Trusts

Paper trusts are very much in form and function like land trusts, except that they are used to hold ownership of paper assets, such as land contracts, notes, and mortgages. Just as with land trusts, the purpose of a paper trust is to provide you with privacy, estate planning and asset protection advantages without restricting your control or your benefits of ownership. After all, paper assets are publicly recorded documents that anyone can see, and since it's really nobody's business who you are, what you own, who you're working with, and what the terms of your deals are, paper trusts help to make sure people mind their own beeswax.

Trust Limits

Land trusts and paper trusts are great utilities, but they definitely have their limits—especially land trusts, which may not be legally permitted in all states anymore. Unfortunately, some investors in the past have made the mistake of assuming that trusts are fool-proof impenetrable fortresses of safety. This is a severe overstatement of both their purpose and their potential. At best, they provide you with a helpful onion-skin layer of anonymity and discretion.

One big drawback to using land trusts is that if you are quick-turning (flipping) short sale deals, you may run into a problem getting your resale transaction closed. Some title companies are not closing transactions or insuring properties that are short sale flips if they are held in land trusts. Their flawed (and in my opinion, *illegal*) reasoning behind banning these types of deals would take too long to explain here. Just be aware that if you are planning to take title into a land trust on short sale deals that you are expecting to immediately resell, you may have some challenges to overcome. If you can't find a title company who will close your deal in a trust, then this is one time when you may have to use your company or some other entity (never your own name) to take title to the property temporarily.

Don't Wing-it... EVER!

When it comes to preparing or using trusts of any kind, never, *ever* go it alone. Always be sure to seek the advice and guidance of a knowledgeable attorney in your area before utilizing trusts—especially since land trusts may not be legal in your area. And always be sure to consult a qualified financial professional (CPA or other financial expert) to make sure that your intended use will benefit you in some manner.

Also... never, *ever* use a land trust or paper trust agreement straight out of a real estate book or course. These documents must meet very specific guidelines to be legal wherever they are permitted. When gurus like myself occasionally include samples of these trust documents, it's only to give your local attorney a head start, and not a short cut for you to trim costs by completely avoiding legal counsel.

And please never forget that land trusts and paper trusts are not miraculous documents scribed into stone by the hand of God. Yes, they're really cool and just as highly effective at making you invisible as Harry Potter's cloak, but just like his flimsy cloth shroud, they are *far* from bullet-proof!

5

M.P.D. marketing
for A.D.D. consumers

Once upon a time, consumers were huddled masses who moved in highly predictable patterns. Marketers found it very easy to reach them, and also discovered that—once reached—these consumers were polite proletarians who listened patiently to every marketing message put in front of them.

Then came today's fractured marketplace, created largely by never-ending advancements in communications technology—which have so far brought us such liberating devices as mute buttons, cable systems with 200+ TV channels, the Internet 2.0, movies on-demand, XM radio, iPods, iPhones, iTouches, iPads, and perhaps the most empowering entertainment device of all, TiVo.

These innovations have rapidly redefined the role that consumers play in the marketing game, turning the tables a full 180 degrees on advertisers in just a few years. Now, the majority of communication power is held by consumers, because they have the capability to choose which (if any) marketing messages they will allow themselves to be exposed to. In fact, today's consumers not only possess the ability to manage whose messages they'll listen to (if they decide to listen at all), but they also get to decide *when* they'll listen to them—and in what format.

However, consumer control is not the only challenge that advertisers have to overcome in today's marketplace. They also have to figure out how to *find* all of these desensitized and extremely picky A.D.D. consumers, so that they can at least try to hit them with a message. This is tougher than ever to do when you consider that the new norm in consumer lifestyle patterns is that there *is* no norm anymore.

And if all of that wasn't bad enough, as a creative real estate investor you have an additional obstacle to overcome. Remember, as we discussed earlier, you are sandwiched in between two completely different kinds of customers; each with diametrically opposed needs to fill. One of them needs for you to *buy* their property in a way that can benefit them as a seller, while the other needs for you to *sell* them a property in a way which would provide them some benefit as a buyer.

Obviously, it would be impossible to create a single brand identity that can effectively reconcile both of these objectives, so you'll need to go "Sybil" and develop multiple personality disorder—except instead of 16 personalities, you only need to create two, along with a distinctly different marketing message to support each one. Of course, this flies in the face of conventional branding wisdom, which is to put all of your eggs into building one brand identity. But remember—you're not in Kansas anymore, Toto. These are not conventional times.

Although many of the techniques featured in this book have their own unique marketing considerations (which we'll cover later), there are still four good reasons to include this general chapter on marketing. The first is to provide you with a basic insight into the primary objectives of marketing. The second is to introduce you to the often-irrational thinking of consumers, and how to shift the context of your message to leverage it. The third is to help you identify approaching market trends, so that you can adjust to stay on the leading edge. And the fourth, of course, is that I simply had to include the obligatory list of basic marketing strategies.

PRIMARY MARKETING OBJECTIVES

Of the estimated 6.8 billion people on the planet, there are (believe it or not) only four things keeping every one of them from being a customer of yours right now:

1. They don't know you exist.

2. They don't want what you're selling.

3. They can't afford what you're selling.

4. They don't trust you.

So what should be the obvious goal of your marketing? To overcome as many of these four obstacles as you can, natch. So let's look at each challenge individually.

1. They don't know you exist. With 6.8 billion potential customers, this one reason eliminates about 6,799,999,900 of them (and yes, I realize that giving some people credit for knowing 100 people is pretty generous). And while you can never reach them all, you can always do better than you are right now by learning how to fully leverage readily available resources; like local business group meetings, investor clubs, social networking sites, neighborhood associations, generous business card distribution, and just opening your mouth to tell people what you do.

2. They don't want what you're selling. The reason that statement doesn't say, "They don't *need* what you're selling," is because I've learned the hard way that most people don't buy what they need... they buy what they *want*.

For example, there are millions of Americans (including myself, and—in all likelihood—you) who really *need* a good retirement plan. And yet, only a small percentage of us will ever invest any time or money into developing one at all; and of the few of us who actually do, most will start too late or simply fail to invest enough into it. Why? Because even though we know that we need to save a certain amount of money in order to live comfortably by the time we reach retirement, what most of us want *more* is to have the absolute best of everything right now.

That's why we live at the edge of (and sometimes well beyond) our means, buying houses that are bigger than we can afford, driving pretentious cars that are newer and more luxurious than we need, using credit to buy 60" flat screen plasma TV's that are bigger than the couches we watch them from (to get the most out of our top-tier HD cable, of course), and wolfing down costly restaurant lunches and dinners 12 to 15 times per week. We don't need any of those things, but we'll continue spending our money on them, because those are the things we want.

Now, I'm not saying that *nobody* ever buys what they need, regardless of want, because it does happen; just not as often as you might think. To prove it, just trace the motivation far enough back on any purchasing decision that you can think of, and you'll find that it will often boil down to a consumer "want" of some kind.

For instance, nobody ever really *needs* a drill bit until they *want* a hole. And on the other end of the spectrum, a patient with late-stage liver disease doesn't actually *need* a liver transplant, unless they've decided that they *want* to live.

Now, this whole *want* versus *need* thing might seem like just a silly argument over semantics, but it's not. It's a lot more. In fact, if you want to be successful selling *anything* in life, it's one of is more important distinctions you'll ever make. Why? Because regardless of how much somebody might *need* what you're selling, if you can't figure out a way to make them *want* it too, they just won't buy it… at least, not from you. So if you want your deals to be truly appealing to your prospects (and trust me, you do), then you need to look beyond the discussion at hand and start negotiating to their bigger "want". *That's* where the real money is.

3. They can't afford what you're selling. This is a tricky one, because affordability is not always a concrete reality. Sometimes, it's just a perception. Sure, there will always be some people who simply cannot afford to work with you at the price or terms you want, whether you're trying to buy their property, or sell them one of yours. But there are going to be others who'll *think* they can't afford to do business with you, when in fact they *can*—and perhaps even *should*.

A prime example of this could be a homeowner in foreclosure. They might initially assume they can't afford to sell you their house at the low price you want, because they owe way too much. But then once you share with them how a short sale works, they'll not only see that they actually *can* afford to sell you their house, they'll also be excited by the fact that selling it to you will stop their foreclosure.

4. They don't trust you. If you've done everything else right—you've let them know you're in business to help them, you've gotten them to want what you're selling, and you've convinced them that they can afford it—but someone is still not willing to do business with you, then there can only be one possible explanation left: They just don't trust you. People need to feel as though they can believe in you before they'll open a business relationship with you. But beware; if you ever feel like you need to defend your motives or convince them of your trustworthiness, it's probably already too late—because you will likely sound defensive doing so. It's best to handle the trust issue subtly in advance.

A great way to do this is with lots of testimonials from real people. The truth is that when you say good things about yourself people rarely buy into it. But when someone else toots your horn it carries a lot of weight. If you've done some deals, get testimonials from your previous buyers and sellers. If you haven't done any yet, get them from community leaders, bankers, professional athletes, celebrities, CPA's or whoever you know. If you don't know anyone who will give you a good reference, it might be time to re-evaluate how you've been living.

LEVERAGING CONSUMER IRRATIONALITY

Consumers don't have to make sense for you to make a profit, which is a really good thing, because consumer irrationality is about the only other thing you can count on as reliably as death and taxes. This is especially frustrating since the number one rule of commerce is this:

The customer is always right... even when they're wrong.

You were probably only familiar with the first half of that statement. But given the full reality, it should be clear that in order to be successful, you'll need to learn how to speak to illogical consumer thinking. That means sometimes you may have to create new contexts and relativities for your business in order to align yourself with their bizarre expectations. Luckily, this can actually be easier than it sounds.

The Relevance of Relativity

Relativity is a key element to every negotiation, yet most people are unaware of it. Relativity is how consumers justify their buying decisions, and the way they use it is by comparing every potential new purchase to a similar past buying decision that they can see or recall. If they can't come up with one, research has shown that they can become paralyzed with indecision—even on the smallest purchases.

This need for *comparative relativity* is so absolutely vital that if you happen to be in a unique business where there isn't much of it for your customers to draw from naturally, then you'll have to create some from scratch using contexts, details, and examples that they can easily relate to.

Exactly how would you go about doing that? Well, perhaps a little coffee talk might help. Let's pretend that you want to start a company that sells 20oz. cups of coffee for $4 each, and let's further say that you want to call this new company Starbucks—after Captain Ahab's first mate in *Moby-Dick* (apparently in our little scenario you are a 98 lb. milky-white literary geek). Some quick math suggests that your venture could be quite profitable, because a $4 price point represents an incredibly high markup on such an otherwise dirt-cheap commodity.

There's only one problem: people are used to getting 20oz. coffees for $1.29 at Dunkin' Donuts, for 99¢ at the corner gas station, or for free at work. That means coffee has a very low price anchor in the minds of consumers. This creates a challenge for you, because if all things appear equal (coffee = coffee), then price is the only aspect a consumer will consider when trying to justify their purchase.

How would you overcome this? It's simple. You wouldn't sell coffee. Instead, you would create a brand new context by offering a unique and exotic-sounding beverage called a *Frappuccino*. Although the name suggests a coffee base, it's not just "coffee" you'd be pitching—so the price anchor would be loosened. To help remove the anchor completely, you could also introduce a new environment, like a friendly counter-culture café, in which to serve your Frappuccino creations.

Now you'd have something totally unique in the marketplace. You wouldn't be just selling coffee like everyone else, but rather serving fun drinks in a boutique atmosphere that can offer consumers a pleasant alternative to the frantically unappealing ambiance of brightly lit donut shops and busy gas stations.

Of course, since you'd no longer be limited by the low coffee price anchor— thanks to your marketplace niche as the antithesis of the coffee context—you'd be free to set your own new price point. But beware, because with this freedom comes a caveat: in the absence of any existing similar products (i.e., $4 coffees), your customers will balk at paying that much for a 20oz. drink of *any* kind, no matter *what*'s in it. They'd first need to see something that somehow validates your $4 price tag before they can be convinced it's okay to buy one. So if no comparable relativity exists for them already, you'll have to make some up and *give* it to them!

How? Well, if your goal was to sell 20oz. coffees for $4, you could create some relativity out of thin air by also offering a 14oz. size for $3.65 and a 32oz. for $4.95. Having three relatively-priced sizes to choose from would give your customers a sensible scale for comparing values; and they'd likely use that scale to decide which size they want, without ever noticing that the context for pricing had been deftly shifted to proportions, and away from the cheap cost of the ingredients themselves.

In other words, they'd be so preoccupied debating size issues, like: *Why settle for a tiny 14oz. drink when the 20oz. is only 35¢ more?* or: *Will that huge 32oz. drink burst my bladder?* that they wouldn't even stop to consider what ought to be their most obvious first question, which is: *Why, in the name of all that's holy am I even THINKING about spending $4 for a freaking cup of coffee anyway?*

But they wouldn't ask; they'd just compare the available choices and buy one. And here's the best part: once they've plunked down $4 for a cup of your java, paying $4 again under similar circumstances would be *normal* for them. In fact, they would actually use their first experience with you as comparative justification for future purchases from you, even though this new context they'd be subscribing to is one that you just dreamed up one day while sitting in your underwear.

REAL ESTATE CONTEXT SHIFTING

So what does all this coffee crap have to do with real estate? Well, if you're buying real estate to resell at a profit, you have to purchase either at wholesale prices or on wholesale terms. Negotiating both on the same deal is great work when you can get it, but that's tough to do without a ski mask and a .357 (which is frowned-upon by your BBB). So let's just see how we can leverage what we just learned about context shifting to make our low price or long term offers appear more desirable.

Context Shifting for a Low Wholesale Price:

When you're buying at wholesale prices you almost have to steal properties. That means you'll want to shift the context of the discussion away from "price" over to something more beneficial, like the speed and finality of a fast closing cash sale.

For example, let's say you're about to negotiate with a seller who's asking $90,000, and you've calculated the most you can pay is $75,000. Typically you might begin by tossing out an offer of $60,000 to give yourself room to negotiate up to your target price. However, starting $30,000 below the seller's asking price virtually guarantees that an air of confrontation will quickly develop between the two of you, forcing you to adopt a weak defensive posture right off the bat.

So what can you do to avoid creating these antagonistic feelings—and the acid reflux that often comes with them? The best way is to proactively set the tone of your negotiation before you ever meet the seller, by branding your offers as beneficial buying programs—such as your *15 Day Cash & Close Program*, or your *Fair Price Offer Program*, etc. Multiple buying programs can help to preemptively establish the benefits of an all cash deal, while giving your seller some comparable relativities to work with; all of which you can leverage by scratching out three escalating offers,* sandwiching the price you want right in the middle—just like Starbucks does:

Offer 1: 15 Day Cash & Close Program: $60K paid in all cash, closing in 15 days

Offer 2: 15 Day Premium All Cash Program: $75K @ 10% down, bal. in 180 days

Offer 3- Fair Price Program: $85K at $850 down, $475 per month until paid off

---

*Notice each type of offer has been branded as a program. You'll learn how to profit from any one of them later.

Just so you know, you're not likely to get offers #2 or #3 accepted. But that's okay, because the only reason they even exist is to help make the fast cash *context* of Offer #1 look more appealing. This strategy also gets everyone's target price on the table immediately, which essentially creates a closed negotiation bubble that neither of you will have to step outside of during the rest of the discussion. Then as you two go back and forth—giving and taking on prices and terms—you can often keep the seller so busy comparing apples to oranges that he just might not realize he could simply reject all your offers and shove you out the door on your keister.

In this scenario, one of three things could possibly happen: 1) The seller may decide to take Offer 1 just as it is, saving you the extra $15,000 you were willing to pay; or 2) The seller may predictably follow your lead and "negotiate" you into paying the middle $75,000 figure (from Offer 2) in all cash (like Offer 1)—which is exactly what you wanted all along; or 3) The seller may just get pissed and jack you in the nose, which means you need to do a more thorough job of qualifying your prospects in the future, or else find yourself an elderly Asian man who can teach you how to better defend yourself. Repeat after me: *Wax on... Wax off....*

Regardless of the actual outcome, you've no doubt enhanced your odds of getting that deal done—and possibly at a better price—by shifting the seller's focus away from your low price, and reinforcing the positive attributes of a fast all-cash closing: such as the speed, convenience, and finality of a completed sale.

By continuing to create new contexts, justified with relativities that you've invented specifically for each occasion, you're likely to get far more wholesale price deals done without upsetting sellers, and without being forced to defend your offers... or yourself...*literally*.

Context shifting for Long Wholesale Terms:

On the other side of the coin, when you're buying on attractive wholesale terms, such as a *subject to* deal with a balloon due in 7 years (you'll learn more about what this is and exactly how it's done in a later section), you don't want the seller to become concerned about the "long wait" aspect. You also don't want him to dwell on the fact that you also need to get a slight discount on the purchase price, because even a relatively small 5% to 10% discount is going to amount to a pretty big chunk of change on a higher value property.

So if you don't want your seller to fixate on either the long terms or the slightly discounted price, what *do* you want him thinking about? Net equity. In a term negotiation, you should always try to shift the context away from the terms and the price, and center your attention on how much of the seller's equity you'll be helping him keep—assuming he has any. If he doesn't have any equity, then your job will be even easier, because a seller without equity doesn't really have anything to sell. But I digress, as that is also a topic for a later chapter.

Getting back to our discussion of switching the context to net equity, let's take a look at a sample scenario: As the scene opens, you're sitting across the table from a seller with a house in pretty good shape, worth about $190,000 to $195,000, and he owes about $150,000 on it. Since he's not going to let you steal it, you know that the only other way you can make a profit is to buy it on long terms with monthly payments. But that's not what you're going to be negotiating—at least not at first.

Your first objective will be to switch the context of the negotiations over to equity preservation, which is advantageous to you since the seller is not likely to have any negative anchors or perceptions about the topic, nor is he likely to have much experience negotiating from that angle. The fastest way to do this is by telling him your goal is to try and net him about the same amount of cash as if he'd hired a Realtor to list and sell his property. Then you pull out a simple one-page equity worksheet from your briefcase to hash out—in writing—approximately how much cash the seller could reasonably expect to net at a conventional closing table.

In our case, we'll say the worksheet shows that starting with an asking price of $199,000, the seller can expect to net about $21,000 of actual cash after paying off his $150,000 mortgage, and subtracting another $28,000 for typical price concessions, closing costs, commissions, and other common deductions, such as seller-paid buyer costs (a more detailed example of this can be seen on page 187).

Now, with his expected net equity cash figure of $21,000 in front of him—in writing—you're ready to proceed with making some offers. Just as you did in our wholesale example, you're not going to make a single offer, but three. This will give him some relative comparisons to help fuel his decision-making process, as well as give him the feeling that he's participating in the negotiations—when in fact, he'll pretty much just be following your lead.

Offer 1: $21,000 equity (all he has coming), payable $2,000 at closing, and the remaining $19,000 when you get cashed out by reselling the property later.

Offer 2: $15,000 equity, payable $5,000 at closing, and the $10,000 balance when you get cashed out of the property in the future.

Offer 3: $10,000 equity, payable all right now, up-front, and in cash—with no more money due when you get cashed out in the future.

Now, don't worry if you don't understand the mechanics of this deal—you'll learn that later. Just know that your objective is to keep your seller busily focused on comparing the relative aspects of each possible transaction (i.e., the more cash he wants today the less equity he'll get to keep overall), rather than arguing with you over price or terms. In fact, notice how price is never even mentioned!

And once again, just as in our wholesale price example, it doesn't matter which deal the seller picks—because if you know what you're doing, you can make money with any one of them.

The High Cost of No Cost

If you really want to leverage consumer irrationality, try offering some stuff for free. There's just something about the concept of "free" that seems to cloud the average person's ability to make intelligent decisions. Most people simply assume that if something is free, there can't be a downside. This is not true.

In his 2008 book *Predictably Irrational*, Dan Ariely explores just how irrational "free stuff" can make people, by citing an experiment which was conducted at the Massachusetts Institute of Technology, in conjunction with members from Duke University and the Joseph L. Rotman School of Management.

This particular experiment involved consumers choosing between two Amazon gift certificates, each of which could be purchased for well below their face value. In the first step of the experiment, a $10 and a $20 gift certificate were priced at $5 and $12 respectively. It was immediately clear to the participants that the $12 investment was the better value—giving the purchaser $8 worth of additional buying power versus only the $5 worth of extra buying power afforded by the lower-priced certificate. Because of this obvious fact, the overwhelming majority (71%) of the test subjects opted for the more expensive $12 investment.

In the second step of the experiment, the researchers reduced the price of both gift certificates by $4 each, making the new price of the $10 gift certificate only $1 and the new price of the $20 gift certificate only $8. Once again, the higher-priced gift certificate represented the better value, and so it was no surprise when a hefty 64% of the consumers chose to pay $8 to get the $20 gift certificate.

Then, something bizarre happened. In the final step of the experiment, the prices of both gift certificates were lowered again by $1 each. This made the $20 gift certificate only $7, but now the $10 gift certificate was free. It should have been obvious to the consumers that paying $7 to get $20 worth of buying power was still better than getting only $10 worth from the free gift certificate—especially when you consider that most things on Amazon.com cost more than $20, and they would have had to dip into their own pockets to make up the difference.

But the test subjects didn't see it that way at all. In fact, 100% of them ended up choosing the free gift certificate, even though it delivered the lesser value.

What happened? Why did the consumers suddenly have such a reversal of logic? After all, just a few moments earlier when the $10 gift certificate was only $1, the majority of them (64%) felt that paying $7 more was still worth it to get the $20 gift certificate. So why did their perception suddenly change as soon as they found out the $10 gift certificate was free? Why couldn't they *still* see that paying $7 more to get the $20 gift certificate was the overall better deal? I'll tell you why— it's because when consumers can get something for free, they no longer feel that comparative reasoning is necessary, so common sense goes out the window.

In other words, people are just stupid for free stuff.

So, if that's true (and it is) maybe you should stop trying to get people interested in your deals by discounting your prices or profits to the bare bones—because most of the time, the only thing you're *really* cutting is your own throat. Maybe, instead of discounting yourself into a lower tax bracket, it might make more sense for you to harness the power of "free", and start tossing bonuses into your deals at no charge to give goofy consumers something to get excited about.

For instance, what if you were to offer a free big screen TV, or HD cable service for a year (or both) as a limited-time bonus for buying your property at asking price by a certain deadline? Of course, this is an ideal "take away" concession item for you to use during negotiations, but even if you ultimately have to give it to them, the $2,000 or so it would cost you beats making three or four extra mortgage payments while you wait around for an eventual offer that'll be well below your asking price anyway. Try it, and you'll be amazed at how much future value buyers are willing to give up just to get something "free" today.

IDENTIFYING MARKET TRENDS

The current real estate trend determines not only what methods you should be focusing on, it also defines what consumers want to hear. Therefore, we need to take a brief look at the three basic real estate market trends.

The 3 Little Markets

Contrary to popular belief, the current national real estate trend should be none of your concern. Whether it's shooting up or crashing down, it just doesn't matter, because by default, all real estate is local. It always has been, and always will be—except for maybe portions of the California coastline west of the San Andreas Fault, which may someday move to a new zip code in the Pacific. Since all real estate is local, it is therefore subject *only* to the market conditions that exist where it lies. So if you want to know what's going on in your marketplace, ignore the national media hype and look no further than your own backyard, Dorothy.

In real estate, the three primary market conditions are: a Buyer's Market, a Seller's Market, and a Balanced Market—which is usually only a temporary transitional phase that the market experiences as it swings between the first two (Buyer's and Seller's market). Of course, there are always micro movements within each broad market trend, but for the most part, you will be more successful selling to the primary needs created by the current trend.

Seller's Market:

A *seller's market* is one in which the demand for real estate is greater than the available inventory. This nearly always leads to higher prices. A seller's market is most often created by an increase in population, local business growth, and/or the introduction of aggressive new lending policies or government mortgage programs. Another term for this type of marketplace condition is *asset-driven*, and viewing it as such can be helpful for you. It reminds you that it is the asset (real estate) which is in demand, and that this demand is what will drive pricing upward as supplies become limited. Therefore, your focus in an asset driven environment should be to acquire as many assets as possible to sell to this hungry marketplace of buyers.

Some real estate investors mistakenly believe that operating in an asset-driven seller's market is always more lucrative, because they know it's easier to sell their properties; which is the necessary final step for realizing their profits. This is not universally true. In fact, a seller's market can be a challenging time for real estate investors to acquire inventory, because sellers can easily liquidate their properties conventionally at retail prices to end consumers, and are therefore less likely to consider selling at wholesale prices or on wholesale terms to investors.

Another concern of creative investors in an asset-driven seller's marketplace is that higher rates of conventional purchasing usually means there are also fewer *buyers* who are in need of the creative assistance that terms can offer. In other words, if buyers are easily getting bank loans, they're not as motivated to purchase properties via riskier methods; like lease-options, lease-purchases, or land contracts.

But even under the best asset-driven market conditions, there will always be buyers and sellers who will encounter situations that will lead to opportunities for investors to generate profits using creative methods. Life is unpredictable. People will continue to die, divorce, and get transferred. Loans will continue to go into default, banks will continue to foreclose, and the occasional dysfunction of human nature will continue to cause people to simply screw things up for no good reason.

Buyer's Market

Whenever the inventory of available homes significantly exceeds the number of qualified buyers in a particular marketplace, this leads to something commonly called a *buyer's market*. This is often caused by falling economic conditions, rising unemployment, market saturation, or any of a host of other negative dynamics. But whatever is causing the buyer/inventory ratio imbalance in your area, constantly referring to it as a buyer's market can compromise your objectivity, because it is a generic label that doesn't provide you with any clues about what you should be doing to help solve it as an investor.

Maybe a better idea would be for you to start viewing this as a *value-driven* marketplace, because doing so will give you the right framing in which to start creating some profitable opportunities. You see, a value-driven marketplace is all about exactly that: value. But since most people are stuck in the mindset that price is the only indicator of value, the consequence is often tumbling property values due to a blood-bath of competing price reductions. The reality is that value has many faces. Price is one of them, but so are convenience, speed, and flexibility.

You see, "value" is a subjective and fluid concept, which, as we learned earlier (in the example of the blind man and the dog), can be tweaked to your advantage with the introduction of some new information. So if you understand the true nature of value, then you can use context and relativity to separate yourself from the rabid wolf pack, and approach potential buyers and sellers with real estate deals that offer more value than they're seeing everywhere else.

Here's an example: In a value-driven buyer's market, you don't have to look too long or hard to find sellers who are highly motivated to get relief from monthly mortgage payments that they no longer want, or can no longer afford to pay. For them, a good "value" wouldn't necessarily mean *selling* the house, as much as it would mean getting rid of the monthly payments *on* the house. But most of them will never know the difference, unless they're fortunate enough to meet you.

In fact, until you come along and introduce them to your term techniques— which can provide them with some attractive "values" (note the plurality) in the form of both reasonable prices *and* mortgage debt relief—they'll probably continue to assume that their only choices will be to either fire-sell the property, or (perhaps far worse) rent it out to a tenant who'll eventually tear it up.

Of course, once you get some properties under contract, your job is only half done. Now you need to move on to providing some value for the buyers who are in that very same value-driven market. You see, sometimes the reason there are so few buyers available in a value-driven market is because many of them can't get typical bank financing, due to poor credit, bad economic conditions, strict lending policies, or some other negative issues. And many of the ones who *can* get financed are often just too scared or unsure to actually pull the trigger.

That means lower prices aren't really going to provide them with much value; because if someone can't qualify for a bank loan, or they're too afraid to commit to one even if they could, then what good is a lower price? However, if you're offering properties that they can buy on friendly terms, with affordable monthly payments and no immediate need for bank financing, you can quickly capture the attention *and* the business of these same people—even if your properties are priced higher than other similar properties. That's because value is not defined by price alone, but rather by the quantity of benefits received in exchange for the money spent.

Balanced Market

As I alluded to earlier when I introduced the three different markets, a Balanced Market in most areas is usually just a temporary phase that each marketplace goes through as it transitions between a Buyer's and Seller's market. That's why our discussion on this type of market is so brief that it's already over; not so much because of the transitory nature of this phase, but more because if you are to remain on the leading edge, you will need to focus on servicing the trend that is on its way in, while phasing out your pursuit of the trend that's dying.

Determining Market Direction

Some people try to measure marketplace trends by simply asking around. This is not always a good idea, especially when you consider how many real estate professionals fail every year because of their flawed opinions on market strategies.

Another way people attempt to determine the market direction is by mere observation. The problem with that method is even if you have extremely broad access to many information sources, sometimes the best clues as to the true direction your marketplace is headed are not readily visible. That means a better bet for determining your current market trend might be to turn to a calculation that's based—at least in part—on quantifiable, real life statistics.

Absorption Rates

One of the best ways to measure marketplace movement is by monitoring something known as the *absorption rate*. Absorption rates are calculations that estimate how long it will likely take for the marketplace to absorb (buy up) all of the inventory that's currently available. A low absorption rate indicates a fast moving, asset-driven (seller's) marketplace, while a high absorption rate identifies a slow moving value-driven (buyer's) market. As you check the absorption rates from time to time, you'll see trends developing; a falling rate indicates a coming asset-driven market, while a rising rate indicates an approaching value-driven market.

So, how do you perform absorption rate calculations? First, you will need access to MLS (Multiple Listing Service) data in your area. This will require the assistance of a licensed real estate agent, broker, or appraiser—unless you happen to be one yourself. While MLS data is not all-inclusive, it can provide sufficiently adequate statistics regarding real estate activity in your target area.

Once you've established MLS access, there are a couple of ways to calculate absorption rates. A common calculation is done by taking the number of properties that have sold in your target area within the previous 30 days, multiply it by 12 to get the annual sales, and then divide that number by 52 to get a weekly sales rate. Then, divide the total number of currently available listings by the weekly sales rate, and you'll have the estimated number of weeks it will take for all of the available properties to be absorbed (purchased) by the market.

For example, if there are 300 properties for sale in your target area right now, and the area had 42 closed sales over the last 30 days, the absorption rate would be 30.95 weeks, with the actual calculation looking like this:

42 sales/month $\times$ 12 months = 504 sales/year

504 sales/year $\div$ 52 weeks/year = 9.69 sales/week

300 properties $\div$ 9.69 sales/week = 30.95 weeks absorption rate

Some people calculate the absorption rate a different way; by taking the total number of sales in a particular target area over the previous 12 months, dividing it by 52 (to get the weekly average), and then dividing that into the total number of active listings. Although this might seem like a more accurate calculation (because it uses the *actual* number of sales in one year as opposed to *estimating* it, as we do in our 30 day calculation), the problem is that this method uses such a long look-back period, it doesn't expose the beginning of new market trends. And these forming trends are the critical first indicators of approaching market phases.

But, perhaps the most common mistake people make when calculating absorption rates is using a target area that's too large. For absorption rates to be accurate, you have to ignore broad statistics, such as the absorption rate of an entire city, and focus on smaller areas, like zip codes, neighborhoods, MLS zones, and subdivisions. Doing this frequently will expose the trends you're looking for.

BASIC MARKETING STRATEGIES

A wise investor once told me that creative deals are made, not found. This, I later discovered (after trying to reinvent the wheel for several years), is absolutely true. However, no matter how much you know, or how good you are at creating deals, if you spend all your time in front of the wrong people, you'll rarely do any business. And the deals you do create will be sucky ones that will inevitably come back to bite you in the butt. In other words, the most important part of marketing for creative deals is digging up the right prospects to put your proposals in front of, because it's the *people* who will make or break your deals—not the *properties*.

Motivating Factors for Creative Deals

Here are just a few circumstances that can turn ordinary people into extraordinary candidates for creative deals:

<u>Sellers</u>

* Divorce	* Layoff	* Death/ Probate
* Transfer	* Bankruptcy	* Can't afford payment
* Foreclosure	* Built new home	* Retiring and moving
* Poor health	* Failing business	* Too much maintenance
* Lawsuit	* Out-of-state owner	* No equity to pay Realtor

<u>Buyers</u>

* Credit issues	* Unreported Income	* Too little time on job
* High debt ratio	* Testing the area first	* Previous home not sold yet
* Short job history	* Prefers anonymity	* No confidence in economy

So now that we know what motivates people to buy and sell creatively, let's move on to the business of finding them.

Marketing for Prospects

Please understand that the following pages contain an obligatory list of basic marketing methods. I know they're not very sexy or edgy, and I realize you may have already seen or used most of them before, but as meat and potato methods, I'd have been remiss to exclude them. However, to make them more interesting, I've tried to infuse each method with at least one unique element or insight you might not find anywhere else. So don't just briefly skim over the next few pages, because you'll miss some really good stuff. Oh… and none of that sliding your finger rapidly down the center of the page crap. You and I both know you've never taken a speed reading class in your life.

A. The Internet

Without question, the Internet can play an extremely important role in your overall marketing strategy. But be aware; it should only be a *part* of your marketing strategy, not the whole enchilada. Because contrary to what you've probably been led to believe, not everyone you'll be marketing to is computer savvy (yeah, I know… it was a shock to me, too).

When you're looking for properties with motivated sellers, don't expect to find too many of them listed on personalized web pages or FSBO web sites. That would be a proactive move, and for the most part, you won't be working with people who have proactive tendencies. In fact, most sellers you'll be doing deals with have become highly motivated because of their complete lack of any genetic predisposition for properly "taking care of business"—get what I'm saying?

When they're online, most of your selling prospects are likely to be exhaustively entertaining themselves Facebooking, You-Tubing, or downloading various forms of porn rather than trying to sell their distressed property. But don't be discouraged. As sad and pathetic as that is, it's actually good news for you—because if everybody lived responsibly, nobody would need your help.

So how do you go about finding motivated prospects online? Primarily three ways: by searching online courthouse filings (looking for sellers), by having an optimized web presence (a website, blog, social network page, etc.), or by using free classified sites like Craigslist (which can sometimes be like a bowl of cereal*).

As far as online courthouse records go, if your county has a searchable database, this can be both good and bad for you. It's nice, because it allows you to search for motivated sellers without leaving your desk. But it's also challenging, in that everyone else can do it too, which will greatly increase your competition.

---

* Meaning even if you can get past all the fruits and nuts, you're still left with a bunch of flakes.

One of the most obvious places to search are foreclosure and NOD (Notice of Default) filings, whichever is standard in your area. However, this applies only to actual online courthouse filings, not to online subscription services which gather courthouse information and post them online several days later. By then, it's too late and you would be better off to go—or send someone—to the courthouse every single day. These are white hot leads which must be researched and contacted daily to stay ahead of your competition. Direct mail can be very effective, but your marketing piece (be it a letter or postcard) must be highly compelling, and your campaign itself, aggressive and consistent in order for your piece to have any chance of cutting through the postal deluge these homeowners will experience.

Another great place to search for potentially motivated sellers at the courthouse is in the probate filings. Probate procedures vary in each area, but essentially, once you've identified the fiduciary (the person who is responsible for administering or liquidating the estate), get them plugged into your preferred contact system and start hitting them right away with a direct mail campaign. Direct mail works well in this venue, because—as I've come to discover—letters, postcards, and flyers can sometimes have freakishly long shelf lives.

This is really important, because for various reasons, many people are not willing or able to sell the property when they are first named as fiduciary. Often, it can be several months or even a few years before they're ready or willing to do something with the property. There have been cases where people have contacted me seemingly out of the blue from letters they received two or three years earlier. Just try to make an impression in a phone call that's capable of lasting *that* long.

Another way to find both buying and selling prospects online is by having a web presence, as I mentioned earlier. But please understand that just having a well-designed web site or social network page is not enough. You have to make sure you've optimized them to get yourself high organic placement.

What does this mean? A couple of things, actually. First, it means whenever a potential customer enters certain key words or phrases into a search engine query box, a link to your site must appear on one of the first few pages of the results. Otherwise, it's unlikely your prospects will see your particular link among the hundreds of pages and countless thousands of other relevant links.

But that's not enough anymore. It's also important *where* your site appears on those first few results pages. If your site shows up on the left-hand (organic) side, most consumers will perceive that your site is highly relevant to their search, which adds the perception of greater credibility to your site. If, instead, your site appears on the right-hand side of the search results page as a sponsored (paid) link, most people understand that you've paid money for the search engine to put you there, and therefore your site comes off more as an advertisement. This means consumers will view your site, as well as your site's message, with greater skepticism—if they decide to view it at all (and these days, they often don't).

There are several ways to optimize your site for high organic placement, but in all honesty, I'm not the guy to teach it. The particulars of this subject go beyond my meager understanding of the process, and besides, search engine algorithms change so often that anything I did try to teach you about it would be antiquated within a matter of months. Web site optimization is probably a job best left to experts who can consistently stay one step ahead of the search engines.

Regardless of how your sites get optimized, one thing that doesn't change is that it's always a good idea to keep your web pages for buyers and sellers separate from one another. This allows you to maintain multiple identities within the same marketplace, so that you can simultaneously convey a unique message to both of your primary customers, each of whom have diametrically opposed needs to fill.

You can separate your messages two ways. The first is obviously by having two completely different sites, each with its own separate vanity URL (such as **www.ForgetBanks.com** for buyers and **www.FairPriceOffer.com** for sellers). If you happen to be a cheapskate who wants to save $15 per month, you can also do this by dividing just one site into two separate, unlinked halves, and then using two separate vanity URL's to forward visitors to the relevant pages on each half.

B. Running Newspaper Ads *(which will appear in both print and online editions)*

Another effective way to get your message out to the masses is through running newspaper ads. This includes not only the major newspapers in your area, but also your community weekly journals, which I've found to be far more cost-efficient and effective. Although these neighborhood papers might not have the giant circulation numbers that the majors do, they can offer you significant advantages that the big papers can't match. Now, I'm not knocking the major papers—they obviously work too. I just happen to prefer the local papers, for several reasons.

First of all, the community publications are smaller. Fewer ads and fewer pages means that your message will have much higher visibility than in the large papers. Another benefit is that the neighborhood papers tend to have a much longer shelf life. Major newspapers usually end up in the trash or at the bottom of the canary cage at the end of each day, while community papers are often kept around the house for a week or more—sometimes even surviving the arrival of the next issue. The reason for this is that local papers are filled with articles featuring neighborhood people (especially children), school activities, and local businesses. Articles about friends, family, and neighbors are far more interesting to most readers than national or world news, to which they often cannot closely relate.

When it comes to getting your message across in these local newspapers, there are actually three different basic strategies, all of which work quite well: classified ads (my least favorite), display ads (my most favorite), and feature columns (I'm kind of on the fence with this one).

Classified ads: These are the most obvious and commonly used newspaper advertising tools, which is why they are my least favorite. But I've used them successfully in the past, so I'll take a moment to cover them for you here.

In many cities, the various individual neighborhood papers have a common central classified ad department. This creates a city-wide network that allows you to target one or more specific neighborhoods with just one phone call.

The only downside to classified ads, in my opinion, is that you are invisibly buried smack in the middle of nothing but advertisements. And while that might sound like an oxymoronic concern, it makes sense once you come to realize (as I have) that many of your best targeted prospects—the ones who need you most— aren't usually making much of an effort to *find* a solution to their problem, due to that whole "failure to be proactive" thing we talked about earlier. And the ones who are smart enough to seek you out in the classifieds will also see ads from your competitors, and (in all likelihood) assume you're *all* full of bull—since many people believe most advertisements are full of misleading lies and half-truths.

As for the ads themselves, they should consist of nothing more than an attention-grabbing headline, followed by brief copy intended merely to generate a phone call or a visit to your web site. In real estate, marketing should always be a multi-step approach, because you're wasting your time if you expect to convince people to buy or sell property using nothing more than a classified ad. Be sure to keep things short and sweet. Classified ads that run on for two or three paragraphs are too cumbersome for people to bother reading—so they usually don't. Here are a few sample ads you could run to attract buyers and sellers for creative deals:

For Buyers: **NO BANKS NEEDED!**
Seller can help with financing.
Job + Downpayment = House!
www.ForgetBanks.com
Or call: (513) 555-7720

For Sellers: **SELL YOUR HOUSE FAST!**
Local company needs to buy
4 houses in the next 60 days.
Fair prices and fast closings.
www.FairPriceOffer.com
Or call: (513) 555-7720
- OR -
WANT TO JUST WALK AWAY?
We can buy your house "as is" and
close very fast! No equity is needed!
www.FairPriceOffer.com
Or call: (513) 555-7720

Display ads: Display ads are the types of ads you see in newspapers and magazines that are anywhere from business card size to full page spreads. Although they are much larger and more visible than classified ads, they are not necessarily more effective at generating business. Plus, their significantly higher price tag often makes them less cost-efficient than just a simple classified ad.

Surprisingly, no matter how big a display ad may be, the fact it's obviously an ad can actually help make it invisible. Why? Consumers are so inundated by marketing messages, they've begun to automatically tune out just about anything that *looks* like an advertisement—even when they should be taking notice.

The way to get around this is to make sure your display ads don't look like display ads. My favorite solution is to make mine look like newspaper articles instead; a technique which has recently found its way into the American lexicon as something called an *advertorial*.

To do this effectively, you must first do some basic research on the newspaper where you'll be inserting your ad. Using it as a guide, you can create your camera ready ad copy using the same font styles and sizes for the headline, sub-headline (if they use them) and body copy. You will also want to duplicate, to the best of your ability, the same layout formatting as their genuine articles.

But don't stop there. Since you've purchased the space, you're allowed to do anything in there you want (within legal, moral and ethical limits, of course), so you might as well take the opportunity to enhance the visibility of your advertorial by inserting a captioned photo. Believe it or not, even a mundane photograph can be *incredibly* effective at drawing a reader's eye straight to your advertorial.

There are at least three reasons to go the advertorial route. One is to keep people from instinctively ignoring your message, as they do with most graphic ads no matter how pretty or professional they look. The second is that you can easily tell people a whole lot more about what you do in an article than you can with a graphic ad. And the third is that most people are highly skeptical about everything they read in an advertisement, but are very likely to believe just about anything they read in an article. Once again, perception trumps reality.

Because of this automatic gullibility factor, many publishers will put your advertorial inside of a box to separate it from genuine articles. They may also place the word ADVERTISEMENT above your article as well. But just like an attorney who intentionally presents evidence to a jury that they weren't supposed to hear, once you see something, you can't *un*-see it. In other words, once people are drawn towards your article by its legitimate first appearance, they will still be more likely to read it and believe what it says, even though they've been informed that it's actually an ad. That's because consumers have a strong worldview about the authenticity of articles that is not easily overcome by simply seeing the word ADVERTISEMENT splayed above the copy.

Below is a very brief and entirely fictitious example of what it might look like if someone were to create an advertorial that seeks potential term buyers. Notice the use of an interesting photo, as well as the presentation of the consumer benefits in an authentic editorial style—as opposed to a blatant, hard sell ad.

Remember—it's one thing to toot your own horn, but when someone else appears to be tooting it for you, it carries far more organic credibility. Notice also how little the ADVERTISEMENT disclaimer seems to diminish the advertorial's interest level or believability.

ADVERTISEMENT

Local company extends a "second chance" of home ownership to grateful citizens of hard-hit Stamford suburbs

By Dawn Michaels
Senior staff writer

Shortly after losing his I.T. position at Dunder-Mifflin Paper last year, Jake Smith and his wife, Laura, received a foreclosure notice from their bank, and were forced to leave their two-story Stamford home.

"That was supposed to be our dream home, the one we were going to live in until we retired—or so we thought," said Jake. "Instead, we had to leave it after only three years."

Even though Jake found another job just six months later, it was too late to save their house. And though they avoided foreclosure, Jake claims, "The whole ordeal bruised our credit and our confidence pretty badly."

"We were devastated and assumed that it would be 8 to 10 years before we could buy another house—if ever," added his wife, Laura.

So when they found out that a local company was selling beautiful homes with financing that didn't require banks, they saw an opportunity that sounded too good to be true. But it was true.

"We have special low interest financing programs that people just like the Smith's can qualify for with nothing more than a job and a reasonable downpayment," said Steve Meyers, president and co-founder of Forget Banks.com, LLC.

Jake and Laura Smith outside their new West Chester home.

"And since no banks are involved there are no lengthy approval processes or closing costs," Meyers said.

"What really surprised me," said Laura Smith, "were all of the choices we had. Every home we looked at was beautiful, and Steve actually offered us up to three different ways to buy whichever home we wanted. It was like an unexpected answer to all of our prayers, and we couldn't be happier."

For details on how you can buy a home today without a bank, call **(203) 555-7720** or go online to: **www.ForgetBanks.com**.

Feature Columns: As a real estate expert in your community, you can try approaching the publisher of your local newspaper about writing a weekly column on the real estate industry in your area. But be aware that writing feature columns can be a double-edged sword. On the one hand, it can provide you with lots of credibility and visibility within your community. On the other, it can make you an easy target for high-profile complaints and lawsuits.

Don't misunderstand, it's not like you're going to be doing unscrupulous or immoral things—unless you *are* unscrupulous and immoral. But the harsh reality is that you'll be dealing every day with people who are motivated and vulnerable, usually due to their own irresponsible lifestyle prior to meeting you. And no matter how hard you might try to do the right thing, they will often continue to screw up their lives and look for someone else to blame. When that happens, you'll have a bulls-eye on your head larger than your neighborhood Target store, and they'll have a free forum in which to publicly execute you: "Your columnist sold me a house and is foreclosing on my family" *or* "I followed the advice in your column, and now I'm broke, divorced, and suicidal", etc.

Frankly, celebrity sucks—which is why I prefer to operate under the radar as much as possible. You don't have to do anything wrong to get sued anymore; just unlucky enough to be in someone's crosshairs while they're feeling über-bitchy.

C. Calling Newspaper Ads

This is my *least* favorite way to look for properties. Why? Well, to begin with, the weekly local and major daily papers only contain ads for a *fraction* of the properties that are available at any given moment. Even the much larger Sunday edition won't feature ads from many of your best motivated seller candidates; like people who've already moved out of the area, financially challenged individuals who can't afford an ad, or lazy deadbeats who aren't proactive enough to run one.

That means most of the people you really want to reach aren't even *in* the paper! This point aside, there certainly *are* some deals to be found in the newspapers, so don't just blow this source off completely. But let's look at where you should focus your efforts, and how you can pre-qualify sellers before you even call them.

First, where should you be looking? Obviously, you should at least peruse the "Homes for Sale" section. Under this heading, you need to quickly weed out all the ads placed by Realtors. This should take about six seconds, because they are generally the lengthy and boring ads with fancy borders, and, due to regulations in most areas, contain a disclosure that the ad was placed by a licensed agent.

Once you've eliminated the agent ads, you need to isolate the ads placed by property owners which show some sign of motivation. Examples of this include ads which contain phrases like: *"Owner relocating and must sell ASAP"*, *"Owner very anxious"*, *"Bring any offer"*, *"May consider owner financing"*, *"Immediate occupancy"*, or *any* ad—regardless of the copy—which contains an out-of-town phone number. Once you've identified all of these potential hot ads, call them. And be sure to develop a follow-up system to contact these same people in another three weeks or so, because their motivations can, and very often do, change.

After you're finished in the "Homes for Sale" section, it's time to head for the "Homes for Rent" section. Why? Because when an individual is unsuccessful at selling their home, often they will resort to renting it out because they need the debt relief. When you see an out-of-town phone number in this section, your knees should get weak. Call all of the ads in this section, except for the ones placed by professional rental companies, investors with several houses, and rentals advertising leases of 12 months or less.

Then where do you go? In some areas, newspapers will even have a section for properties being offered as "Lease Options". At first glance, you may think that this would be a great section to look for deals. The truth is, however, that most of the people in this section are investors who are either offering sandwich lease-option properties with high downpayments, or using the lease-option approach to get higher rents and deposits on their rental units. Still, don't automatically assume there are no deals in this section. Look at every ad before moving on.

Now that you know the *where*, let's talk about the *how*. How do you call all of these people? Well, actually, maybe *you* shouldn't, but you need to make sure that *somebody* does. You can get a friend or relative to do it, which I highly do not recommend. Instead, you should more seriously consider hiring someone part-time and making it their job. That way it will get done, and if it doesn't, you can fire them without forever ruining Thanksgiving and Christmas.

You can provide your "prospect engineer" with a simple call flow sheet to follow, and then pay them either a flat hourly rate, or—even better—pay them a couple bucks for every call sheet they submit. These call sheets would provide you with information as to if or why the seller is or isn't interested at this time. You can then follow-up personally right away, or time-activate a future follow-up. I highly suggest that you also incorporate a *generous* bonus into whatever pay scale you create to keep your call person motivated, i.e., paying them an extra $50 or $100 every time you buy a property. Don't be stingy with this! Being tight sometimes costs you a whole lot more than it can save you!

D. Realtors

I strongly advise that you cozy up to a good Realtor (not *literally*—although even as I say that, I'm actually sleeping with a hot one), but not just to find actively listed properties. In fact, about the only time you'll be looking through actively listed properties is when you're searching for potential wholesale deals, which represents only a portion of what you'll be doing as an investor overall. More often than not, you'll be utilizing your Realtor as a resource for helping you establish property values through comparable sales, and sifting through printouts of expired listings in search of potential term deal candidates.

So, why not have them looking through actively listed properties for potential term deal candidates as well? Well, that strategy doesn't usually work well very often, because when you're buying on terms, you'll generally be offering very little or no up-front money. And since the listing Realtor will probably want to get paid, this could be problematic. It's pretty hard to get a Realtor to accept a two to five year deferment of their commission while they wait for you to cash out—and even harder to find a term deal that will be so profitable you'd be willing to put enough money down to enable the seller to pay their Realtor today.

When utilizing printouts of expired listings, there are a couple of things to keep in mind that will help you get the most out of this incredible resource. The first is that you'll want to establish a set of parameters for your Realtor to stay within. Pick a targeted price range, a few ideal areas or zip codes, and work them with a consistent campaign. This is one place where you don't want to dilute your time, efforts or marketing budget by chasing every possible lead, just because they're so easy to find.

The second key is to set a regular schedule for pulling these expired listings frequently. This may be far less time-efficient than sitting down to do it once or twice a month, but in this case, efficiency takes a back seat to effectiveness. A list like this is obviously going to change daily, and if you space your searches too far apart, you'll effectively be giving your competition a two to four week head start on the good prospects that expired right after you ran your last monthly or bi-weekly list. When it comes to mining expired listings, time is of the essence.

So… what would you do with all of this valuable expired listing information? You would use it to create a database for launching a relentless letter and postcard assault (check out the *Direct Mail* section for some great tips on this). After all, it's your job to put your "value" in front of as many highly motivated sellers as possible—and doesn't it stand to reason that a database full of recently expired MLS listings could contain just a few people who might be extremely anxious to sell their properties? Absolutely.

You may be wondering approximately how many expired listings you might expect to find each time you pull a list, and whether or not there will be many leads to process. Well, this will certainly vary quite a bit, depending on your market and specific target parameters. But I can tell you this, the last time I had my agent run my list (in Cincinnati), there were about 200 expired listings in just a one month period—and that was just in my targeted price range and preferred areas! That represents about 2,400 prospects per *year* to process!

Now, another reason you'll want to establish a good working relationship with a respected Realtor is for referrals. Realtors are a great source for referrals, because they often run into sellers who have some issues they aren't really sure how to handle. When that happens, the professional relationship you've established with your Realtor will not only position you to receive a referral, but it can also help lend you instant credibility with the potential seller, which will make your job of closing the deal that much easier.

E. PR Pack/ Special Report

If you've ever heard your favorite guru talk about "credibility kits" you can thank me, because I'm the one who introduced the concept to our industry in the late 1980's. Back then I called mine a PR Pack, but when I shared it with one of the real estate educational titans in the early 1990's he rebranded the concept and ran with it… while forgetting to give me any credit, btw. Since then, I've reformatted mine into a *Special Report* to give it a broader appeal and make it easier to mail.

What are PR packs and special reports? They're simply packets, folders, or booklets of information designed to showcase the benefits of the products or services you offer, as well as some testimonials to enhance your appeal. These are among the most powerful marketing tools in existence, because if they're done right, they can instantly remove three of the four obstacles that are theoretically keeping you from doing business with everyone on the planet (see page 56).

What makes them so effective? They provide a cost-efficient and proven format for building an emotional desire for your offerings within the minds of your prospective consumers, while simultaneously removing any doubts they might have as to your abilities or professionalism. You see, two of the biggest concerns your potential customers will have upon meeting you are: 1) whether or not they *want* what you're proposing, or 2) whether or not they can *afford* what you're proposing; and both of these concerns can be extremely difficult to overcome if your prospects don't know exactly what it *is* that you're proposing.

A PR pack or special report lets you take your time to educate your consumers on the facts and benefits of your buying and selling methods with left-brain content, while entertaining their right-brain emotional side with images and artistic page layouts. Of course, no good PR pack or special report is complete without testimonials. In fact, a good publication leads with several of them right up front.

But the credibility enhancement power of PR packs and special reports goes beyond just the positive influence created through the right combination of information, entertainment and third-party endorsements. There is also the general marketplace perception that these are the kinds of advanced promotional materials that only successful companies are resourced and capable enough to design and utilize, as well-produced PR packs and special reports (and by that, I don't mean poorly photocopied pages haphazardly stapled into "reports" or stuffed into cheap Office-Max folders) are not typically associated with amateurs, wannabees, or fly-by-nighters. Even more, is that these marketing elements can help brand and separate you by raising the appearance of your professionalism far above everyone else in your marketplace. After all, how many of your competitors even *have* professionally-designed promotional materials to distribute in the first place, let alone are successfully putting them into the hands of consumers?

F. Direct Mail

Another very effective way to get your message out is through direct mail campaigns using postcards and letters. One thing I've found to be very effective is bumping postcards up to oversized proportions. It's great to put something in a potential seller's mailbox that stands out far and above everything else.

Oversized cards have enough space for you to give lots of details in large type font, yet they cost the same to mail—and less to produce—than letters. Best of all, postcards don't have to get opened, which means you can use printed labels to address them quickly and easily. Just try getting 100% of your letters opened when they're addressed with labels. It won't happen. People can spot junk mail with labels from across the Grand Canyon—and clinical tests have shown that they can pitch them in the garbage so fast that they don't leave enough forensic evidence on the envelope to prove they ever even touched it.

One of the most effective uses I've found so far for postcards is in direct mail campaigns sent to expired listings. The first step is to enter the addresses of all the expired listings you get from your Realtor each week into a database, and then merge the database into new label document file, using the mail merge function of your word processor. It's a good idea to create a new database with each new set of expired listings to keep each database manageable for editing (I use the date as the database file name).

Now, I realize that you may have already tried something like this and had results that were not exactly stellar. But this is where you get to learn something new. Most people will print that label file directly onto a set of labels, and then send just one postcard to each prospective address, hoping that the property owner will call. That's just not enough. You need to hit them repeatedly, and in a regular, predictable pattern at least five times.

Here's an easy way to do that: Go ahead and print your new label file onto labels, but also print another copy of that label file onto plain white paper. Then add a cover sheet which shows the dates of at least 4 more mailings for that list, beginning in 7 days, with additional mailings scheduled for every 7 days thereafter until all 4 mailings are checked off.

There are two reasons to print the list on white paper; one is to save money, the other is to save time. You see, my assistant creates the label file with the word "Homeowner" on the top line, followed by the database file name, which is usually the date (e.g., 03.31.10), in very small letters. This way, it's easy to figure out which database the card came from. Then, when the postcards come back because the property was vacant, or there was no mail receptacle, or it was a bad address, etc., we can go to our plain paper copy of the list and just cross that address off. This keeps us from resending postcards to the same dud addresses four more times, but not so much because we're concerned with wasting another 50¢ or 60¢ each on postage and fulfillment (which *can* actually add up over the course of a year, by the way). More importantly, crossing out the bad addresses saves us a great deal of time by keeping us from researching the same property more than once, as you'll see in a moment. Then, when it's time for the next mailing, we simply use our copier to reproduce the cleaned list onto new labels.

Sometimes postcards come back because the seller has already moved, and the post office cannot forward cards that are addressed to "Homeowner". When this happens, you might be tempted to count up all the returned postcards to see how much money you wasted: "Let's see... 25 cards came back today at 60¢ each.... hmm... I just threw away $15 bucks!" But actually, you're holding a gold mine of potential deals worth *way* more than $15, because you now have the addresses of 25 vacant properties that are in the exact price range and areas you want, with MLS listings that have recently expired. Could you *get* a hotter list? Say no.

Your next step would be to research public records for the names and tax mailing addresses of the owners of these vacant properties. In most cases, the tax mailing address will be the same as the vacant property, but don't worry, because now that you have the owner's name, the post office can forward your correspondence to them wherever they've moved.

The next step is to put those names and addresses into a new "vacant property" database, and then merge it onto labels and a sheet of white paper (just like before) with a cover page for three more mailings. Then, use this new database to send a personalized form letter, mailed in a *hand-addressed*, physically-stamped envelope—that means no labels or postage meters. Follow this with a multiple mailing postcard campaign like the one you did to "Homeowner", and hit them again and again at least every 7 to 10 days.

When it comes to designing your letter, it's a good idea to put your photo on it. This helps people to feel more as though they're dealing with a real person, rather than just the ambiguous, disembodied voice they'll hear in their heads while reading your letter. Of course, this is not true for everyone. For instance, if you look like this:

...then you might be better off just letting your prospects stick with the ambiguous, disembodied voice in their heads. You might also want to consider putting Dr. Dorfman and his *Extreme Makeover* staff on retainer...and speed dial...like, *today*.

G. Radio

Radio advertising is no longer a marketing strategy that's reserved for just the "big boys" anymore. In fact, most people are unaware of just how relatively inexpensive and cost-effective a good radio campaign can actually be for a small business like yours. That's because beyond delivering your message repeatedly to literally hundreds or even thousands of people on a consistent basis, radio also projects a couple of misperceived notions that can work to your advantage.

First of all, your competition is likely to be among those who mistakenly believe that radio advertising is universally cost-prohibitive. This is good, because it'll scare them away from radio faster than the musical stylings of Lady Gaga. And if your rivals aren't busy clogging the airwaves with their own commercials, the lack of any competing "noise" will make your message that much more unique and noticeable.

A second advantage to radio's cost misperception is that it can create the illusion among your targeted prospects that your company is much larger than it really is. This can score you a lot of credibility points, as I discovered first-hand one day when a man signed over his beautiful property just because he'd heard my ad on the radio. Turns out it was a done deal before I had even gotten to his house, because (he assumed) if I wasn't an expert, how could I have afforded such an extravagant form of advertising? This credibility enhancement is even more pronounced in Christian radio, where listeners can develop a blindingly fierce loyalty to advertisers who provide financial support for their favorite religious programs—especially if they perceive that it is a faith-based organization.

Of course, if you're thinking of launching a radio campaign, you need to be aware that if you just start carelessly throwing money at it, it can become an extraordinarily costly proposition. Plus, there are no guarantees it will ever be successful, no matter how much you spend. A bigger budget doesn't necessarily equal bigger returns. With radio, prudence and deck-stacking are key elements.

One of my favorite strategies for improving the odds of success is to exploit some of the hidden advantages that only talk stations and Christian radio can offer. What is it about these formats that can make them a more efficient platform for advertisers? There are several reasons, but chief among them is this: people who are tuned in to these stations are usually *listening* to what's being said, rather than regarding the broadcast as ambiance. This is called *active listening*.

You see, for most music station listeners, the programming is often little more than just background noise. These consumers listen to music so passively that they sometimes barely even register that it's there. And the only thing they tend to notice less than the music are the commercials; because as soon as the music stops and talking begins, they're instinctively programmed to either ignore whatever's coming out of the speakers, or begin channel surfing to find another station that's playing music which is equally suitable for barely listening to.

Another benefit to most talk and Christian radio stations is that they tend to feature a lot of local programming, which is more appealing on a human level. Some of the larger broadcast companies, by contrast, have moved away from operating their network of music stations individually. Rather than having each station staffed by local personalities, they've adopted a "satellite" approach of simultaneously broadcasting the exact same music program to all of their stations from a single studio (located God knows where), which can give these stations an empty, vacuous feel. Of course, talk and Christian radio stations also carry many nationally-syndicated programs as well, but they almost always feature plenty of local experts, which can help these stations maintain a more neighborly feel.

Ironically, even though listeners of music stations are more likely to tune out commercials, these types of stations generally have much higher advertising rates. The reason is because they can usually produce quantifiably higher Arbitron ratings, which isn't really all that impressive when you consider that these ratings measure only the *quantity* of listenership, without respect to the *quality* of listeners. And after all, it's the *quality* of the listenership that counts, right? I mean, what good does it do someone to spend truckloads of money putting messages in front of a whole bunch of targeted listeners if these people aren't even actually *listening*? Is that where you want your message? Nah...me, neither.

Now, having said that, I'm not suggesting that you should completely ignore ratings. Quite the contrary, in fact. I've found that the #1 stations in the talk, sports, and Christian formats can often generate a pretty good share of listenership among certain ideal demographics, like homeowners, which explains why their advertising rates can sometimes exceed those of some music stations. So my strategy has generally been to look at the market ratings data for my preferred genre, and then shoot for advertising on the #2 station in the marketplace.

The reason I like the #2 stations is because they can get my message in front of a pretty good chunk of listeners for a lot less money than a #1 station, because like everyone else in the media business, their advertising prices are driven purely by ratings. But even though a #2 station might quote you a significantly lower price per spot, your overall campaign costs can still get out of hand very quickly, which is why I always negotiate to run my ads on remnant space.

Remnant space is the term to describe any commercial airtime or physical space that is unsold. Beyond radio, this would also include television ads, all forms of print media ads (newspapers, magazines, etc.), and even things like retail mall space.

In radio, every programmed commercial slot that passes without a paid advertisement is a revenue opportunity that's been lost forever—because once it's gone, it's gone. So in order to at least partially monetize an otherwise dead commodity, nearly every radio station will offer to insert your advertisement into available remnant spaces at deeply discounted spot rates. This allows for you to get your ad on the air at spot prices that are well below market. But the trade off is that you can't choose when your ads run—which can actually be a devastating concession, because theoretically you could end up having your ad run sixteen times in a row beginning at 2:40 a.m. with no spots at all showing up during daylight hours. This might not be a bad thing if you were, say, marketing a hot single's chat line. But since we're buying and selling real estate, we need our message to reach a more targeted, qualified, and *awake* group of prospects.

That's why if you're going to create an ad campaign that utilizes a run of remnant space ads, it's a good idea to negotiate for those ads to run only during unsold slots that fall within certain limited time parameters, such as between 5:00 a.m. and 10:00 p.m. These are sometimes called *rotator runs*, although the stations in your area may have a different term for this. If you happen to want a little more control over when your ads run, but still don't want to pay card rates (the station's full published price for advertisements), some stations will even offer to let you run your remnant space ads within an even narrower, more desirable time frame, such as between 6:00 a.m. and 7:00 p.m. (sometimes called a *prime rotator*), in exchange for a slightly higher per-spot rate.

As if utilizing remnant space to enhance the value of your radio marketing wasn't good enough already, you can make it even better by leveraging the natural retail gaps that exist between seasonal changeovers and major holidays. Scheduling your ads to run when retailers aren't fighting over each other for airtime would not only mean less clutter for you to cut through, but the smaller demand for radio advertising will further drive down the price of remnant runs.

But don't stop there. After you've negotiated your best deal on an ad campaign, tell your station sales rep that you're still going to need them to toss in some overnight spots for free. When you ask for this, your negotiating posture will suggest that you're fully expecting them to toss in a bunch of virtually worthless spots that they already assume nobody else is going to buy anyway (except maybe a few chat line owners). Your true aim, however, is to maximize every dime you're spending by getting as much exposure for your campaign as possible—especially since there are always some highly motivated people in every market who are saddled with insomnia over the fact they can't sell their properties.

Example: A few years back, there was a high-profile local talk station in my area that was charging $250 to $400 per one-minute spot during drive-time, but I negotiated a one week Monday-Friday prime rotator (between 6 a.m. and 7 p.m.) of 20 spots for only $1,350, which is equal to just $68 per spot. In addition to that discount, I also got them to "bonus" another 5 overnight spots *per night*, which meant 25 additional spots for that week. Even better, by committing to run a second week's worth of ads, I got them to throw in a third full week's worth of ads for free. They also let me divide my runs into a *"one week on, next week off"* schedule. That means for a total investment of only $2,700 I got my message delivered 135 times with excellent frequency over a five week period at an effective cost of only $20 per spot! And in case you were wondering, during that campaign I ended up getting dozens of highly-coveted morning and afternoon drive-time airplays—as well as a few spots during the most highly-rated syndicated talk show on radio, the Rush Limbaugh program.

What did I do with all those radio spots? I ran a two-step campaign that drove listeners to order a special free Special Report on how I could buy their properties quickly for a fair price. Every week this campaign ran, my average response was between 70 to 100 valid, unique requests per week for reports. From just one of those weeks, I ended up putting together four deals that netted about $60,000 in total profits over the subsequent year and a half.

Think things couldn't have gotten any better? Think again, because the radio station didn't bill out the ads until nearly two months after the spots ran. And since they also billed on a net 30, this gave me yet another month before I had to pay the invoice—which I did using just the downpayment I'd received from one of the properties I'd already resold. In case you don't get the full magnitude of this, it means I not only managed to get four no money down deals from a single radio ad campaign, but I also got the radio ad campaign *itself* for no money down too! Nothing down radio advertising... sounds like the subject of a new course!

Now, I'm sure you've noticed that many new radio-style options have come along recently which can offer consumers a lot of ad-free listening; alternatives such as XM Radio, cable audio channels, and online streaming radio for computers and cell phones. Because of all these new consumer choices, standard over-the-air radio advertising has got to be an even better bargain now than it was back when I ran my last campaign a few years ago. So don't forget to check into radio advertising as a marketing strategy, and don't be afraid to play some hardball when you negotiate. After all, they need you right now far more than you need them.

H. Public Access Television

Cable TV can offer some interesting opportunities to market yourself in ways that can help you quickly separate yourself from the competition. The cost can be anywhere from absolutely free (including production) to insanely expensive, but what's really ironic is that the free alternative can actually be the most effective.

Free cable public access television is one of the most underutilized marketing strategies available. In most areas it will cost you nothing at all to have a program professionally produced and then aired repeatedly for several weeks. The only downside is that you usually cannot mention your costs, fees, or pricing structure, nor are you permitted to promote your product or service in a commercial fashion.

That's okay, because this strategy isn't a hardcore direct sale approach. It's rather more like business foreplay; a deliberately subtle and indirect way of getting what you want... and by that I mean *customers*, not sex—unless you're a guy, in which case that's probably the only thing you ever *really* want.

Public access is a terrific platform that allows you to generously, and cost-effectively (it's free after all), share your expertise with the community. Over time, your consistent visibility—coupled with your apparently unselfish motives to help others—will give rise to somewhat of a minor celebrity status for you. This can easily lead to some tremendous business opportunities (as well as some creepy stares in the produce aisle) that you wouldn't have gotten otherwise. And although celebrity has a potentially nasty dual nature, as I alluded to earlier in the section on newspaper ads (how *ever* does Johnny Depp do it?), anyone who wants to directly challenge your opinion on television will have to work a lot longer and harder to do it, thanks to some of the natural hindrance aspects of this particular format. This can reduce the risk or likelihood of some kook or past unhappy customer waking up one day and deciding on a whim to wage a smear campaign against you.

Given all the benefits of public access television, it blows my mind that such an awesome resource like this can exist—free of charge—and yet so few people will ever take advantage of it; the obvious exceptions being city council members, little league coaches, and every kitchen table evangelist within a hundred miles.

Now don't get me wrong. I love God. I really do. And as a Christian, I absolutely love that these home-grown evangelists feel a burning desire to spread the Gospel. But let's face it, not since the Ninth Crusade of 1272 has the world seen anything with the potential to set Christianity back so far and so fast as some of these TV programs. The problem, you see, isn't so much with their knowledge of scripture. It's really more often about their... well... *delivery* of it.

Look, I'm sure these sincere souls have forgotten more about the Bible than I'll ever know. It's just that some of them tend to forget it *while* they happen to be preaching it. But that's not all. Production failures and mechanical mishaps can sometimes turn these well-meaning shows into perfect storms of unintentional comedy—or worse—epic disasters on par with Amtrak derailments or 15-car interstate pile-ups. Gruesome and horrifying, yet strangely... *mesmerizing*. And as loathe as I am to admit it, there are moments when no one is around that I actually find myself channel surfing to score another quick fix of it (is that bad?).

Perhaps this is exactly what concerns you. Maybe your fear of becoming someone's secret guilty pleasure has kept you from even considering this resource as a viable marketing option. But it doesn't have to be that way, because if you prepare yourself adequately, study your dialogue, and opt for the recorded show format (so that you can edit as needed, versus a live show where anything can—and usually *will*—go wrong), you can end up coming away looking like a true professional. And a fully coherent one at that.

Free public access is not the only form of advertising available on cable. One cost-effective paid method is to run crawler ads along the bottom of your local weather channel, if that's still available in your area (it's not in mine anymore). This can be effective because watchers of this channel are captive and actively reading what's on the screen. It's also one of the very few stations on the 200+ cable lineup that you can reasonably expect many targeted households to click onto at least once every day—or several times per day during episodes of bad weather.

Another marketing alternative is to run fully-produced TV commercials, but that can get expensive and may not yield proportionately better results. First of all, good commercial production isn't cheap, and neither are the best spots to run them. Sure, you can get an ad rep to throw in some bonus remnant spots for you, just like with radio ads. But with 24 hours in each day, and 200+ stations on each tuner, a few random extra airings won't get you much notice. Besides, TV viewers don't want to see your commercials (or *anyone's* commercials for that matter), and they're fully armed with the technology to avoid them; from remotes which can mute and change channels, to DVR's which can fast-forward right through them.

I. Business Cards/ Flyers

Your business cards and flyers should be designed as mini-billboards. They need to quickly state what you can do for potential buyers and sellers. The best way to accomplish this is to create a good headline for each type of prospect (yes, that means as a multiple-personality real estate marketer, you'll need two different business cards), followed by a concise and convincing argument for your services. In other words, put your sales pitch right there on your business cards and flyers.

Whatever you do, don't try to save money by creating some kind of generic one-type-fits-all-customers-and-occasions type of business card or flyer. You know the kind I mean—it says something useless and insanely simple like:

Joe Smith, Investor
(513) 555-7720

What good is that? It doesn't tell people *anything*, and it certainly doesn't give anyone a reason to call you—unless they have OCD and simply cannot rest until they know exactly *what* you invest in, or they're a festering psychopath looking for a random target to stalk. Good luck with either one of those, by the way.

As for fancy logos, cool artwork, or brightly colored paper, don't waste your time on them. All you need is a good message. So when you sit down to design a business card or flyer, downplay who you are, and focus mainly on what you can do for people. Also, be sure to give interested prospects as many ways as possible to reach you, including a local direct number, a toll-free number, a fax line, an email address, and a web site if you have one (if not... *get* one).

J. Drive Prospective Neighborhoods

There's no reason at all why you can't get yourself out into the field every so often and visit some of the neighborhoods in your area that appeal to you. In doing so, keep your eyes peeled for properties which appear to be vacant or distressed. Properties that are empty, in obvious states of disrepair, or which are showing signs of significant neglect might be indications that the owner is in trouble financially, which means they may be open to the idea of selling.

Another possibility is that the owner may simply be too old or frail to maintain their property. If you come across an owner like this who just can't keep up, and you find that they're not ready to sell their property yet, then I have another suggestion for you; but brace yourself, because it's way out there. What if, perhaps, you stopped looking at every property as a potential opportunity for helping yourself, and every so often view one as a really good opportunity to help someone else instead? Why? Well, in case you don't know it yet, stepping up to help someone when you have no hidden agenda and absolutely nothing to gain is not only a good thing to do, it's also rewarding beyond words. Try it sometime.

PARTING THOUGHTS ON MARKETING

Repetition works: When it comes to marketing, little can compare to regularly-spaced repetition. Potential customers in every industry have ever-changing life circumstances, which will lead to needs and motivations that are highly fluid in nature. Therefore, a message which might not be of much interest to them today might suddenly seem extraordinarily compelling to them just a few weeks later. This is especially true in real estate, and doubly true when it comes to real estate *sellers* So if you've already paid to get a seller into your pre-qualified database of prospects, keep working that seller until one or more of the following occurs:

  a) They sell their property;

  b) You buy their property; or

  c) One of you dies… preferably not you.

Multi-pronged attacks work: Utilizing several different marketing methods simultaneously can work on two levels. For one, it obviously gives you more exposure, and hence a better likelihood of connecting with someone at just the right moment they need to hear your message. And two—less obviously—when consumers see your message in multiple locations, they will sometimes attribute this to something beyond random chance or coincidence; often going so far as to interpret it as some kind of sign from above, or from fate…or karma…or even Shirley MacLaine—depending on whatever form of paranormal or supernatural communication they happen to be subscribing to at the moment.

So don't fight it, embrace it. Use the force, as it were. Because when people encounter your message unexpectedly, especially if it's the second or third time they've heard or seen it, they'll often feel as though there's a greater force at work compelling them to at least call you to see if there's something to the apparent coincidence. I know this because some of my past customers have told me so.

The illusion of destiny is an extremely powerful motivator. It is so influential, in fact, that it can actually drive a potential customer into developing an emotional commitment to make a deal happen with you, when they might have otherwise had only a passing interest in your offering. That means if you can manage to create a marketing crusade that projects just a fraction of the serendipity found in, say, a typical Nora Ephron screenplay, you'd be able to live the rest of your days like a rock star doing whatever you want; from sunning yourself on a private Hawaiian beach, to astral planing with Ms. MacLaine on the forest moon of Endor.*

The only downside in attempting to engage serendipity as a marketing catalyst is that it has a highly subjective and organic nature that can be very difficult to create synthetically on demand. However, the more marketing strategies you employ simultaneously, the better your odds of stumbling onto just the right combination of messages to create the *appearance* of serendipity to your prospects; which in turn would be, ironically, a wonderfully serendipitous discovery for *you*.

Advantage goes to the initial contactee: The negotiation advantage usually goes to the party who is the *recipient* of the first communication. There are two subtle, but very real reasons for this. First, it's generally presumed that the person who initiates contact is the one who is more motivated to consummate the deal. And second, the person who makes the first contact bears an unspoken burden— regardless of how slight—of defending their reason for opening the dialogue.

Therefore, your best prospects for good deals will usually be the people who were motivated enough to make the first move and contact you. Ironically, this also includes respondents to your direct mail campaigns, even though your direct mail piece technically represents the first official communication between you.

How is that possible? Well, even though your postcard or letter creates the *illusion* of being a first contact, the reality is that it was just a cleverly-disguised blanket inducement for any one of your prospects to request some additional information; which, in doing so, would make *them* the actual initiator of the dialogue. The perception that your letter or postcard opened the discussion first is somewhat disarming, and can help encourage a response. But it's not until one of them feels motivated enough to literally pick up the phone and call you that the *true* initial contactee is established; and that will be you—not them. This gives you the advantage of being in the driver's seat, even before the negotiations begin.

---

* By the way, if you happen to know *what* and *where* the forest moon of Endor is without having to look it up on Google, you might want to keep that to yourself—because it means you're probably a flaming geek.

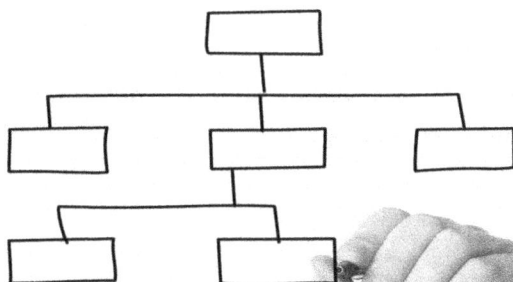

systemization is
a four-letter word

kay... so it's got 13 letters. It's *still* a dirty word. That's because most people would rather be waterboarded at Gitmo for two weeks, than be forced to sit through just one brief talk on systemization. Look, the process of systemizing is a real drag, I get it. But *having* a systemized business? *That's* a beautiful thing.

So before you go running for the hills screaming in horror over the mere mention of that unholiest of words, please take a moment to first consider the following two highly relevant and inescapable facts:

Fact #1: Ferris Bueller did it. Even as the 1980's foremost icon of laziness and frivolity, Ferris managed to successfully systemize a highly elaborate ruse that incorporated two friends, three answering machines, and a couple of audiotape loops. Of course, this didn't get him any good deals on real estate, but it did allow him to realize his near-impossible goal of ditching school for the ninth time in one semester without getting busted by his arch nemesis, Principal Ed Rooney.

Now, am I suggesting that if you systemize your business you'll get to spend a sunny day driving a California Spyder around Chicago while taking in a Cub's game, perusing an art gallery, visiting the Sears Tower Skydeck, hijacking a parade float, and eating pancreas at Chez Quis? No. But it sure does improve your odds of being able to do all of that if you *wanted* to (except the Chez Quis part, since it doesn't actually exist). That's because unless you systemize your business, you'll probably never have enough time or money to slip away anytime you want just to spend a day playing hooky as though you were a carefree 18 year-old kid again.

And yeah, I know Ferris was just a juvenile figment of the late writer/director John Hughes' imagination, but it's not *what* he gets away with in the movie that matters, since most of the plot requires too great a suspension of disbelief (that's Hollywood for you). The lesson is in *why* he got away with it, and it's as simple as this: Ferris first took the time to design the system that would help him accomplish his goal (however deviant), before he ever stepped out his front door to go hustle his unwitting buddy, Cameron. So if Ferris Bueller can do it, you can too.

Fact #2: You're already systemized. Another sobering fact you've probably never considered before is if you have a business, you're *already* systemized. The only question is whether a depiction of your system looks like a well-oiled machine:

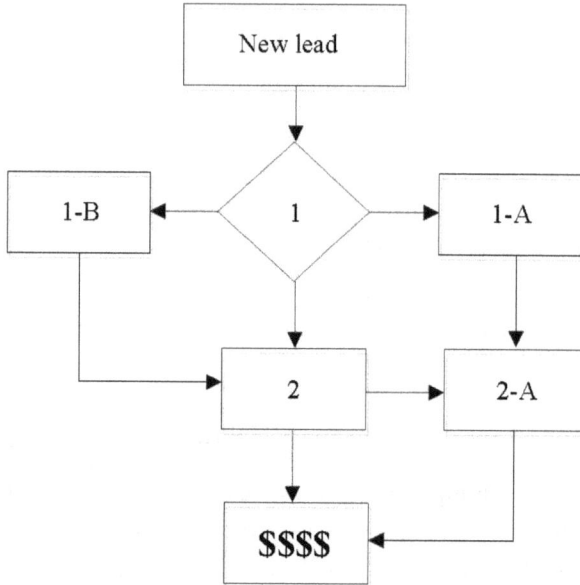

... or a CSI crime scene:

Scary... yeah, I know. Now that I have your attention, I must confess that although I'll be using this chapter to share with you some reasons *why* you need to systemize your business, and some basics on *how* you can do it, unfortunately I won't be able to tell you exactly *what* your particular system will look like. That's because just like leaving your lover, there are at least 50 ways to make money in real estate. Therefore, if we're all doing something different, your system isn't going to look like my system, which won't look like Donald Trump's system, and so on. So let's start at the beginning and look at a few reasons *why* you need to systemize.

FOUR REASONS TO SYSTEMIZE

There are at least four really good reasons to systemize your business. You will get the first three, but the last one will probably fly right past you.

1. A system can help you succeed in spite of a flawed business plan.

If you're serious about getting somewhere in this business, you'll be using some of the information in this book, and from other sources, to create a very basic business plan. In fact, a business plan is the first step towards systemizing. You won't do it right the first time, but don't feel bad—I didn't either. In fact, nobody has ever designed a business plan in the beginning stages of a new venture that didn't need to be revised; because no plan, regardless of how well it was thought-out, has ever fully survived contact with unpredictable consumers. Therefore, it doesn't make sense to keep trying to perfect a business plan that's going to change anyway.

A better idea would be to create a series of actionable steps based on the components of your initial plan, because simply moving forward will expose where your plan needs to be tweaked—even as it's uncovering other profit opportunities that you didn't foresee in the planning stage. I experienced this phenomenon personally, when my very first plan was supposed to generate profits of $60,000 in six months, but produced $90,000 instead. Oh well...crap happens.

2. A system gets everything done when it *needs* to get done.

In real estate, just like in any business, *when* something gets done can be just as critical as *what* gets done. By creating your business plan, you will be forced to identify a series of actions and events which will ultimately bring revenue for you (God willing). Once you know what these actions and events are, you can begin to construct a system of steps to execute them in the proper order at the proper time. This will help to ensure that everything gets done, when it *should* get done.

Consistent follow-up with potential sellers is a good example of this, as their moods and circumstances change frequently. The only thing that can guarantee your marketing pieces will get placed in front of them on a regular basis is a good system, so if you don't systemize for any other reason, do it for this one.

3. The big money is always in the system, not the business.

Don't believe me? Then come to Cincinnati and let me buy you a beer and gourmet burger at Terry's Turf Club. After we're done, we'll buzz over to McDonald's on Beechmont for a Coke and McBurger; and then you can share with me some other reason as to why Terry's can have such a superior product, and yet *McDonald's* is the one who's serving 47 million customers in over 31,000 locations worldwide.

There's no question about it, systemizing any business is the key to maximizing its potential for profit and growth. The reason is because it positions the business for duplication. And, while it's true that simply systemizing a business does not by itself guarantee that the company will be successful or even duplicatable, it does however enhance the odds of both—especially since you can't duplicate a business without systemizing it first.

For instance, everyone recognizes McDonald's as one of the ultimate examples of success through systemized duplication. But most people mistakenly believe that it was due to McDonald's finely-tuned system of preparing hamburgers and other fast food products; when in fact, the real secret behind McDonald's massive profiteering has been the systematic acquisition of prime real estate. You see, after only 5 years in the fast food business, Ray Kroc discovered that even though his duplicatable system of food preparation routinely generated millions of dollars in gross revenues, actual profits were being measured in mere thousands—which kept the huge corporation perilously close to bankruptcy at all times.

So Kroc decided to enhance his company's profitability by creating a new system; one that focused instead on acquiring prime real estate, which he could then lease out to the franchisees who would be the actual owners and operators of the McDonald's restaurants. This brilliant strategy worked, bringing the company back from the brink of its own premature death, and allowing it to continue contributing to the premature death of the consumers of its products instead.

Today, the McDonald's Corporation still owns and operates some of its locations corporately, but the vast majority of their US restaurants are franchise locations, most of whom pay McDonald's not only franchise royalties, but substantial rent payments as well. Can you say "double-dip"?

4. A system can get you out of the way, so your business can *really* grow.

Hmmm. Now there's something you've probably never thought about; actually getting out of your own way. Obviously I'm not suggesting you give up control of your business, but you might want to at least consider extracting yourself from the simple daily tasks that a chimpanzee could perform—maybe even better than you.

Many small businesses struggle, and frequently fail, because key people are wasting too much of their time and talents on mundane activities; resources that could have been put to better use generating revenue or raising capital.

Sometimes, this is due to an entrepreneur's inability to recognize or prioritize those tasks which are most important. But far more often than that, it's because many entrepreneurs ironically suffer from a paralyzing psychological fear of success. This fear can literally cause them to intentionally bury themselves in unimportant busywork as a subconscious ploy to avoid tackling the substantially more important tasks that could result in the very success they're secretly afraid of.

Systemizing can actually help both types of entrepreneurs overcome their issues. For the first entrepreneur, systemizing requires that they identify all of the necessary tasks. As soon as all of the tasks have been reduced to writing, the entrepreneur will find it much easier to prioritize them by importance.

For the second (more common) entrepreneur, creating a system gives them the ability to extract themselves from the aspects of their business to which they are not well-suited. This is critical, because you can be in the right industry, at the right time, with the right product or service, but if you're personally occupying the wrong position at your company, you'll end up killing it. And it will be ugly.

THE BASICS OF HOW TO SYSTEMIZE

Now that I've made what should have been a thoroughly convincing argument as to *why* you should systemize, it's time for me to show you, in basic terms, *how* you actually go about doing it. Unfortunately, I can't be too specific on the "how" aspect, because as I mentioned earlier, everyone will have a unique plan depending upon a variety of factors; such as their abilities, goals, and resources, etc.

STEP 1: Create a Business Plan

The first step in systemizing your operation is to figure out what your operation actually *is*. The way you do this is by developing a business plan. Contrary to popular myth, creating a business plan does not have to be a laborious process, requiring months of collaboration with expensive attorneys and CPA's; resulting in a 300 page masterpiece of capitalistic literature, complete with pie graphs, an alphabetized index, and numerous bibliographic citations.

Fortunately, your initial business plan can consist of as little as just one page. I know this, because that's what my first one looked like. I started by identifying a few parameters, such as the period for which I was planning, my revenue goals for that period, the scope of my plan (which in project management terms means a breakdown of the various elements of the plan), and the plan's basic execution timeline.

Now... don't start sweating or swearing. This is a whole lot simpler than it sounds, as you'll see in the example on the following page. You may also notice that my one-page plan contains some of the beginning stages of a system as well. These were more fully identified in my action systems that followed.

ONE PAGE BUSINESS PLAN

Period: **7/1/95 - 12/31/95** (6 months)

Revenues: Minimum of **$60,000** by year end

Scope: Develop a monthly, weekly, and daily plan of action to accomplish the revenue goals set within the time frame of this plan.

Strategy: Contract 5 term deals, and wholesale 10 properties averaging revenues of approximately $10,000 per month, as follows:

Term Deals:

*Expecting to realistically close a Lease-Purchase or Land Contract deal that will generate an average of **$6,000.00** upfront cash with 1 out of every 20 pre-qualified prospects receiving a Special Report, the requirements will be to:*

Place 200 Special Reports by 12/31/95, averaging 33.3/month (or about 7.6/week).

Wholesale Deals:

Assuming realistically that 1 out of every 15 offers made on pre-qualified properties will be accepted, generating a wholesale profit of at least $3,000 each, the minimum requirement will be to:

Make at least 150 offers by 12/31/95, averaging 25 per month, or about 6 per week.

MONTHLY OVERVIEW:

Methods to generate term deal leads: (avg. of 34 per month)

1. Mail "Special Report" postcard to expired listings.
2. Run "Special Report" radio spots.
3. Place "Special Report" flyers.
4. Mail "Special Report" to FSBO newspaper ads showing motivation.
5. Send "Special Report" letter to out-of-town property owners.
6. Mail "Special Report" postcards to targeted area lists.
7. Place "I Buy Houses" business cards w/ Lease-Purchase/Land Contract solutions.

Methods to generate wholesale leads: (avg. 25 per month)

1. Make offers on MLS properties
2. Mail "Cash For Your Home" postcards to expired listings.
3. Mail letters to owners of vacant, ugly houses, focusing on out-of-town owners.
4. Process leads from other sources- ants, referrals, etc.

WEEKLY OVERVIEW:

Week 1 and Week 3:   1. Create, fine-tune, and implement term deal lead generators.
2. Follow-up on all leads generated.

Week 2 and Week 4:   1. Create, fine-tune, and implement wholesale deal lead generators.
2. Follow-up on all leads generated.

Please understand, a really simple business plan like this isn't going to cut it if you're looking to raise capital from an investor or a bank (and remember, any capital you raise must qualify as non-recourse, otherwise I will personally hunt you down and unleash a verbal assault on you worthy of a Marine drill instructor with Tourette's and a flaming case of hemorrhoids). For serious capital efforts, you'll obviously need a much more comprehensive business plan.

As you can see by looking back over my first plan, the point was merely to keep breaking every objective down into smaller tasks. For example, I took my overall revenue goal, and divided it by the number of months in the timeline to get a monthly revenue target. I then took a couple different buy/sell strategies, estimated their approximate revenue potential, and used simple math to figure out how many of each type of transaction I'd need to do to reach that monthly revenue target. Once I knew how many deals I needed to do, I estimated how many offers I'd need to make to get that many deals accepted. I then came up with some tasks for getting my message in front of those prospects. After all that, I then created a series of weekly task groups, within which I could execute those tasks on a regular basis.

In other words, the entire plan was reverse engineered; starting with my end goal, and then working backwards until I had developed a series of easily identifiable specific actions. It's like planning a very long road trip: you look at your destination, then plan a series of one-day driving spans, which you further break down into a sequence of possible fueling stops and points of interest.

STEP 2: Design a system to execute your plan

Once I'd completed my basic plan, I took a separate sheet of paper and created a daily plan of action template, which I called my Daily Plan of Action (weird). Anyway, the idea was to create a checklist of daily tasks in consideration of my weekly and monthly objectives, making sure everything got done, and in the right order. Each template was for a one month period, which I then used to generate six hand-dated monthly checklists, one each for July thru December of 1995.

As I worked out my system of alternating weeks, focusing on term deals one week and wholesale deals the next (see the following page), a few interesting facts I hadn't considered before began to surface. First, I noticed that if I followed this plan, I would only have to work 20 days per month, which is fewer than the 22 day average month most people have. Second, I also noticed that most tasks didn't take very long to perform, so each day that I *did* work was likely to be short. And third, it occurred to me that most of the tasks on the list could be just as easily done by someone else, which would free me up for far more important things; like finding more deals, making more offers, or having more time to annoy my wife.

Win-win-win.

DAILY PLAN OF ACTION
FOR MONTH OF July , 1995

WEEK 1
Days 1-5

Day 1: Tues. 7/1
[ ] Order expired listings from Nancy and Cindy
[ ] Follow-up last month's Day 16 Report mailing.

Day 2: Wed. 7/2
[ ] Mail Special Reports to motivated FSBO ads
[ ] _____

Day 3: Thurs. 7/3
[ ] Place flyers in target neighborhoods, grocery stores, carry-outs, laundromats, etc.
[ ] _____

Day 4: Fri. 7/4
[ ] Research out-of-town owners (internet)
[ ] _____

Day 5: Mon. 7/7
[ ] Send letters to -out-of-town owners.
[ ] _____

WEEK 2
Days 8-12

Day 8: Tues. 7/8
[ ] Order MLS junker printouts from Nancy.
[ ] Mail "Cash" postcards to expired listings.

Day 9: Wed. 7/9
[ ] Review MLS printouts, edit and fax back.
[ ] Review Ohio Offer Tracker & re-submit.

Day 10: Thurs. 7/10
[ ] Schedule appt. for MLS junker properties
[ ] _____

Day 11: Fri. 7/11
[ ] Look at Ohio MLS properties, make offers.
[ ] _____

Day 12: Mon. 7/14
[ ] Log previous day offers in Ohio Offer Tracker.
[ ] _____

WEEK 3
Days 15-19

Day 15: Tues. 7/15
[ ] Mail postcards to expired listings.
[ ] Process all leads from other sources

Day 16: Wed. 7/16
[ ] Mail Special Reports to motivated FSBO ads.
[ ] Follow-up on Day 2 Report mailings

Day 17: Thurs. 7/17
[ ] Create and run Special Report radio spots
[ ] Send second letter to out-of-town owners.

Day 18: Fri. 7/18
[ ] Place flyers in target neighborhoods, grocery stores, carryouts, laundromats, etc.

Day 19: Mon. 7/21
[ ] Brainstorm new ideas, tweak ad materials.
[ ] _____

WEEK 4
Days 22-26

Day 22: Tues. 7/22
[ ] Order MLS junker printouts from Cindy.
[ ] Send Special Report to radio respondents.

Day 23: Wed. 7/23
[ ] Go over MLS printouts and edit. Fax back.
[ ] Review KY Offer Tracker and re-submit.

Day 24: Thurs. 7/24
[ ] Schedule appointments for KY MLS properties.
[ ] _____

Day 25: Fri. 7/25
[ ] Look at KY MLS properties, make offers.
[ ] _____

Day 26: Mon. 7/28
[ ] Log previous day offers in KY Offer Tracker
[ ] _____

STEP 3 (Optional): Identify specific job descriptions

Once you've outlined a basic business plan, as well as a daily, weekly, or monthly task checklist to execute it, the next step—which is optional—will be to figure out who's going to be performing these tasks. The easiest way to do this would be to group several similar tasks together into a handful of sensible categories, and then assign each category a title—or in more familiar terms: a job description.

This is the first step in extracting yourself from the equation of your business system, and although this exercise is not required, it is, however, mandatory if you ever want to be able to position yourself for any real success in this business—or any other business, for that matter. Here's an example of what it could look like:

Secretarial: Filing, clerical, envelope stuffing, database management, postcard mailings, phone work

Office Manager: Choosing, implementing, and monitoring all lead generating and follow-up systems to find prospective buyers and sellers

Property Acquisition: Negotiating with prospective sellers, coordinating funding sources, attending closings

Property Disposition: Negotiating with prospective buyers, attending closings

Administrative: Ordering title work, switching utilities, running keys, placing signs, processing payments, etc.

STEP 4 (Optional): Assign someone to fill each job description

Once you've identified these different job descriptions, put a name next to each one that identifies the person who is responsible for completing the tasks. If you're like many small business owners (and virtually every real estate entrepreneur), your name will be next to every single job description. That's okay, at least in the beginning. Unfortunately, I can look at people who have been in this business for 20 years, and their name is *still* next to every job description.

Of course, if that's the way you want to keep things, who am I to argue? It's your business. But, once again, if you ever really want to get somewhere with your business, your next objective must be to seek out people who have the time and the skills to fulfill each position better than you can, and hire them.

At first you might think it's impossible to find someone who can do *anything* better than you (you little business-strangler). But that's crazy talk and you know it. So therefore, it shouldn't be hard at all to convince you that you need to get someone else to handle some of the mundane busy work once your business is up and running—even if it's only on a part-time basis at first.

And yet, as sensible as all of this reasoning is, far too many people will still have a difficult time even considering the idea of turning *any* aspect of their business over to someone else. Maybe you know this feeling. If so, it's usually because of one or more of the following three reasons:

1. You really don't have confidence in anyone else's abilities, probably because you've bought hook, line, and sinker into all that saccharin-sweet purple dinosaur crap that says, *"You're special, because no one else can do things exactly like you can"*. The real truth is that there are a multitude of people who can do absolutely *anything* you can do, and many of them can do it far better and faster than you could ever hope to. Get over it.

2. You're either too busy or too lazy to teach someone else what to do, in which case you'll be forever resigned to perpetually having to do it all yourself. This usually results in exactly what you don't want, but which you ultimately deserve: smaller paychecks than possible and longer workdays than necessary. Oh... and you can forget about going on any *real* vacations; you know, the kind that don't involve taking your laptop and cell phone so you can check voice mail and email every two hours.

3. You're paranoid that if you teach someone else how to do some of the things you're doing, they'll just quit and go on to be your competitor. Here's a news flash: Contrary to what you might believe, everyone is not out to steal business from you. You will be training people only on small portions of your overall business, so without all of the pieces of the puzzle, they're not likely to be a real threat to you. However, it's still not a bad idea to exercise caution. A great deterrent to employee defection is to require them to sign a 5-year non-compete agreement before you ever disclose a single thing. That way, if they ever decide to mutiny or go solo, they won't be able to legally engage in real estate investment transactions anywhere near you.

Look...what it comes down to is this: If you don't have the very best person possible fulfilling each job position your company has, then you're not generating anywhere near as much revenue as you could be. But be careful. Don't go out and hire a bunch of people you like, and then try to create a job position to fit their talents; that's a recipe for insolvency. You must first create the *system* that will run your company, *then* you can go out and find the people to run your system.

Ideally, your goal should be to have the ability to extract yourself entirely from the process at some point if you should ever want to. That way, you'll not only have a money machine that can crank out cash while you're napping topless in your thong on a beach in Rio (even if you're a girl), but you'll also have a highly marketable business that you can sell for many times more than you're being paid to own it.

How's *that* for a little something to think about?

In fact, maybe this would be a good time for me to take you on a little side trip into deep left field. You'll see why in a moment, so just be patient and read on:

Back in the 1980's, a friend of mine noticed that people in small towns and villages were being ignored by the incoming cable television companies who were installing their new systems. Due to the economies of scale, these cable companies focused only on densely populated areas to keep their customer acquisition costs as low as possible, i.e., running a mile's worth of cable in a crowded city or suburb netted them far more paying customers than a mile's worth of cable in a small outlying village.

My friend saw this as an untapped niche opportunity, so he combined his legal training and his skills as a federal government liaison (between government officials, small town leaders, and general contractors) to begin building small municipal cable companies—one for each village—from the ground up. Within a few years, he had created a chain of fifty-four little independent systems that were serving (as a whole) thousands of customers, and generating about $900,000 per year in annual profits.

That would have been a great end goal for most people, but not for Alan (yes, that's his real name—there was no need to change it since he's not all that innocent). Instead, he sold the parent company which owned all fifty-four systems for about a $20 million profit. Why? Well, because he could. After all, at $900,000 per year, it would have taken him over 22 years to collect $20 million. So let me ask you: If you had a choice to work for 22 years to make a certain amount of money, or get it all in cash today and take the next two decades off, what would you do? Yeah... me too.

*   *   *   *   *

In an unrelated story, I knew another man who went out one day to buy some good quality home fitness equipment, but couldn't find any. Back then, most stores only sold cheap, flimsy machines that were awkward and didn't last long. He was miffed, but looked at it as an opportunity rather than as a problem. So he borrowed $2,000 on his Visa card, and opened a specialty store that featured high-end home gym equipment (rowers, treadmills, etc.). The consumer response was incredible.

He spent the first six months of his store's existence identifying and documenting a system based on the individual tasks that were running it. Then, he took his proven new system and duplicated it over and over again until he had opened ten stores in just 2-1/2 years. He then sold half of his shares in the parent company to the H.J. Heinz Corporation (that's right, the ketchup people) for $1.6 million. If you've heard this story before, then you may already be familiar with T. Harv Eker—which is quite possible because he's gotten a lot more popular since I first met him back in 1995.

Anyway, by now you're probably wondering if I went off my meds or something, since I've just led you down two completely tangential paths with a pair of stories that appear to have no relevance to one another—or to real estate investing, for that matter. While that may be true (about the divergent nature of my discussion, not my meds), they do, however, have a great deal of relevance to the concept of how you can build wealth by creating a business that is systemized—because in doing so, you are effectively building a brand new money machine from scratch.

Money machines are marvelous little creations that can attract serious attention from large corporations who are always on the lookout for cash cows that they can buy to boost their bottom-line profits. In fact, these companies often have entire divisions (mergers and acquisitions) devoted to the task of finding and acquiring successfully systemized businesses. They also have deep enough pockets to make a deal happen when they find one they like (I've since learned that lots of people have deep pockets, but unfortunately most of them also happen to have short arms).

"But," you say, "I'm a real estate investor, so there's no way to systemize or duplicate what I do". Yes, it appears that you have regrettably stumbled into the only business on earth that can't be automated or replicated. Apparently, no one else but you can find or evaluate real estate deals, or figure out how to buy and sell them profitably—this, despite the fact that there are over 2.5 million trained and licensed real estate agents in the United States. Granted, only about 20% of them actually know what they're doing; but that still leaves half a million capable individuals.

If, in fact, real estate investment companies can't be systemized or duplicated, somebody forgot to tell Ken D'Angelo before he went and developed a system of buying and rehabbing properties, and then franchised it nationwide as Home-Vestors. And if real estate investing is supposed to be a mom-and-pop thing, Richard Davis of Trademark Properties (from A&E's *Flip This House* and TLC's *The Real Estate Pros*) must have goofed up, because he systemized a work-force of about 40 people, and then established duplicatable revenue in the form of both real estate profits *and* television syndication fees. And, of course, fully defying the typical one-trick pony mentality is the real estate brand champion himself, Donald Trump; who not only has an army of people buying, selling, and operating his multi-million dollar property portfolio, but who has also mastered branding so well, he can duplicate himself simply by licensing his name alone for millions of dollars to all the developers who just want to display the name *Trump* on their own projects.

"But," you insist in a whining tone (apparently you bitch a lot), "no one would be interested in buying *my* real estate business". That may be true, but only because your business probably has nothing to sell. After all, if you're like most investors, you're doing everything yourself, so you can't very well expect to sell out and move to a beach-front bungalow in Oceanside, California. Nothing would get done. And even if your company has some real estate holdings, they're probably leveraged to the rooftop in mortgages, and whatever cash flow they may be generating, if any, would dry up as soon as you're no longer there to babysit the tenants every day.

In other words, unlike my friend Alan in the first story, you have no system to sell—or the system you have doesn't generate much revenue. You see, you might think Alan sold a *company*, when in fact, what he really sold was fifty-four *systems*; and the only reason the big cable company wanted to buy his parent company was so that they could integrate all fifty-four of his little money machines systems into their one big money machine with a single stroke of a pen.

The purpose of the second story with Harv Eker was to illustrate why you wouldn't necessarily have to worry about the other challenge you might expect if you wanted to sell your real estate investment business: overcoming the almost ridiculous frugality of real estate investors. If you've been around awhile, you already know that we real estate investors don't buy *anything* unless we absolutely have to. And when we do, we always choose the thriftiest alternative possible— which is a polite way of saying we're a cheap bunch of bastards who would've figured out how to put Neil Armstrong on the moon with only $168 worth of duct tape, spray paint, and PVC had *we* been running NASA in 1969. Real estate investors are a stubborn lot who usually prefer to reinvent the wheel over and over, rather than pay for a proven, profitable system. Go ahead… ask me how I know.

So don't limit yourself to the idea that you would have to sell your real estate company to someone who's already a real estate investor (thank God!). As Harv's story proves, your potential buyers don't even have to be in the same *industry* as you. Did you ever wonder why a huge company like G.E. can offer thousands of different products and services; ranging from light bulbs, to international consumer credit cards, to jet engines—and just about anything else in between? They got that way by literally buying up a bunch of small, profitable, *systemized* businesses.

Oh… one more thing: If you like the idea of selling your company some day, don't expect to get a lot of cash if you only have one systemized money machine— unless it makes a crapload of money, of course. Most of the time, as our stories show, you will need to duplicate your system several times over in order to attract the big boys (or girls) with the big bucks. And if you're concerned about competing against yourself, you could always replicate your business model in other cities with just a handful of support staff at each location. Or perhaps you could develop a passive system, like maybe a web site that generates leads, advertises properties, and drives prospects to an inbound telemarketing company (the fewer employees you would need, the better), which you could then expand *virtually* into other cities.

Look, it doesn't matter *how* you replicate; just *that* you replicate. Otherwise when you get ready to sell, instead of negotiating with Halliburton, you'll be sitting down with Hal E. Burton, D.D.S., who's looking to give his bored wife something to do, or a project to keep his college drop-out son busy enough to stay out of trouble. And by the way, Hal will have shallow pockets *and* short arms.

So why am I telling you all of this—especially when I know almost nobody who reads this will ever seriously consider systemizing their real estate investment company with the objective of perhaps selling it later? Because I wanted to expand your mind and broaden your "box", so that you'll be more likely to create or entertain profitable new ideas that can't be found in any book—not even this one. I also did it because I know that at least one person who reads this will be inspired enough to actually do something really big with it. All the resources you need to do it are out there; you just have to want it badly enough to go and find them.

7

the
complementary techniques

I f you're a guy, chances are pretty good this is the first place your eyes went immediately after laughing at that hot mess on the cover. Am I right? Of course I'm right. I'm a guy, too. But this chapter appears near the end of the book for a very good reason; it contains some of the least important stuff in here.

This probably sounds counterintuitive, especially since this is a book about creative real estate investing. But that's what makes this book different than most any other ever written on the subject. More than two decades of real life experience has taught me what is truly important, and so this book was designed to cover topics in a declining order of importance; with the most essential aspects being covered first. This is called "putting your ducks in a row", and it's a far better strategy than the one we men subscribe to, which generally has us trying to put interesting carts in front of boring horses. Maybe someday we'll catch on.

For a time I actually considered calling this book *The Full Frontal Instruction Manual*, just to make sure no guys would buy it. That way, I could assure myself that everybody who did buy the book would get the most out of the great information in it—mostly because they'd all be women who would take the time to read it in the correct order from front to back.

So if you're a guy who's just been busted for skipping chapters, head on back to the *Introduction*, and you can catch up with us here again later, okay?

For everyone else, there's just one more thing I'd like to mention before launching into the meat of this chapter: I'm going to pull back on some of the irreverent silliness, and try to be a little more serious for awhile. This is not because I've suddenly lost my sense of humor, nor is this because I don't want you to have any fun. I'm just a little concerned that you may not always know when I'm kidding, and I don't want you showing up to any of your appointments with rubber chickens dangling from your briefcases, or whipping out contracts that contain crude references to excessive flatulence or no-no special body parts.

The Right Way to Use Nothing Down

Nothing down is the essence of most creative real estate, and will therefore be an overriding theme throughout this chapter. However, please understand that it's not the techniques themselves which will make your deals "no money down" transactions, but rather how they've been adapted and engineered for use as nothing down strategies. In other words, none of the techniques in this book are nothing down by default. You have to tweak them first, and then utilize them in just the right way to make them effective using little or none of your own money.

So before we move on to the techniques themselves, I'd like to take a moment to point out a couple of important issues, so that we can be certain we're both starting from the same page—literally and figuratively.

Let's begin with the obvious; the definition of a nothing down real estate transaction. A nothing down transaction is simply when the buyer receives 100% of their funding from sources other than their own pocket. This sounds like a universally good thing, especially to new investors. However, there's more that needs to be considered beyond just where all of your funding comes from—especially if you intend to operate as a professional real estate entrepreneur who would like to make a profit and stay in business.

You see, getting 100% of your funding the wrong way can not only be extremely dangerous, it can also remove virtually any opportunity for you to create either cash flow or resale profits; two of the most critically important aspects of real estate investing. Most of the nothing down gurus of the 1980's were either blissfully unaware of this fact, or just criminally negligent when they preached that it didn't matter how or where you got your 100% financing, just so long as you got it on every single deal, sensibly or otherwise. In fact, one famous TV guru used to boast, "Just buy all the properties you can, and worry about the payments later!" This goes beyond terrible advice. In fact, it's borderline unconscionable (last I heard, he'd gone bankrupt and had to pay a $200,000 fine to the FTC).

Some of these 1980's gurus advised investors to scam banks into giving them 97% FHA loans by posing as owner-occupants, and then completing the nothing down deal by having the seller hold the 3% balance on a second mortgage. Even more scandalous, they also taught people it was okay to over-finance those deals by giving their sellers a 10% second mortgage behind a 97% first (for a total of 107%), which netted the investor a check back at closing for the 7% overage.

Worst of all were the gurus with the balls to tell investors to pay clueless people to front for them as owner-occupant buyers; the idea being the patsy would assign the freely-assumable loan over to the investor as soon as it closed. I was once approached to be a straw man for a deal like that myself, back when I was too dumb to know how risky *and* illegal it was. Some guy offered me $1,000 bucks to get a loan on a property he wanted, just so I could assign the mortgage to him.

I was about 25 years old at the time, and for two solid weeks all that I could think about besides big boobs and cheese coneys (usually in that order) was getting my hands on that pile of cash. I applied for the loan without hesitation, and thank God I didn't qualify for it. Of course, I was really upset at first, because I felt like I'd just lost a grand. But I found out later that this was not only an illegal transaction, but that assigning the mortgage to him wouldn't have released me from liability on the note. In other words, I almost tied up my credit with a crook for up to three decades—risking default, foreclosure, and deficiency liabilities—with no way to prevent or stop a worst case scenario from happening. Luckily, I dodged that bullet. But many other good people I know were not so fortunate.

Common sense should have told people that financing any property for up to 100% (or more) of its value doesn't leave any equity with which to make a resale profit, and if the financing was done at prevailing rates—and it usually was—then how were people supposed to create any positive monthly cash flow? The truth was that many of these duped investors rarely had any positive cash flow at all, and what little they did have always got chewed up in repairs, taxes, expenses and vacancies.

So without either of these two profit centers, about the only thing left for these people to rely upon was the appreciation of the property's value, which—as I've been touting for years—is a dangerous assumption. Appreciation is an ancillary benefit to real estate investing; like icing on the cake. It cannot and should not *ever* be used as a fulcrum for leverage, because, as we've all recently seen, appreciation is obviously not automatic.

In fact, any real estate transaction that relies solely on appreciation to make it profitable is not actually an investment—it's a gamble. So if you're ever tempted to bet the farm on a nothing down deal that requires appreciation, just drop what you're doing and head to Vegas instead where the odds are better, the food is cheaper, and your inevitable losses, smaller.

Nothing Down is a Point of View

Here's a question: If someone is traveling in the back of a glass-enclosed pickup truck travelling 70 mph, and they're tossing a tennis ball straight up and down in their hands, what is the actual path the tennis ball is taking? The answer is: it depends on your perspective. If you're watching from inside the truck, the ball is traveling straight up and down, but if you're watching from the curb as the truck passes by, the ball's path is in the shape of a mathematical sine wave. So, which observation is correct? Both... but *your* perspective is the only one that matters to you. You see, perspective is what can make a deal nothing down, even though it may not be a nothing down transaction. Confused? Then look at it this way: If a deal is nothing down from your point of view, and you're the investor who engineered the transaction, then it simply qualifies as a nothing down deal.

Look again at the earlier definition of nothing down; the one that says it's whenever the buyer gets all of their funding from other sources. If you get a partner to put up a large downpayment for a deal, and the rest of the money is provided by a bank, then it wasn't a nothing down transaction for the seller, because they got all cash at closing. Neither was it a nothing down for the lender who put up the bulk of the money, nor for your partner who put up the large downpayment.

The only person it was nothing down for was you.

Of course, Real Estate 101 says that in order for any deal to be legally binding, some initial consideration (a.k.a. earnest money) must change hands. But it doesn't say anywhere that this consideration has to be cash. Consideration is usually interpreted to mean cash, but it can technically be anything of value; such as a pair of Nike cross-trainers or a Michael Bolton CD (although a compelling argument could be made either way as to whether or not a Michael Bolton CD actually *has* any value).

There is also no clear requirement that the binding consideration has to be paid by the buyer. Couldn't the seller just as easily pay it to the buyer? Why not? After all, the entire purpose of binding consideration is that it represents an inducement to draw someone into an agreement, by demonstrating a show of the payee's good faith intent to fulfill the covenants of the subsequent contract.

So isn't it fair to assume that in some situations the *seller* might be the one with the greater need to induce the buyer into signing? Of course—especially if the seller owes more than the property is worth, and will be expected to bring money to the closing table to clear the deed. Auto manufacturers offer people cash to buy their cars all the time (mostly because they have to). So, why can't a seller do the same? That's something new to chew on, isn't it?

But even if you have to give the seller some cash, the idea is to keep your cash outlay low enough as to make the deal *virtually* nothing down. You'll learn how to do this later, but it doesn't matter because you won't be leaving your money in the deal, anyway. You'll be getting it all back quickly—and more—once you've resold, leased out, or refinanced the property (with a non-recourse loan, of course).

And P.S.: Don't ever let anyone poke fun at you or make you feel inadequate because you're trying to do a nothing down deal. Just remind them that nothing down deals are only kind that banks ever do. From the smallest corner bank making a personal loan, all the way up to the biggest bank in your town funding a multi-million dollar commercial mortgage—banks *always* have to borrow 100% of the money they need to do their deals. Always!

So the next time someone hassles you, pick the most respected bank in your city and tell the bully that you're doing deals no money down because you choose to. But XYZ Bank doesn't have that choice, because they can't get their deals done any other way! *Now* who looks like the 98-pound weakling?

LET'S TALK TECHNIQUES

It's finally time for us to move on to what most people incorrectly believe is the most important part of this book—the techniques themselves. In total, there are six different buying and selling methods. If you can master these six core strategies, you can make a really good living despite whatever direction your real estate market goes—up, down, or sideways.

So here are the six techniques. They're not listed in any particular order, because their importance will vary based on your market conditions at any given moment. And as for preferential order, there is none, because they're all simply tools that I use whenever necessary (at least that's what I tell everyone out loud, but just like any other parent of six uniquely different siblings, I secretly have my favorites). Anyway, they are:

1. Wholesaling
2. Options
3. Lease-Purchase
4. Land Contract
5. Subject To
6. Short Sale

As I go through these techniques over the next 120+ pages, I'll be giving you mostly the basics of each one, while tossing in a few unique ideas every so often to spice things up. I won't be going into exhaustive details or including actual agreements, because that's too much work for what you've paid me. If you want to buy something with 700 pages for less than $30, get a Tom Clancy novel.

However, as a favor to you for purchasing this book, I did create a special link where you can get a detailed course that I wrote on all of these techniques called *Real Life Nothing Down*, at a significant discount of 75% off list price.

Just go to: **www.FullFrontalRealEstate.com/RLND** (write this down; this link can't be found anywhere else), and you can get an e-version of the entire course manual with an in-depth, line-by-line analysis of each technique. I'll also throw in a bonus file containing digital versions of all the forms and agreements I use today. These documents are already formatted in Microsoft WORD, which means you can easily customize them to make them your own in just a matter of minutes.

Of course, I have to advise you not to use the agreements in that course straight out of the box, but having them in digital form can save you lots of time and money—since it would take your attorney far fewer billable hours to tweak them for you, as opposed to drafting them all from scratch. Plus, the language of my agreements can provide insights into unique ways you need to be protected that your attorney might not have otherwise considered. Trust me... I've been to *that* seminar.

WHOLESALING

WHOLESALING

A QUICK OVERVIEW

> **What it is:** Wholesaling is the act of buying or contractually tying up properties at a very low price—usually below wholesale—and then reselling the property "as is" at a wholesale price or assigning the contract for a fee.

> **What it does:** Wholesaling provides you with an opportunity to generate a profit whenever you encounter a property owner who is willing to sell at prices that are well below market. Professional wholesalers specialize in providing inventory for retail investors who are too busy to look for deals.

> **How it's done:** The idea is to search for distressed properties (often with equally distressed sellers) that can be purchased for well below market value. Once you find these properties, you can put them under contract at a very low price, and then do one of the following:

   a) Close the purchase and resell the property at a slightly higher price, or;
   b) Enter into a contract to resell the property before you even close your purchase, usually during the escrow/inspection period, or;
   c) Assign your purchase agreement for a fee.

Although these properties are typically put under contract at below-wholesale prices, and then marked up to the wholesale level, this is not always the case. Anytime a property is bought, or put under control, for a price that is less than what it can be immediately resold for constitutes a wholesale deal.

> **How it generates revenue:** Wholesaling generates revenue through contract assignment fees, or by allowing you to capture the difference between your low buy price and your higher sell price.

> **Best market cycle:** Wholesaling works all the time. In up markets, the high demand for retail inventory makes deals a little harder to find, but often more profitable when you do. In economic downturns, the average deal is usually less profitable, but deals are easy to find, and even easier to sell since the investor market often flourishes when the retail market falters.

> **Caveats:** Wholesaling is sometimes referred to as "flipping", and although it is a perfectly legitimate process, significant negative publicity and increasingly ridiculous restrictions placed by lenders, government authorities, and title companies can sometimes end up complicating deals unnecessarily. These issues can often be minimized or overcome with advanced planning, and may also result in additional costs for temporary transactional funding.

The Basics

Most everyone is familiar with the process of buying properties cheap, fixing them up, and then reselling them for top dollar. This is known as *retailing*. Wholesaling, on the other hand—also known as *quick-turning*, or more frequently (and nefariously) as *flipping*—involves putting that very same property under contract at a price that is below the wholesale level, and then instead of fixing it up, immediately reselling it "as is" at a wholesale price to another investor or an end buyer. The spread between the below-wholesale buying price and the at-wholesale selling price represents the wholesaler's profit.

The practice of wholesaling real estate is no different than the wholesaling of goods to any retail outlet or department store, such as Walmart or, at the other end of the spectrum, Nieman Marcus. Retail consumer outlets of every pedigree buy their inventory from wholesale suppliers at wholesale prices, because it's easy and profitable. The same goes for many retail real estate investors, who are often so busy with the process of fixing up and selling their inventory that they just don't have the time or the energy to track down their next project.

That's where wholesalers come in. The objective of a wholesaler is to find the motivated property owners who are willing to sell their properties at below-wholesale value. Then, just like department store wholesalers, they simply mark the price of the properties up to the wholesale level and sell them to investors or ambitious homeowners who are willing to tackle the repairs that the properties will nearly always need—which brings us to property condition.

It's very rare for a property owner to knowingly or willingly sell their property for far below its market value unless it's in extremely bad condition. Therefore, a wholesaling investor must be prepared to deal with ugly properties, and have a good idea on estimating not only the property's future retail value, but also the approximate cost of the repairs needed to get it into retail shape; one that will allow their wholesale buyer to either rent it out or resell it at full market value.

Wholesaling in the Real World

Retailing is generally far more lucrative than wholesaling, since the retail investor typically has the greater investment of time and money. But this is not universally true, as I've occasionally wholesaled properties to investors for a greater profit than they were able to generate by fixing it up and reselling it at full price. This was not due to any fraud on my part, but more often to a combination of me getting a very good buy price, and the investor screwing up the repair process through carelessness, lackadaisical execution, or just good old-fashioned ineptitude. And even when my retail investors do make more money than me, it takes them several months to collect their profit, and only a few days for me to collect mine. This often makes the additional revenue less worth the pursuit—at least in my eyes.

As for finding properties to buy below the wholesale level, it's a lot harder than it used to be, but that doesn't necessarily mean it's hard to do. The truth is that it just used to be a lot easier than it *should* have been. All you had to do was team up with a Realtor, and go page-by-page through the MLS books (that's right—in the old days listings used to come out weekly in a thick paperback book), looking at the "remarks" section of each listing for signs of motivation.

Without the benefits of computers back then, this was tedious work. But it paid off handsomely, as I would routinely find three or four good prospects per week, and get about 25% of my offers accepted—wholesaling either the property or my contract within a few days, for an average profit of $3,000 to $6,000 each.

Needless to say, it wasn't long before the unusual ease and profitability of wholesaling caused the Efficient Market to engage with a vengeance; forever diluting the earning power of the strategy as it drew a tremendous number of brand new people into the loop until we were all literally tripping over one another. This is not to say that wholesaling is dead, because you can still find lots of great deals—even in the MLS. But now, you just have to look a little harder, dig a little deeper, and be ready to pounce a whole lot faster than everybody else.

Unfortunately, I don't have enough space or time to go into all of the ways of finding good wholesale leads—especially since most of the advertising strategies in the chapter on marketing can be so easily adapted for this. But I do want to take a moment to share an important concept that can help give you a leg up on the competition—and here it is: One of the best ways to minimize or eliminate your competition in any business is to be the first one to reach your potential prospects.

Now, this does *not* mean meeting the paperboy at 5:00 am every day so that you can scan the classified ads before the rest of the world wakes up, nor does it mean installing speed-dialing software on your fax machine so your offers can get to the listing Realtor faster. And although I do strongly recommend having your Realtor set up an immediate response system for whenever new properties within your parameters are entered into the MLS, what I really meant by getting there first was that you should try to preemptively reach these prospects before they even offer their properties for sale. In fact, some of your best deals will probably come from owners who weren't even expecting to be sellers, until you showed up to plant the idea in their heads.

Good candidates to approach for a possible distressed sale include: a) out-of-town property owners and landlords, who can be found through property records or list brokers; b) frustrated landlords, who can be found through eviction court filings; c) owners of vacant, ugly, even condemned properties*, who can be found through posted legal notices or by driving through neighborhoods; and d) heirs, executors, and administrators of estates, who are listed in public probate filings.

---

*Being condemned means a property is unfit for human habitation—not necessarily that it has a date with a dozer.

So far, all of this talk about wholesaling has still left a pretty big question unanswered: *Exactly how much is the wholesale value of any particular property?* This will vary for each one, and there are no concrete rules that can nail it down precisely. But there is a reasonable calculation that goes something like this:

$$ARV - WM - RC = WV$$

What does this equation mean in laymen's terms? It simply says: *The After Repaired Value* (ARV) *of a property, minus a Wholesale Margin* (WM), *less any Repair Costs* (RC), *equals the Wholesale Value* (WV). So let's walk through the wholesale calculation process by looking at each variable individually.

ARV = After Repaired Value: This variable is self-explanatory, representing what the property will be worth once it has been repaired to excellent condition. This is nearly always a future value estimate, since most properties that are prime wholesaling candidates are usually in really rough condition when you find them.

The best way to estimate a property's future value in excellent condition is to have the property professionally appraised. But that is neither practical nor prudent, since you would have to pay for this on every property before you could even make an offer. A reliable alternative would be to use sales data of similar properties in close proximity to your subject property. If your county's property records happen to be online, this would be a good start. But to do it right, you really need access to the MLS (Multiple Listing Service) in your area. That means if you are not a Realtor, you'll either need to get one on your team, or hack into your local Board of Realtor's system (which I strongly discourage).

Once you have a couple of good comparable sales to go by, be sure you remember to adjust the future value of your target property if, after being repaired, it will have (key operative words being *"will have"*) somewhat nicer amenities than your comps; such as a brand new kitchen, new carpet and flooring, all new windows and doors, etc.

In other words, if your property will look, feel, and even smell brand new, while your comparable sales were for properties that were in just "pretty good" condition, perhaps with outdated kitchens and baths, then it's okay to inflate the future value of your subject property just a little to account for the like-new condition. This, of course, assumes that all other aspects of the properties you're comparing are similar, and that your local market is stable and/or appreciating.

Just be aware that one of the biggest mistakes new wholesalers make is keeping their ARV estimates intentionally too low in an attempt to be safe. This can be problematic, because the wholesale margin is a pretty generous deduction, with some built-in additional safety cushions. So don't be too cautious or conservative, because if you keep your ARV artificially low, then your resulting offers will be too low as well—leading to too many rejected offers.

WM = <u>W</u>holesale <u>M</u>argin: This is the margin you need to deduct from the ARV, in order to allow for your buyer's net retail profit, as well as their inevitable purchase, holding and selling costs (excluding real estate commissions). This margin also includes a small "fudge factor" error cushion, which is intended to account for slight miscalculations of the property's future value, as well as repair cost overruns and unanticipated fees or delays.

Most often, the WM is expressed as a percentage of the ARV, in order to keep it appropriately proportionate for every deal. Usually this percentage runs from 25% of the ARV on higher-priced properties, to about 35% on lower-priced properties, i.e., the higher the price, the lower the WM percentage. Although using a lower percentage on higher-priced properties may seem counterintuitive—especially since higher-priced properties require greater investments of time and money—it makes perfect sense when you apply the economies of scale to price.

Here's what I mean: A realistic WM (wholesale margin) percentage for a $100,000 property would be around 35%. That would equal a $35,000 spread, which would provide both a reasonable investor profit and a sensible safety cushion to cover all of their purchase, holding and sale costs (without a Realtor), as well as a few additional costs due to minor mistakes or sudden surprises.

However, on a higher-priced property worth, say, $300,000, using that same 35% margin would provide a very large WM of $105,000, which is quite ambitious and not very likely to result in your ability to calculate a reasonable offer for your potential seller. Therefore, in order to generate more attractive offers on higher-priced properties, it's necessary to reduce the WM percentage proportionately. In the case of a $300,000 property, a 25% WM should suffice, as it would allow for a $75,000 spread in actual dollars, which should be more than enough to cover your investor buyer's profit and cost requirements.

So how do you know exactly when to use 25% or 35% or... *whatever* for your WM percentage? You'll just have to use your gut, because there's no exact science or universal formula. However, if it helps to know my general philosophy, I use a sliding scale that starts at 35% for properties with an ARV of $100,000 or below (although it's rare when I consider properties with ARV's below $100,000 anymore), and then drops 5% for each one hundred thousand dollars in increased value—never going below a 25% WM. In other words, I use 35% for $100,000 properties, 30% for $200,000 properties and 25% for properties $300,000 and up.

Of course, you're free to do whatever you want, because there are no right or wrong formulas; only those which are more and less efficient. Just be aware of two common WM mistakes, usually made by investors who are new, or who have been burned too often: 1) trying to be safe by using WM's that are too big, which makes it hard to buy properties because their offers are too low; and 2) trying to get offers accepted by using WM's that are too small, making it hard to sell properties to wholesale buyers, because the potential net profit is too low.

RC = Repair Costs: This is another self-describing variable, which represents the estimated costs of bringing the property from its current status of disrepair, into a state of excellent condition; suitable for selling at retail price, leasing at retail levels, or simply occupying. Repairs will obviously vary greatly from property to property, so there is no way to apply any type of standard percentage formula or spread, as we were able to do with the wholesale margin (WM) figure.

Repairs have to be estimated for each property on an individual basis. There are three ways to do this. One is to get estimates from professional contractors, but this is highly inefficient as you would have to do this on every property prior to even submitting an offer. Another way would be to go through the property and make an exhaustive list of every single item that needs to be repaired or replaced; after which you would need to price each item individually at nearby stores before adding an estimated labor cost for installing them. This takes forever.

The third method, which is by far the fastest and most efficient, involves creating a repair estimation form containing a handful of standard major repair categories—each with its own specific calculation formula. The form would also provide for the inclusion of any additional atypical major repair items, as well as a place to calculate a proportionately relevant cost cushion factor. This cushion would account for all of the various miscellaneous smaller repairs, plus provide a buffer to cover the costs of any hidden repairs, mistakes, or budget overruns.

To illustrate this concept for you, I'll share the two repair estimation models I created at the very beginning of my career. They've worked so well I still use them today. The only changes I've made have been to the cost factors of each category; reflecting price increases over the last two decades. The reason I created two models was to represent two basic types of properties; each with slightly different socio-economic end buyers. One is a 1,200 square foot bread-and-butter ranch, generally purchased by lower- to middle-class buyers, and the other is a 2,500 square foot two-story, often purchased by middle- to upper-class buyers.

Model One (avg. size = 1,200 sq. ft. ranch):

1. **Roof:** Tear off and replace $5,000   = $_____
2. **Floors:** $3.50 per sq. ft.   = $_____
3. **Heating/Cooling:** Total Replace $4,500   = $_____
4. **Kitchen:** Total replace $3,500   = $_____
5. **Bathroom(s):** Total replace $2,000   = $_____
6. **Windows:** Replace _____ @ $350 each   = $_____
7. **Electric:** New panel w/lead-in $1,250   = $_____
8. **Painting:** $2.50 per sq. ft.   = $_____
9. **Other Major Repair:** _____   = $_____

Total of Major Repairs = $_____ x .33 = $_____ Misc

Total of Major Repairs + Misc = $_____

Model Two (avg. size = 2,500 sq. ft. two-story):

1. **Roof:** Tear off and replace $7,500   = $_____
2. **Floors:** $3.50 per sq. ft.   = $_____
3. **Heating/Cooling:** Total Replace $5,000   = $_____
4. **Kitchen:** Total replace $5,000   = $_____
5. **Bathroom(s):** Total replace $3,000   = $_____
6. **Windows:** Replace _____ @ $350 each   = $_____
7. **Electric:** New panel w/lead-in $1,500   = $_____
8. **Painting:** $2.50 per sq. ft.   = $_____
9. **Other Major Repair:** _____   = $_____
10. **Other Major Repair:** _____   = $_____

Total of Major Repairs = $_____ x .33 = $_____ Misc

Total of Major Repairs + Misc = $_____

As you may have noticed, some of the categories in the two models above use square footage as a factor in estimating repairs. In those instances, it means you should use the square footage of the property being estimated, not the square footage of the basic model you're using. The additional *Other Major Repair* lines are for identifying unique and case-specific major repairs, such as driveway replacement or foundation problems. You can often get an experienced friend or contractor to give you an approximate repair costs for these items on your first few offers. Eventually, you'll develop a pretty good idea of what to budget for them.

Of course, there may be times when you'll come across a major item for which you have no idea what to estimate on repair costs. Don't let that stop you, even if you don't have anyone else with which you can consult on the matter. Just plug in a number that feels good to you at your current level of understanding, and move forward. If your offer gets accepted, either you or your wholesale buyer will have plenty of time to confirm all of the repair estimates prior to closing.

If the actual repair costs turn out to be much higher than you expected, you can always just walk away. Although this could mean forfeiting an occasional earnest money deposit now and then (assuming you don't make your offers contingent on your satisfaction of repair cost estimates), the few deposits you might lose over the years will be minuscule when compared to all of the revenue you would have missed by being too afraid to make any offers.

WV = Wholesale Value: This figure represents a reasonable estimate of the property's wholesale value, but not necessarily the *exact* or *only* possible wholesale value of any given property, since there is no such thing. This value can be calculated in a matter of seconds once you fully grasp the three simple variables we've just covered. But remember, this is a calculation of a property's approximate wholesale value—not a formulation of your actual offer.

Formulating Wholesale Offers

A common error many investors make is to treat the approximate wholesale value (WV) in the equation above as their maximum allowable offer—often referring to it by the popular acronym *MAO*. This is incorrect.

If you're going to be a true wholesaler, then you have to remember that your wholesale buyer will be expecting to buy properties from you at the WV (wholesale value). Therefore, the WV can never be the same as your MAO (maximum allowable offer), otherwise, you will be trying to buy properties at the same prices you would expect to sell them for. That kind of goofy business logic leads to rapid insolvency—not only in real estate, but in any industry.

Therefore, you must first remember to deduct a reasonable profit from the WV (wholesale value) before you make an offer to your seller. What is a reasonable profit? Once again, there's no hardcore answer. Much of that will depend on how bad the property *looks*; not necessarily how bad it really *is*. In other words, the right ugliness can actually provide an advantageous smokescreen behind which you could easily hide a very nice profit. For example, repairs that cost only $20,000 sometimes look to the average seller like $40,000 or $50,000 worth.

An even better indicator of how low to make your initial offer is to consider how motivated the seller appears to be. Most often, this will be reflected in the asking price. For example, if you're looking at a property with an ARV (after repaired value) of $100,000 and it needs $20,000 worth of repairs, a seller who is asking only $60,000 or $65,000 is likely to be a lot more open to entertaining your below-wholesale offer than another seller with a similar property who's asking a ridiculous $85,000 or $90,000 (you'd be amazed at how many sellers do this).

So, let's take a look at how you might formulate an actual offer for a property like the one in our example. First, we'll use our formula from page 124 to calculate the WV (wholesale value):

$100,000 (ARV) *minus* **$35,000** (WM) *minus* **$20,000** (RC) = **$45,000** (WV)

Next, you'll have to decide the minimum profit (MP) you would be willing to make for doing this deal. If you want to make at least $5,000, then your real-life MAO (Maximum Allowable Offer) would be $40,000, calculated as so:

$45,000 (WV) *minus* **$5,000** (MP) = **$40,000** (MAO).

But that's still not your initial offer amount. It's a good idea to come in below your $40,000 MAO to give yourself room to come up during negotiations. How far you start below the $40,000 mark will, again, depend upon how bad the property looks, and how reasonable the seller's asking price is. Unfortunately, there's no way to create a formula for this, because there are just too many market and deal-specific variables. This is one figure you'll have to arrive at using the SWAG principal: you know... Scientific **W**ild-**A**ss **G**uess.

By now, it should be no surprise that your offers, as a wholesaler, will have to be very low indeed. Unfortunately, there's not a whole lot you can do about this, because the process simply *is* what it is. But there are some things you can do to help nudge the odds in your favor.

The first thing you can do is to make sure you're dealing only with highly motivated sellers. This is the foremost issue above all others, because no matter how bad a property looks, if the seller isn't anxious to unload it, you'll be wasting your time trying to convince them that they *should* be anxious to unload it.

Another thing you can do is focus your efforts on vacant, ugly properties that need—or *appear* to need—lots of repairs. And when I say ugly, I don't mean properties with nasty carpet and paint. I mean Butt-Fugly properties that definitely need re-carpeting and repainting, but not until after you've replaced some of the floors or walls first so that you actually *have* something to re-carpet and repaint.

How bad do properties need to look? Here's a clue for you: most experienced wholesalers find cat urine to be an aphrodisiac. Raw sewage is an acceptable substitute, as are odiferous dead animals (raccoons, squirrels, etc.), provided they've been dead only a few days so that the smell is still ripe.

Now, I know what you're probably thinking—especially if you're new to real estate, or if you're a wholesaler who's getting a little tired of dealing in crappy properties every day. You're wishing: *Just once, I'd love to find a seller with a really nice property in a really nice area who is willing to sell it to me at a low wholesale price. That would be so cool!*

Am I right? Well, guess what? If that ever *does* happen to you—and it very well could someday—the truth is you're not going to like it one bit. In fact… it'll freak you out. How do you think I know this? Because it happened to me once, and it made me a nervous wreck. So, please pardon me for a moment while I temporarily hijack this train to tell you about it.

TRUE STORY: One afternoon my phone rang, and before I could get my bearings, the caller—who identified herself only as Candis—asked me point-blank if I could really pay all cash for her house and close quickly like my postcard said.

I immediately launched into my standard reply, which was designed to lead people into selling me their properties on terms. I said, "Yes, I can pay cash for your house and close quickly—but if I tell you how much I'd have to buy it for, you'll get mad at me and hang up. Instead, how about if I tell you about some of my other buying programs where I can pay you a fair price for your house?"

"Nah," she replied. "I'd rather hear your cash offer."

"Well, I don't have any idea what to offer over the phone, since I haven't seen your house yet and don't have any idea what it's worth," I told her.

"Oh, I can tell you exactly what it's worth," she blurted. "It's worth $140,000 to $145,000 as it sits. So based on that, how much can you pay me for it?"

"Okay-y-y," I said slowly. "Umm… Look, I really don't like making offers over the phone without looking at the property first. But if you're going to press me to give you ballpark, then I'll also need to get a feel for what shape it's in. How much work does it need? In other words, if I wanted to jam it up into perfect shape, about how much money—in your opinion—do you think it will take?"

"Oh, the property doesn't need anything. It's only 4 years old and literally in perfect shape right now. I just had all the carpets professionally cleaned, and I just finished painting the entire inside yesterday. So… again, how much can you pay me for it, and how fast can you close?"

"Well, Candis, based on what you're telling me, and as long as the house is everything you say it is, I can probably pay you about…" my voice trailed off as I whipped out my calculator to find out what 70% of $145,000 was. Seeing that it was $101,500, I continued "…Ummm, it looks like I can do about $100,000 cash, max. But honestly, I just wouldn't feel good about buying your house that cheaply. How about if we explore how much *more* I can get you with my other programs, okay?"

Of course, I was assuming that once she received the shock of hearing such a low price, she'd shake her head, come to her senses and be ready to hear about my subject-to or land contract programs. Instead, she came back with: "Nope. Let's just do all cash. Can you meet me today?"

Well, I decided that it couldn't hurt to humor her and at least go look at the place, so I said, "Okay," and headed out the door. When I got there, this is what I found:

As I pulled up to the house, I felt my car slowing down at about the same rate my jaw was falling slack. I couldn't believe what I was seeing. The house was everything she said it was—at least from the outside. This was quite surprising, because in my experience sellers lie… *always*. Not so this time. It was nicely landscaped all around, had a newer garden shed out back, and was on a small cul-de-sac of very nice homes, some worth $185,000 to $200,000 or so.

I didn't know whether to crap my pants, do somersaults, or look for hidden cameras.

I opted to play it cool. So as I knocked on the front door, I did my best to appear nonchalant, acting as though this kind of thing happened to me at least once a week. *That* was not easy. When Candis answered the door, I could see beyond her that the house was vacant, except for a sleeping bag on the living room floor. Apparently, everything else she owned had already been packed tightly into her little covered pickup truck in the driveway. She was ready to go.

She took me on a quick tour of the house, which didn't take long. It had three bedrooms, two full baths, a wood-burning fireplace, and a full walk-out basement. With the exception of some paint on a few light switch covers, a very small stain on the dining room carpet (the size of a penny), and a cracked toilet seat (she had stood on while painting the bathroom), the interior was in absolutely perfect condition.

After we finished walking through it, I turned to her and said, "Look, Candis. I'm going to be honest with you. I really don't feel good about buying this house from you so cheaply. Why don't you go ahead and let me buy it from you on terms for a much higher price? Or better yet, I can give you the number of a really good Realtor who handles this area. He can get you a much better price than I can pay you. What do you say?"

"Well," she said, "will any of these other choices cash me out within the next 10 to 15 days, like your all cash program?" When I said no, she pressed on and insisted, "Then I just want to sell it to you outright for all cash. I really don't care about the price."

Now... in all the fantasies I've had about a seller uttering *that* magical phrase to me someday, the one thing I *didn't* count on was the paralyzing panic that would come with it; a combination of fear that I might be taking unconscionable advantage of someone who was naïve or incompetent, blended with dread over the fact that the house might be sitting—unbeknownst to me—on a sinkhole. Regardless of my concerns and convictions, Candis got me to write up the contract anyway.

After I had filled out the agreement in its entirety, I turned the document towards her and proceeded to go over it line-by line. At the end, I showed her where to sign, but just as she was about to autograph it, I grabbed the agreement back and quickly jotted down a handwritten disclosure at the bottom of the front page. It basically said that she was fully aware that her property was being purchased well below market value at a wholesale price, and that it was going to be immediately offered for resale at its full retail value. The disclaimer also said that she has considered and declined the idea of selling the property through a professional Realtor for considerably more money, and that her decision to forego this option was done of her own free will.

I turned the agreement towards her and asked her to initial next to the disclaimer before signing on the back page. She bent down to read what I had written, but after a few seconds she froze and said, almost to herself, "Oh... okay.... *I* see what's going on here."

For the next few moments, she said nothing while remaining perfectly still, which I found incredibly unnerving. Then... ever so slowly... she lifted her head until her cold blue eyes made contact with mine. Suddenly, I could no longer feel my knees. She continued her hypnotic, unblinking stare. Then, in a chilling voice that was eerily similar to one I'd heard only once before in a TV interview with Charles Manson, she simply said, "You think I'm crazy... *don't* you?"

And I didn't answer right away.

Naturally, my delay in responding was due in part to the fact that I wasn't so sure she really *wasn't* a couple french fries short of a Happy Meal. But my bigger concern was that my throat had just constricted, and any attempt to speak would have probably resulted in nothing more than a series of incomprehensible squeaks.

Her icy stare soon melted into something between sympathy and compassion as she watched rivers of sweat erupt on my forehead, belying my heroic efforts to maintain a poker face. This prompted her to immediately assure me that everything was okay, although I'm not sure if she did it to ease the tension in the room, or to avoid what she feared might be an impending heart attack.

"Relax, Nick," she said. "I'm perfectly sane and capable of understanding what's going on." I must have appeared unconvinced, because she went on to say, "Look, if it makes you feel better, my ex-husband and I used to own apartment buildings in Hyde Park (one of Cincinnati's most prestigious neighborhoods). So trust me, I'm smart enough to know what's going on. You're not taking advantage of me."

This was, needless to say, and enormous relief to hear. But it was nothing compared to what she told me next, which once again left me speechless.

She asked me, "Nick, do you know why you're here today?" I was hoping she was going to say to buy her house, and not that she intended anything involving my liver and some fava beans (I immediately glanced around for a bottle of Chianti). But before I could reply, she went on, "I'll tell you why. Unlike most people, you clearly aren't driven by greed. Now, don't get me wrong, I'm not saying there's anything wrong with money, because I used to chase it, too. But no longer. I'm moving to a religious community where I won't *need* money, so I don't really care how much I sell my house for, so long as I get enough to at least pay off my $95,000 mortgage.

"You see, I called a bunch of other investors with newspaper ads, flyers and postcards, and told them all the same story I told you. And you know what? Every single one of them was ready to come and steal my house... except you. You were the only one who tried to actually steer me away from fire-selling it to you.

"You bent over backwards trying to talk me into doing terms so that you could pay a more reasonable price. You were even willing to walk away and help me find a Realtor to sell it for me at full retail price, because you were worried about taking advantage of me." She paused for my reaction, but the look of slight confusion on my face told her I wasn't 100% sure where she was going with all of this.

So she continued.

"It's simple. You were the only person I talked to who actually cared more about doing right by me than about making a big fat profit for yourself; so that's why *you're* here and they're not. I figured if someone's going to make a killing from my house, it ought to be you—because in my opinion, you were the only one who deserved it."

I was stunned.

"You know what else?" she added, "The Realtor I had it listed with until last week called me yesterday with a $135,000 buyer." When I asked why she didn't take the offer, she said, "Because I don't want anything to do with that ass-face agent or his buyer. The whole time he had my house listed he was a jerk to me. So there's no way I was going to let him make a commission on my house. No way."

With that, she bent down and initialed my disclaimer, signed the back page, and sent me on my way. I was so exhilarated about the great deal I'd just struck, that it took about ten minutes into my ride home before it suddenly dawned on me that I had just committed to buying a house for $100,000 cash within 15 days, and I only had access to about $40,000 or $50,000 in available cash and credit lines.

I panicked for about 30 seconds, then calmed down and called a friend of mine who was a fellow investor in my real estate group. Fifteen minutes later, Harold had agreed to buy the house from me for $110,000 cash, closing in 7 to 10 days pending an inspection of the property. That put me right back on Cloud 9, where I'd been just moments earlier upon leaving Candis' house.

Ten days later, I walked into my title company's office to collect my check for $10,000. As I opened the door to the conference room where the closing was being held, my heart stopped. Sitting at one end of the conference table with his arms crossed was Harold, and sitting at the other end with a great big smile was Candis. In between them were 8 or 9 people, none of whom I recognized.

My first reaction was to bolt, assuming that half of the strangers were undercover detectives conducting a sting operation of local real estate fraud, while the other half were probably members of a production crew from *Dateline NBC*, looking to expose predators of a different sort (other than those with pedophilia tendencies). When a quick scan of the room confirmed that neither Stone Phillips nor Chris Hansen were among those present, I realized that I was probably just being paranoid.

So I relaxed, took my seat, and waited for the festivities to begin; thankful that they would be orchestrated by the title agent who apparently knew everyone's identity; but who had also decided for some reason to forego any introductions.

The closing began with me assigning my contract to Harold in exchange for a $10,000 check—that much I expected. But I didn't foresee what would happen next. Turning to his left, Harold assigned the agreement again, this time to an investor named Jim for another $10,000 check. Jim then turned to his left, and assigned the agreement yet again to his sister and brother-in-law in exchange for yet another check. At that point, Jim's sister and brother-in-law, as the actual buyers of the house, proceeded to sign all of the loan and closing documents with Candis.

When the dust finally cleared that day, four people walked away from the closing table with checks. Ironically, it was Candis, the actual owner and seller of the house, who got the smallest check by far—which really made her day. It pleased her not just because she no longer had a need or desire for money, but rather because she also had to split whatever money she *did* get from the sale with her ex-husband. And she was determined to send him the smallest check possible as a final *"Screw You!"* for having left her alone and heartbroken. She succeeded.

Now, please keep this story in perspective and remember that it's an example of a wholesaling anomaly, not a typical deal. That means you cannot and should not use it as a justification for creating a business model that specializes in finding the extremely rare, once-in-a-blue-moon sellers like Candis, who are both willing and able to give away their pretty properties for a song. You'll starve.

Your best bet is to stick with what works, which—as we were discussing before I started rambling on about Candis—is dealing primarily with vacant, ugly properties owned by highly motivated individuals who are anxious to unload them.

However, there's one more very important piece to the wholesaling puzzle, and that's learning how to frame your really low offers in the best possible light. Now you don't absolutely need this skill in order get deals done and make some money. But, if you'll take some time to develop a presentation that makes your offers *appear* more attractive—by shifting context and perception to adjust the seller's fluid opinion—you'll generate a lot more cash with a lot less effort.

There are at least three ways to improve your offer acceptance rate:

Method 1: Take my Uncle Guido with you when you visit sellers. He doesn't actually do any negotiating, he just stands in the background clearing his throat and patting his violin case occasionally. For some reason, this always seems to make really low offers suddenly irresistible to even the most cynical sellers. However, despite its effectiveness, I do not endorse this method—particularly if you happen to be negotiating with any member of the Soprano family.

Method 2: Negotiate on-site at the property in the ugliest room you can find. Doing this makes it very easy for you to remind the seller how nasty their property is by merely glancing around from time to time. This strategy is especially effective if you also happen to be wearing a disposable dust mask to "protect" yourself from mold and odors. And yes... I'm serious.

Method 3: Make multiple offers, just as we had looked at briefly on page 60 in our discussion on context shifting. The idea behind making multiple offers is to create some comparative examples that will not only help to frame your preferred offer in a more positive light, but will also help keep the seller so preoccupied with mulling over their sudden abundance of choices, that they may forget to be insulted enough to punch your lights out.

As an example, let's assume you're trying to put a deal together on the $100,000 (future value) property from our earlier scenario a few pages back. Let's also say that your seller is asking $60,000, but you need to get him to agree to sell it to you for a maximum of $40,000.

Starting your negotiations by simply tossing out a $40,000 offer is not a good idea for two reasons. First, it creates an instant $20,000 chasm, which can cause your offer to fall flat on the table and die a horrible death amid peals of hysterical laughter—or worse, filthy expletives. Second, it represents your maximum offer, which paints you into a corner by removing your flexibility to increase your offer a little during negotiations; something that the seller will be expecting you to do.

Instead, you can open your discussion by taking out a piece of paper and presenting three offers that you've hopefully remembered to preemptively brand as beneficial "buying programs" (see page 60) before you ever met the seller:

Offer 1- 15 Day Cash & Close Program: $30,000 paid in all cash, closing in 15 days

Offer 2- Premium Cash & Close Program: $40,000 at 10% down, bal. in 180 days

Offer 3- Fair Price Program: $50,000 at $1,000 down, $500 per month until paid off

What are we doing here? Three things: First, if you recall the substance of our context shifting chat back on page 60, you'll remember that what we're trying to do is establish a new set of parameters (a.k.a. *comparable relativities*), so that we can frame our desired offer in a better light by surrounding it with two other offers which appear to have some relevance. By the way, if you think this isn't an effective strategy, remember that this is the same basic premise under which Starbucks created three different, but relatively similar drink sizes in order to get you (and millions of other people) to spend a ridiculous $4.00 for a cup of coffee that costs about a quarter to make.

Second, we're trying to give the seller a series of choices in an effort to avoid starting out on opposite sides of the figurative negotiating table, with the offended seller and his high price sitting on one side, and cocky you and your really low price sitting on the other; each bent on defending their point of view to the death (of the transaction), if necessary.

And third, using multiple offers with a variety of prices and terms allows you to construct a closed negotiation bubble; one that is flexible, yet doesn't require stepping beyond its confines because you can volley back and forth—giving and taking on price and terms—using just the three offers that are already on the table, i.e., the more money the seller wants, the longer you want to pay it back, etc.

Ultimately, you'll be shooting for the seller to feel as though he has "negotiated" you into paying the higher price of $40,000 from Offer #2, while agreeing to give him the fast closing benefits of Offer #1, which is what you wanted to do all along. Starbucks would be proud of you.

But—and with all due respect to Kim Kardashian, this is a *pretty big but*—what if the seller decides to pick one of the other two offers you made, such as the split-funded deal in Offer #2, or the long term payment deal in Offer #3? How do you make any money wholesaling these?

It's actually pretty simple and, in fact, easier. Why? Because when you're reselling it to your wholesale buyer, Offer #2 gives them six months before they have to come up with most of the money that's needed to pay off the seller. They can easily get this cash later on by refinancing or reselling the repaired property.

For example: you want to wholesale the property for $45,000 and your seller picks Offer #2 ($40,000 with $4,000 down, and the $36,000 balance in 6 months). That means now your wholesale buyer won't need to cough up the entire $45,000 all at once. All they would need today to buy the property is $9,000 cash ($4,000 to the seller, and $5,000 to you), and it's pretty easy to find a wholesale buyer who'd prefer to pay only $9,000 up front and the rest later, as opposed to all $45,000 at once.

Offer #2 also gives your buyer enough time to actually fix up the property and resell it, so that they can simply use their end buyer's money to pay off the seller's balance. Or, they could repair the property and use its new $100,000 value to get a quick equity line or hard money loan of $36,000 to pay off the seller.

But what if the seller picks the $50,000 all-payment option in Offer #3? How can you wholesale a property for $45,000 when you're paying *$50,000* to buy it? Well, if you buy the property using Offer #3, you're getting wholesale terms, so you don't really need a wholesale price anymore.

What do I mean? Think about it: if your seller only needs $1,000 down, that means now your wholesale buyer would only need $6,000 cash to buy the property instead of $45,000, or even $9,000. Then once they've repaired it, they'll have a $100,000 property with a small $49,000 loan balance and only a $500 monthly payment. Besides enjoying $51,000 in equity, do you think your investor could also set up some nice cash flow with only a $500 payment to service? Sure!

But there's more. On top of that, Offer #3 says that the payments are $500 per month until paid, with no mention of any interest charges. Therefore, 100% of every $500 payment will be principal, which means it will all go towards reducing the $49,000 balance. With that kind of paydown, your wholesale buyer will own the property free and clear in only 98 months! So while they're enjoying excellent cash flow, they'll also be building even more equity in the property very rapidly. Do you think you'll have any trouble getting a wholesale buyer interested in a deal like this? Please say no, otherwise I'll be worried about you.

Here's one more thought, which I'm only going to explore *very* briefly: If you can access enough cash through partners or private hard money lenders (including friends, family members, and acquaintances), you could keep these deals and all the profits for yourself, rather than waste them on wholesale buyers. End of point.

Wholesaling Caveats

There are only a few caveats that you'll need to be aware of while wholesaling. Some of them are authentic issues that warrant genuine concern, while others are just a bunch of nonsense hassles concocted by the a-holes who run most banks, title companies, and government agencies for the express purpose of creating unnecessary hardships for legitimate, hard-working, and honest real estate investors like you and me (*ooops*...is my bitter contempt showing?).

The first thing you need to realize is that it's critical for you to fully identify and limit your liability to both your buyers and your sellers in the event you are unable to perform for any reason. I know we covered this briefly in our earlier discussion on managing risk in Chapter 4, but this is important enough to bear repeating here.

When you're buying, you absolutely must limit your full obligation in the event of a default to the forfeiture of your earnest money. Because if you put a property under contract and discover later that you can't close due to something unforeseen, such as the lack of sufficient funding, or seriously underestimating repair costs, or perhaps an inability to locate a wholesale buyer in time, your contract had better protect you from excessive seller recourse. Otherwise, you could find yourself praying to God that your losses will be limited to just the thousands you'll waste defending yourself in a nasty lawsuit for damages.

Similarly when you're selling, if you're unable to deliver a clear deed and you haven't limited your liability to your buyer, your buyer could end up driving away from the courthouse in your car—perhaps even on their way to your *house*, if the judge was so inclined to give *that* to them as well. I have always been careful to clearly identify and limit my buyer's recourse to a refund of their earnest money as fully liquidated damages. That way, I've never had to worry about any of my assets becoming the subject of random judicial redistribution... if you know what I mean. You and I are already getting enough redistribution from our federal government. There's no need to make it any worse.

Beyond limiting your exposure to liability, the only other natural caveat to wholesaling is that you may not find a wholesale buyer in time to close your deal with the seller. The only way to ensure that this won't be a problem for you is to have a list of qualified, capable wholesale buyers in-hand before you ever go out to make any offers to sellers. You can do this at least two ways, even before you make your very first offer.

One way is by joining a local real estate investment club, and letting them know that you're a wholesaler looking for cash buyers. Another is to run an ad or post a website looking for all cash buyers. Whichever method you choose, take the time to capture the contact info of interested investors, and find out what their investment limits and preferences are. That will let you assemble a list of qualified buyers who will be standing by just waiting for you to bring them deals.

But don't stop there, because no matter how good you are at qualifying potential cash buyers, some of your list members will pick up deals before you can contact them, a few others will have a change of circumstances, and the rest (read: majority) will have just outright lied to you about their ability or desire to ever actually buy *anything*. Flakes come in all different shapes, sizes, and professions.

That means every time you put a property under contract, in addition to contacting your investor list, you should also advertise each specific property for sale in every form of media you have at your disposal. This will help you build a larger and more varied buyer's list, and possibly even uncover a few really hot retail cash buyers. The great part about advertising properties cheap for all cash is that it's like a box of chocolates; you never know what you're gonna get.

So basically, those two strategies—limiting your liabilities to buyers and sellers, and making sure you always have a list of buyers—are the only two things you need in order to protect yourself from the few, naturally-occurring concerns that can arise while wholesaling. After all, wholesaling should be simple and uncomplicated, just like it is in every other industry on the planet.

Unfortunately though, you're not *in* every other industry on the planet... you're in real estate. So let's look at how to handle a few of the extraneous challenges that have been heaped upon us by a minority of duplicitous dumbasses (apparently, I'm still bitter...) who seem bent on destroying real estate investing as a career choice. As you'll soon see, every headache we're about to discuss is traceable back to one thing: the reckless determination of this handful of numbskulls to vilify and permanently ban the legitimate practice we know simply as *flipping*.

Flipping Challenges, and How To Overcome Them

Every wholesale deal, by definition, will involve a flip. That means whether you like it or not, you're eventually going to have to flip something—either a property or a contract—in order to make a profit. So now might be a really good time for you to find out what's behind all the nasty hype associated with flipping, so that you can figure out in advance how to avoid any potential problems.

First and foremost, let me make it perfectly clear that flipping real estate is not only fully legal, it's absolutely legitimate as well—regardless of what your favorite title attorney or real estate guru has told you. In fact, flipping is an acceptable and integral part of nearly every industry in America... except real estate.

So what went wrong? Well, it all started with the buyer and lender fraud that occurred during some flip transactions in the late 1990's and early 2000's. The way it worked was dishonest investors would put properties under contract for very low prices, and then immediately flip them at the same closing table to ignorant buyers for far above market value, using fraudulent appraisals to validate their inflated sale prices, and fudged loan apps to get the overleveraged loans approved.

When the media caught wind of these illicit transactions, they labeled them as "illegal flip deals", and then focused their full efforts on denigrating the crooked investors who orchestrated them—while generally giving a pass to all of the appraisers, title companies, mortgage brokers, and (occasionally) Realtors who were the indispensible co-conspirators on those very same deals.

Of course, zero blame was placed on the ignorant buyers who were viewed rather conveniently as victims, even though they were often just as responsible for their predicament as the immoral investors were. I mean, if someone is willing to blindly sign anything you put in front of them, without conducting any due diligence whatsoever because they're too ignorant or lazy to do it themselves, or too cheap to hire a professional to do it for them, then it's their own damn fault when they get ripped off. Now, don't misunderstand, I'm not defending the perpetrators of the fraudulent deals. But let's not forget the doctrine of Caveat Emptor. Buyers should clearly have some responsibility for their own actions.

Anyway, as the flipping drama continued to unfold over the subsequent years, the terms "illegal flip" and "illegal flipping scheme" became very popular catch phrases. Unfortunately, this led to the majority of Americans linking the two words *illegal* and *flip* together—perhaps forever—in the wrong context. The end result was that although the phrase "illegal flip" was originally intended to describe a flip deal that contained fraud, the public (and many others among the generally smug and uninformed press), misinterpreted the phrase as an indictment of the entire flipping process—as though the flip itself is what made the deal illegal, not the fraud that was committed *during* the flip.

HUD, in a typical knee-jerk government agency response that was both ill-conceived and ineffective (big surprise, there), immediately refused to underwrite any purchase money loans if the seller had not been on title as an owner of record for at least 90 days.* This was called *title seasoning requirement*, and the obvious purpose of this flawed policy was to prevent FHA borrowers from getting duped into participating in any more fraudulent flip deals. But HUD's methods were utter overkill, because fraudulent flips were actually pretty rare, despite their high profile visibility—kind of like shark attacks. The unintended consequence of this new restriction was that it prevented an overwhelming majority of otherwise fully qualified buyers from getting loans for their perfectly legitimate purchases, simply because their transactions met the definition of a "flip" deal. Dumb, dumber, dumbest. It was as if Jim Carrey had taken over as the chairman of HUD.

A much easier and more effective solution would have been for HUD to require multiple appraisals from two randomly selected HUD-approved appraisers for any deal in which the seller had been on title for less than 90 days. Then, they could have just taken the lower of the two values, or averaged them together.

*As of this writing, HUD has temporarily suspended its 90 day title seasoning rule to help aid economic recovery, which begs the question: If flipping is *good* for economic growth, why did they even ban it in the first place?

Either approach would have guaranteed that lenders or buyers would never again be compromised by greedy investor/appraiser collusions, since it would be impossible for any one investor to have *every* appraiser in town conspiring to inflate values for them.

This simple solution would have also preserved the right of investors to buy and immediately resell their properties without any unfair interference from the government. In fact, by creating the title seasoning restriction, HUD stomped on our constitutional rights by placing undue restraints on alienation. What this means is by refusing to lend money to otherwise qualified buyers based on the irrelevant length of the seller's ownership, HUD was obstructing the core right of all citizens to sell their properties to whomever they wanted, whenever they wanted, for whatever reason they wanted. Thomas Jefferson would be displeased.

This began a domino effect, as more and more lenders decided to adopt the same ridiculous seasoning requirements under the assumptions that: a) HUD knew what they're doing; and   b) perhaps flip deals may actually be sinister after all. Fortunately, some lenders were intelligent enough not to go down that path.

Of course, if you're wholesaling to a cash buyer, then title seasoning won't be a problem for you—although you're still not out of the woods, as you'll see next. But if your buyer does happen to need financing, as most do, they may just have to shop around a bit to find a lender that does not require title seasoning.

Another hurdle you'll have to overcome is finding a title company that will even close a flip transaction for you, because many of them are worried that the FBI will raid their offices and shut them down, just like some of the title companies who were egregiously complicit in fraudulent flipping schemes.

You see, although the media may have initially chosen not to scrutinize many of these co-conspirators within the public forum, title companies, appraisers, and mortgage brokers were routinely being investigated behind the scenes by federal agencies; later leading to raids and shut downs. And every time that happened, it made big news from coast-to-coast. Just like every shark attack.

This scared the crap out of most title and escrow attorneys, who decided it was probably best to err on the side of caution, and just stop closing flip transactions altogether. Thankfully, there were still a few title and escrow companies who were smart enough to see through the hype and continue doing them, so long as they were comfortable with the terms of the deal and the investor behind it. Those are title agencies and escrow companies you need to seek out. But even when you do find them, you'll still have one last obstacle: funding your purchase portion of the flip deal without using your own money—assuming you don't have any.

Ever since I began wholesaling back in the early 90's, I've always been able to let my buyer bring their cashier's check to the closing table, which my title company would then use to pay my seller for my purchase, and then cut me a check for whatever was left over as my profit.

For example, if I had a contract to buy a property for $100,000 and another contract to sell it for $120,000, I would just send both contracts to my title company, and they would set up two separate closings scheduled for the same time in two separate rooms. In one room, my buyer would bring a check for $120,000 to close his purchase, which the closing agent would then take into the next room and use to fund my purchase deal. Using the $120,000 funds from my buyer, the title company would cut a $100,000 check to my seller, and a $20,000 check to me. Because of this arrangement, I never had to bring money to closing. Ever.

But for some reason that I can't wrap my brain around—even with an I.Q. approaching 145—most title companies just won't do that anymore. Nearly every single one of them, even the few sharp ones who will still close flips, have adopted a new policy of requiring both halves of a flip deal be stand-alone transactions. In other words, your purchase half and your selling half must be completely separate transactions, each with its own separate funding.

This can create a significant challenge to you as a wholesaler, because it means that in order to flip a property in today's world, you will need to come up with the cash to purchase each property on your own without using your buyer's money.

So now what do you do? You have three choices. Your first choice is to bring your own cash to closing, which is a problem for most wholesalers because they don't have any. Your second choice would be to locate a cash partner to put up the money. This is also not an extremely attractive option, because it will typically cost you 50% of your profits, which are usually not all that big to begin with on most wholesaling deals. Your third, and most reasonable choice is to use something called transactional funding, which I both love and hate at the same time—to the same passionate degree.

Transactional Funding

Transactional funding is temporary financing that provides the money you need to close your buying side of a quick-turn (flip) deal. In addition to providing the cash you need, they can also furnish you with a POF a.k.a. VOF (Proof of Funds/ Verification of Funds) letter for you to submit to the listing agent or your potential seller, if necessary. This can be extremely helpful, because many Realtors and sellers these days are requiring proof of your financial capacity to close.

Most transactional funding companies charge two to three points (a point is one percent of the amount borrowed) for lending you the money. As for qualifying, they usually don't even bother to look at your credit score or your income, because the only thing they're usually concerned with is the loan-to-value ratio of the property they're lending against. If it's low enough, you're automatically qualified.

But there is a potential problem with borrowing money from a transactional funder to flip properties. What if you were to buy a property, and then for some reason your selling side of the flip transaction doesn't close? What then? How would you pay the investor back? What would your payment and interest be?

Fortunately, there is a simple procedure that can prevent this from ever becoming a reality, and many transactional funders use it. What is it? They will often require your title company or escrow agent to refrain from releasing any of the transactional funding for your purchase until after they have completed a "dry" closing of your selling side of the flip (a dry closing is one where all of the documents are signed, but no funds are released).

Doing this accomplishes two things: 1) It ensures that you won't ever get stuck with a property because you won't own it until after you've already technically sold it; and 2) It guarantees the transactional funder that their money will never actually be at risk—not even for a minute. If that's the case, then why do they even care about the loan-to-value ratio of your pending deal? Beats me.

Overall, my feelings on transactional funding are both mixed and highly-charged. On the one hand, it's a critical and indispensible tool for overcoming the bass-ackwards thinking of most title agents, allowing you to get your flip deals done when you wouldn't have otherwise been able to. On the other hand, it bites because you're paying thousands of dollars for the privilege of pseudo-borrowing money to complete a ten minute transaction—I say *pseudo* because in reality TF is just about as functionally useful as the Queen of England... or nipples on men.

In case you were curious, 2% interest for 10 minutes is equal to an annual interest rate of 105,120%, which is not only depressing but also an apparently massive violation of usury laws. I haven't wasted any time trying to figure out how they get away with that. Instead, I just write it off as one of those great mysteries of life, like *What is the meaning of life?* or *How does gravity work?* or the most puzzling mystery of all: *Why did William Shatner think it would be a good idea to cut an album?*

How to Circumvent Funding and Seasoning Issues

Would you be interested to learn how you can make wholesaling a lot easier by completely removing all the hassles of the ridiculous seasoning requirements? What if I could also show you how to make your deals more profitable at the same time, by removing the cost of transactional funding and double closings? Have I got your interest? Then pay attention, because there are two easy ways to do this.

The first way is to flip your contract instead of the property. This is done by assigning your purchase agreement to your end buyer for a fee equal to the spread you created between your original "buy" price and "sell" price. This allows your buyer to purchase the property directly from your seller at your low price.

But what if you don't want your buyer to know how much you have the property under contract for? Then a second way to do this would be to get a contract to sell the property, and then create a cloud on the property's title by filing a memorandum of contract at the courthouse. Then, let your seller deed the property straight to your buyer, while the title company cuts you a check to release your recorded interests in the property for an amount equal to your profit spread.

Both of these techniques remove the seasoning obstacle, because in each case your buyer would be purchasing the property directly from your seller, who is already a seasoned owner of record. Both of these methods would also increase your profitability, because they do away with the need for transactional funding or a double closing, saving you points plus two sets of closing costs.

Removing Chain of Title Risks

Another nice feature of the last two methods we just talked about is that they both reduce your exposure to liability by keeping you out of the official chain of title. Many people don't realize that if you appear in the chain of title (even for only one minute) you can be held liable for title problems for many years after you've sold the property—as long as 40 to 50 years or more in some states.

You see, both a general warranty deed and a plain deed—which is assumed to offer general warranties unless otherwise noted—are guarantees from you to your buyer that the title to the property is not only clear now, but has also been clear for all of the previous years that it's been in existence (although some states have limits). Additionally, you're promising that if a past title defect or claim against the property should ever pop up later, you will pay for whatever it takes to clear that title up—even if it means paying off some long-ago spouse or child who's interests were never properly extinguished from a *previous* title. Ouch.

Of course, the purpose of an owner's policy of title insurance is to protect you from these liabilities, but there are some downsides to title insurance. For one, policies are expensive, and they don't cover every defect, such as fraud or misrepresentation. Plus there are no guarantees the title company you bought the policy from will still be in business down the road should you need to file a claim.

So once again, the best way to minimize your risk of exposure is to eliminate it completely; and the best way to do that is to use the strategies above to avoid appearing in the chain of title at all whenever possible. But when that just can't be done, your next best bet is to transfer ownership using a limited warranty deed, or—if you're holding title in a trust—using a trustee's deed or fiduciary deed.

Any one of these deeds would accomplish the same thing for you, because they all greatly limit the promises that you would be making to your buyer. That's because with these deeds you would only be warranting the title to be free from defects during the period in which you owned the property—not before, or after.

Actual Wholesale Case Study

One day, Tammy, a 30 year-old mother of three from South Carolina, called me about a house she had inherited from her mother in a nice area near my office. She said of all the *I Buy Houses* phone numbers she found in the newspaper, mine was the only one that had the same area code and exchange as her mother's, so she called me because she thought I'd probably be as nice as her mom was (God's honest truth!). She asked if I could meet her at the house soon—and by soon, she meant now. Fortunately, I was not too busy to drop everything and get out there.

I knew the area pretty well, so when I got to the house it was exactly what I had expected. It was worth about $80,000 repaired, and after walking through it, I figured it would need about $15K in repairs. I was using my 30% wholesale spread formula at the time, which gave me a WV (Wholesale Value) of $41,000 ($80K less 30% = $56K, minus $15K in repairs = $41K). I wanted to make at least $5,000 wholesaling it, so that made my MAO (Maximum Allowable Offer) $36,000 ($41K less $5K = $36K).

Tammy told me she had originally wanted to move back into town and live in her mom's house, but her husband had literally gotten tired of rehabbing it, and had told her as much just a few hours earlier. So on a whim, she had decided that afternoon to just sell it and go back to the coast. I asked her how much she would be willing to take if I could pay her all cash and close in 7 to 10 days. She said if I could give her $25,000 she'd be tickled pink. Funny... I felt the same way.

Of course, since that was her first offer, I tried to negotiate a little to get an even better deal. But she wasn't budging, and I didn't push it. I didn't need to. In fact, I was concerned that if I pushed too hard, she just might decide to start shopping around for a better price.

So we wrote the deal up on-the-spot for $25,000, and on my way home I called a cash investor who specialized in buying homes in that area. He was an expert who usually closed within three to four business days, and he estimated the same $36,000 as his MAO, which meant that I was looking at an $11,000 payday in about 72 hours or so.

Prentiss (my wholesale buyer) was true to his word and closed the deal for $36,000 in just three days, with the deal being expedited by the fact that we both used the same title company for all of our deals. He went on to spend $20,000 in repairs (not $15,000 as I had estimated), and sold the house quickly for $89,900 (not for the $80,000 I had estimated).

Now... does this mean I made mistakes in estimating both the ARV (After Repaired Value) and the RC (repair costs)? Not really. Prentiss suspected that if he spent an extra $5,000 to tap into the public sewer system, he'd be able to eliminate the undesirable septic system, thereby enhancing the property's market value to more than just $80,000. He was exactly right, and that's why he's an expert.

OPTIONS

OPTIONS

A QUICK OVERVIEW

> **What they are:** An option is an agreement that gives a potential buyer (optionee) the right, but not the obligation, to purchase a property from the owner (optionor), at a negotiated price for a specific period of time.

> **What they do:** An option provides you with temporary control of real estate without any rights of occupancy, giving you time to conduct due diligence, and/or to identify or create a profit opportunity.

> **How they're done:** Typically, the optionee (you) will pay the optionor (property owner) an upfront, non-refundable option fee for the right to buy the property at an agreed price and terms. If the property is purchased, the upfront fee is usually applied to the purchase price. If the property is not purchased within the designated time frame (the option period), the option expires and you would typically forfeit your option fee. However, since you were never required to purchase the property, the forfeiture of your option fee is the seller's only remedy against you.

> **How they can generate revenue:** Options can be used to tie up properties at a particular price, in anticipation of: a) finding a subsequent buyer to purchase it for more; or b) waiting for the property to appreciate in value—either slowly over time, or quickly via an upcoming event, such as a zoning change or an impending eminent domain acquisition.

> **Best market cycle:** Options can work quite well in either up or down markets. In my opinion, they are much better suited for up markets, because having a greater quantity and quality of potential buyers greatly improves the speed and likelihood of a successful resale. Some people argue that options are better during down markets, because tougher conditions lead to higher numbers of motivated sellers being open to optioning their properties at lower prices. Although they do work in down markets, the trade-off is that there are far fewer willing and qualified end buyers for you to choose from.

> **Caveats:** Using options strictly for reselling properties at a profit may require licensure in some areas, although this is a debatable issue. Due to increasing "anti-flip" policies by lenders and title agencies, options may also create some closing challenges similar to those in wholesale deals. These issues will require some advance steps to minimize or overcome, and may also lead to additional costs for temporary transactional funding.

The Basics

Option agreements are unilateral, which essentially makes them binding on only one party—the seller (optionor). The buyer (optionee) has a choice as to whether or not to buy the property; but if they decide to do so, the optionor must comply.

As a control method, options are frequently combined with lease agreements to create the ever-popular Lease-Option (which we'll cover shortly). But options do not have to be tied to any other document or transaction. Straight options have a number of beneficial uses all by themselves.

In commercial real estate, options are common. They help companies make intelligent buying decisions by allowing them to tie up one or more prospective properties until extensive (and often *expensive*) due diligence can be performed, such as feasibility studies, confirming build-out expenses, etc. If the research looks favorable on a particular of property, the option on that parcel can be exercised, while the options on any others can be allowed to expire. This results in a forfeiture of the option fees, but the trade-off is there are no other liabilities for non-performance. That makes options an efficient strategy, because randomly conducting due diligence on properties before knowing for certain that they can be bought at a suitable price is a gamble most companies simply cannot afford to take.

Options are also used on residential properties, most often by investors. The drill is pretty much the same as in commercial applications. After a property is optioned, the optionee (investor/buyer) conducts his or her due diligence. If it appears that it makes sense to proceed with buying the property, the option is exercised. Exercising an option is as simple as sending written notice to the optionor (seller) prior to the expiration of the option period, stating that the optionee intends to buy the property as provided in the agreement. At that point, the option agreement is essentially transformed into a purchase agreement that is bilateral, meaning both parties are now obligated to perform. The optionee then aligns his/her/their funding for the purchase, places the paperwork into the hands of a title agent for the preparation of the closing documents, and closes the purchase.

The Agreements

As far as the contract itself goes, options can be done several different ways. The first is obviously by using a straight option agreement. A Letter of Intent (LOI) can also be used, but a pretty common trick is to take a standard purchase and sale agreement, and just tweak the language a little. By simply giving the buyer much longer to close, and limiting their liability to a forfeiture of their earnest money, you can instantly turn your favorite LOI or purchase contract into a viable option agreement.

A very common option question is, "How much are option fees?" That's like asking, "How high is up?" There are no set standards, but commercial option fees can typically run from $1,000 to $10,000; while residential properties, by contrast, can often be as low as $100 to $500. But the real answer to that question is this: Option fees are as much as you can *get* when you're selling, and as little as you can *get away with* when you're buying. A great way to keep your option fees low would be to use the earnest money negotiation tactics coming up on page 144.

Using Options in the Real World

A few years back, I used options nearly every day as part of my short sale deals; but no longer, since I've re-worked my short sale agreements to utilize the *subject to* strategy instead. These days, I've pretty much relegated options to bastard step-child status, i.e., I keep my option agreements locked away in my briefcase and avoid mentioning them whenever possible. And although I'm aware that they're lurking inside, I seldom bring them out into the light of day for anyone to see—except on those rare occasions when it looks as if I don't have any other choice.

Overall, I've found that options work best in the following two applications, both of which I rarely encounter in the wild: 1) on high-end properties that can be fire-sold at auction, and; 2) on bread-and-butter properties that can be tied up and shopped to a small list of qualified retail buyers. Here's a closer peek at each type.

1. On high-end properties: Options are an effective tool for tying up very high-end properties at hundreds of thousands—or even millions of dollars—below their market values, with the intent of quickly auctioning them off at aggressive prices that are considerably higher than the option price, but well below market value.

Auctions are fast becoming a popular and profitable means for selling very high-end properties, often in the multiple million dollar range. Here's how the process works: an investor gets an option to purchase a very high-priced property at a significant discount, and then advertises it for sale by auction. Then, they fire-sale it at a price that's slightly above their option price (by percentage) but far enough below market that consumers will pounce on it. Of course, the actual prices and percentages will vary immensely from deal to deal, but the general principle is this: even small percentages on very expensive properties can amount to quite a bit of money, in actual dollars and cents, for the investor middleman.

In fact, just for fun, let's take a look at an extreme example. Let's say you find the owner of an $8 million mansion that's been for sale for two years, which is not unusual in that price range. Let's say that the seller happens to be highly motivated to get rid of it fast, because he has an opportunity to discretely jet to the French Riviera with Jessica Alba. As a result, you're able to negotiate an option to buy it for only $5.2 million cash, which is about 65% of the market value. Then, let's say you hold an auction a few weeks later and end up selling it for $5.5 million, which is 68.7% of the market value. As you can see, you've only generated a 3.7% spread (by percentage), but that small spread is equal to $300,000 in cash!

Now, you're probably wondering if owners of $8 million mansions ever *really* agree to take 35% discounts for quick all-cash offers. The answer is: not always… but sometimes. In fact, depending on what's cooking in their lives at the moment, they'll occasionally take even less—and they often have enough equity to do it. I once met someone who optioned an $8.6 million property for—believe it or not—only $4 million! He auctioned it off in a few weeks for $5.6 million, which, in case you don't want to bother with the math, is an 18.5% spread that equals a $1.6 million dollar profit—just on the house alone! He made another couple hundred thousand auctioning off the contents and the boat out back that very same day!

The closest I ever got to something like that was when I optioned a $1.2 million house for $720,000 a few years back—although I never got the chance to actually exercise my option. You see, three months before I came along, the seller had already accepted a non-exclusive purchase offer from another individual. The contract had about 20 contingencies in it, but since it was also non-exclusive it allowed the seller to continue looking for another buyer, which is where I came in. Sadly, as soon as the contingent buyer caught wind of my option, he immediately waived all of his contingencies and bought the property before the ink was dry on my contract. A couple of years later when it came up for sale again during a tougher market, it still went for $921,000—that's $201,000 over my option price!

Do you know how incredible it feels to make $200,000 on the sale of just one house? Well, don't feel bad… I don't either. The best I've ever done with an option was $15,000, and I've only made a total of $25,000 with the two options I've done in my career (not counting the $128,000 I made when I used options on my short sale deals). This is not due to any lack of understanding the option-to-auction technique, nor to any fear of dabbling in high-end properties. It's mostly because Cincinnati just doesn't *have* many multi-million dollar properties for me to work with. Also, there aren't too many people standing in line to pay millions of dollars to live here—not even if it means getting to buy a property for considerably less than what it's worth. So basically, that leaves me—and most other people in similar markets—with the bread and butter option approach.

2. On bread-and-butter properties: Options also work well as a means of tying up several properties in a particular price range and specific area, for when you have a qualified retail buyer (or list of buyers) looking to purchase in that area.

Even though options can work on any type of property in any area and any price range, this particular strategy is ideal because it positions you for a faster, easier, and more likely paycheck. The reason is because you'll be in possession of what would be tantamount to crystal ball enlightenment; you already know who your buyer will be, and how much they're willing to pay for a particular property. Unfortunately, *actual* crystal ball enlightenment—such as how long you're going to live or whether your spouse is fooling around—will continue to elude you.

Anyway, these "known" buyers can come from two sources: buyers you were already working with on another property you had for sale, or a list of buyers you've built in advance of looking for properties to option. The first strategy simply takes full advantage of a valuable resource you already have; one which most investors are sadly unaware of. After all, you've probably paid lots of money to find some good qualified buyers. So if you already have 'em... use 'em!

Building a buyer's list in advance is a guerilla tactic that we discussed previously in the section on wholesaling. Not only does it give you a stable of buyers to draw from, it also helps you identify and measure the demand for your intended niche before you even bother to exploit it. In other words, if hardly anybody is interested in buying properties in the particular area you want to target, wouldn't it be nice to know that *before* you commit to spending a lot of time and marketing money buying or optioning properties there? Of course!

However, if you do this, you have to be a careful about how you market for buyers when you don't have a product for them yet, i.e., you can't say something like "Stunning 4 bedroom, 3 bath contemporary in desirable Coldstream Woods", unless you already *have* a 4 bedroom, 3 bath contemporary in Coldstream Woods under your control. But even if you don't have one there, but want to work with buyers in that area, you could say something like, "Looking for a good deal on a gorgeous contemporary home in Coldstream Woods? Then please call me today! If I don't have exactly what you're looking, chances are I will very soon!"

Regardless of where you get your qualified buyer prospects (qualified meaning seriously ready, willing and able to buy, not just tire-kickers), once you have them, go to the areas they want to buy and start optioning some properties that match their preferences. After you have some under contract, you can simply walk your buyers through each property in rapid succession, and then let them decide which one they want. If all of the properties meet their criteria—which you already know they do—chances are pretty good that they'll want at least one of them.

And because you had built-in buyers ready to rock, and knew what they were looking for, as well as how much they were willing and able to pay in advance, optioning some properties for them would be pretty easy to do. Think about it: you only have to market to a small area, you won't have to ask the sellers for long option periods, and you can generally offer them pretty reasonable all-cash prices that are often much higher than a property wholesaler would offer.

As my cousin Vinnie would say, "Badda-bing... badda-boom."

Of course, some gurus will teach you to go out and option a whole bunch of properties anywhere and everywhere you can, simply because it's risk free to do so. Then, they'll tell you to go looking for buyers for all of those properties, and sell whichever ones you can, while letting the rest of the options expire. I don't generally like this strategy; it can be time-intensive and full of potential problems.

First, if you're optioning properties before you know how much you can resell them for, then your option offers will involve some guesswork. Sometimes you'll paint yourself into a corner by offering more than you should have. This can lead the need for a last-minute discount, which can be both embarrassing and highly unprofessional to ask for.

However, the more likely scenario is that since you have no idea how much you can resell the properties for, you'll usually be offering far too little in an attempt to be conservatively safe. This will make you look greedy to the seller, and as a result, many sellers you might have otherwise done a deal with will flat-out reject your low offers. This will create more work and marketing costs for you than necessary, because you'll need to submit more offers to make the same amount of money.

And the challenges continue. If you've got a bunch of various properties in various areas and various price ranges under contract, your marketing for potential buyers will have to be very broad and general in order to encompass all the variety you have to offer; and this lack of niche focus will make your marketing far more expensive—and far less effective—than you'd probably like.

Plus, when you market a seller's property for sale at considerably more than what you've just agreed to pay them for it, they'll sometimes have a problem with that. You see, even if a seller is likely to net about the same amount of cash whether they option it to you or sell it themselves through a Realtor, the difference in how they surrender their hard-earned equity can actually become a hot topic.

Why? It all boils down to the perception of *commission* versus *profit*. Sellers perceive a *commission* as something that's been earned. But when they see you taking a *profit* from their equity, even if it's for the same amount they would have spent on commission and closing costs, they may suddenly feel as though you're taking something away from them. So if you're planning to option properties first, and then begin a marketing campaign to find buyers at higher prices, you can expect some of your sellers to pitch a major bitch fit.

Here's an example: If a seller offers a property for $250,000 through a Realtor, they're likely to net roughly $220,000 or so before deducting closing costs and tax prorations. This figure comes from a $250,000 asking price, less the following costs, which are pretty standard in today's marketplace: a 3.2% price concession ($8,000), a 6% Realtor commission ($14,500), and another 2.8% contribution towards the buyer's closing costs ($7,000). Most sellers won't have too much trouble accepting these costs as being reasonable, and possibly even inevitable.

However—and here's the weird part—if that same seller were to let you option their property for that identical $220,000 net, and then discovered the very next day that you're trying to sell it for $250,000, they might suddenly feel as if they're being screwed because it looks like you're taking a $30,000 chunk of their hard-earned equity as your "dirty" profit. This precise concern, coincidentally, makes a perfect segue into a discussion on our last challenge of the day; circumvention.

One last issue we'll cover about optioning properties is to figure out how you can prevent all of your sellers from circumventing you, and selling directly to the buyers you're digging up for their properties. Simultaneously, you'll need to keep your buyers honest as well, since they'd all love to circumvent you and go straight to your sellers to pick up properties at the lower prices you're optioning them for.

One way you can protect yourself from circumvention is by recording a memorandum of option on all of your optioned properties. But if you're running around optioning lots of properties everywhere, this can get bothersome and even dangerous—because when each option expires, you're legally obligated to file (at your own time and expense) a release for it at the courthouse. Otherwise, you will leave yourself open to potentially nasty litigation down the road for something called *slander of title*—and that is not an area to tread casually.

Does that mean I'm against filing memorandums? No way! In fact, I think it's crazy not to record *something* before taking buyers through properties you've optioned. But since memorandums require much care in their recording and release, it's a safer strategy to option properties in smaller numbers to meet the needs of your buyer's list, rather than trying to option every property in town.

Why Options?

Now, just so we're clear, I'm not claiming that I've ever set the world on fire with my option prowess. In fact, as I mentioned before, I've only used them a couple of times as a stand-alone method (excluding about the dozen or so short sale deals I used them on). But I still felt it was imperative to include them in this book—especially since they've helped me generate $25,000 in profits that I couldn't have gotten to any other way, given the nature of those two particular deals.

Another plus regarding options is that as far as speediness is concerned, they can be pretty tough to beat as an investment approach. The $15,000 deal only took me five days to complete from the time my seller signed the option agreement to the moment I was sitting down at the closing table to flip the property. At only eleven days, from start to finish, the $10,000 deal took slightly more than twice as long, but that's still pretty fast by any standard.

But here's the main reason I included options: they are a great way to take control of properties at reasonable prices with very little risk to you or the seller. Your risk is minimized by the fact that you haven't committed to anything except possibly forfeiting your option fee. There are no monthly payments to service, and no requirements to ever buy anything. The seller's risk is minimized by the fact that if you perform, the price is likely to be decent, since the you don't necessarily have to steal it as in a wholesale transaction. And if you don't perform in the short period of time you have, the option simply expires and the seller is free to start looking for buyers once again.

Licensing Challenges

As you may have noticed in some of the option examples, there are times when an option deal seems to closely parallel that of a "list and sell" transaction done by a licensed real estate agent, in that the investor takes control of the property—just like an agent might get an exclusive right to sell—and then collects a profit for successfully finding an end buyer for it—in the same way that an agent collects a commission for successfully selling a property. The apparent similarities of these two processes have not been lost on many state legislators, who have ignorantly passed laws requiring licensure for anyone who "deals in options" on real estate. Apparently these legislators are too stupid to grasp the simple notion that two transactions which may *seem* similar could, in fact, be vastly different.

The most glaring difference between them is that in an option deal the investor is a principal member of the transaction, while in a commissioned sale the licensed agent is a third party who's been hired to advise and protect the buyer and/or the seller. This is not a minor discrepancy, but rather a massive disparity. As the principal member of a transaction, an investor is acting solely on their own behalf *as* the buyer or seller, whereas a licensed real estate agent acts as a representative *of* the buyer or seller. Do you get the difference? Of course you do. It's a clear distinction that is patently obvious to everyone except (apparently) lawmakers, most of whom are too busy playing God and diddling 20 year-old pages to notice.

Even more distressing is that many states with these option laws are content to leave vague as to what "dealing in options" actually means, ensuring inconsistent interpretation and potentially broad applications. This could lead to witch hunts wherein even the most casual optionee could be classified as a wanton violator of state licensing laws. After that, it would only be a matter of time before some radical judge sets a precedent by ruling that wholesaling properties constitutes "dealing in options" too. Don't scoff, because a ruling like that could easily be justified under the frequent legal interpretation of "function over form", i.e., something *is* what it *does*, no matter what you call it. And after all, isn't wholesaling at its core a form of optioning? Of course it is. And such a ruling would eventually lead to licensure being required for wholesaling any properties that you don't physically buy first. Can you feel the noose tightening?

Ohio, Wisconsin, Louisiana, and Colorado are four states I know of with laws on the books that identify dealing in options as a practice which requires licensure in certain applications. However, Louisiana and Colorado both go on in almost identical language to further define exactly what "dealing in options" means; and in their statutes it includes anybody (or entity) who options a property with the intent to resell it, even if the property passes through their own name. This means even when an investor is a principal member of a deal, acting only in their own interests and providing no fiduciary advice to other people (which is the opposite of what real estate agents do), they are still required to be licensed. To comment on this in the most polite language possible: that's an absolute crock of bullshit.

You see, the whole point of licensure is to provide a process of accountability for individuals who advise or represent *other people*. In other words, if an individual is going to advise someone else on critically important matters, such as buying or selling real estate, there should be a system in place to make sure the person giving the advice is qualified to do so, and that the advice they give is in the client's best interests. This makes perfect sense to any sane individual.

However, when you're negotiating for the right to buy a property, and you have made it clear to the seller that you are representing only yourself and that they are responsible for their own representation, licensure should NEVER be required, even if you are planning to resell that same property seven seconds later. I mean, how the hell can any government justify interfering with free will by restricting your right to negotiate for the purchase of a piece of real estate—regardless of how long you intend to own it? That's nonsense. As long as you are acting on your own behalf as the buyer and the subsequent reseller, and you haven't provided any advice to your seller or your subsequent buyer, then no state or federal government should have the right to regulate you. After all, reselling something you've just bought for more than what you paid for it is the basic platform for all American commerce. Why should it suddenly be restricted just because the commodity is real estate instead of paper clips... or bananas... or window shades? If a process is legitimate, it's legitimate—regardless of the industry or price point. Period.

All of that aside (he said, as he finally descended from his soapbox), and with the laws on the books being what they are, what do you do? Do you tuck your tail and forego options altogether? Well, that is one choice. Another would be to get licensed yourself, or hire a licensed agent to work for you either part-time or as an occasional contractor (check with your attorney first) just for your option deals.

Or, you could decide, with your attorney's blessing, to just plow ahead and do options with no regard for the laws which apparently seem to restrict them. Some attorneys are still of the opinion that these laws don't apply if you're a principal member of the transaction. And many seasoned investors—contrary to the advice of both myself and of their counsel—believe that operating ethically and below the radar can reduce the risk of discovery to the point where it is too unlikely to be a concern. Either way, you wouldn't be alone in your decision to move forward and option properties anyway. Thousands of people are doing it every day

Whatever you decide, just remember that if something is really worth chasing, it's always worth taking a little extra effort to position yourself properly for the pursuit. This is especially true when seemingly large obstacles like licensure requirements, which appear insurmountable to the average lazy real estate investor, can actually serve to clear out the competition for you so that you can work the leading edge profitably and peacefully.

Keeping Downpayments Low

When it comes to options, the bulk of your money for purchasing the property will be coming either from your buyer in a contract flip, or from a transactional funding company in a "deed-in, deed-out" quick-turn double closing. That means your only actual monetary investment in the deal will be the up-front option fee you agree to pay, so let's look at how to keep that as low as possible without sending up any red flags or pissing anybody off.

The trick to doing this is all in how you present it; both in your framing and your negotiating posture. Let me explain. First of all, your previous discussions with the seller should have already established the attitude that you are someone with a potentially valuable solution for them, and that you are not by any means a Desperate Housebuyer (which is *not* the name of a new reality show coming to A&E this fall). Second, it's important that you approach the option fee as a standard, almost bothersome, aspect of the agreement that you are discussing only because it's necessary—as opposed to framing it as a critical financial commitment that you are trying to cheap out on.

For example, as you're going over the agreement with the seller, when you get to the option fee, simply explain that it's merely a deposit required to make an agreement binding, which is why you're putting up the $10, $100 or whatever minimum is required by your state. Then, without hesitation, you casually move to the next line in the agreement, being sure not to rush too quickly, lest the seller may become wary; but also being sure not to leave an awkwardly long pause, which the seller may take as an invitation to challenge the small amount you've just offered.

If you learn to time it right, sellers will instantly form the perception that the amount of the option fee is an inconsequential detail, and will obediently follow your lead into the next paragraph; much the same way an audience follows a street magician's conspicuously active left hand, as his right hand slips covertly up his jacket sleeve to retrieve a hidden playing card.

Of course, sometimes a seller will want to back up the train and take a closer look at the small option fee you're suggesting. What then? Well, the last two things you want to do are: a) get defensive about it, or b) suggest that it's all you can afford—even if it is.

The best tact is to gently remind the seller that you're offering the amount that is required by your state (almost as if you're deferring the blame to the state legislature), and then assure him that you will be otherwise heavily invested in the deal's success by virtue of all the time, money, and energy you'll be expending in the process of getting them cashed out of their property. Besides, in the general business world, people usually pay others for providing solutions for them, not the other way around; so it just doesn't make much sense for you to be expected to pay

THE COMPLEMENTARY TECHNIQUES

someone a lot of money for the privilege of utilizing your resources to help them resolve a situation. That's usually more than enough to satisfy the seller. If it isn't, you're sitting in front of the wrong seller.

This low downpayment negotiation strategy works exactly the same way, and for the same reasons, in virtually any other nothing down transaction—whether you're looking to limit an option fee or an earnest money downpayment. So as you learn about the other techniques covered in this book, just remember the lessons you learned here: that you are in control, that you are not desperate, that the seller is the one with the problem, that you are the one with the solution, that it never makes sense to pay dearly for the right to help someone out, and that—above all things—refusing to pay a large downpayment should never be framed as a matter of affordability (even if it is), but rather as a sensible business decision based on sound reasoning. If you can convey this well, negotiating miniscule downpayments will be a breeze, regardless of the technique you're using at any given moment

Actual Option Case Study

When Troy scored me that coveted Red's opening day ticket, I thought he was just looking to hang out for a few hours. And maybe he was. But eventually, the talk turned to real estate investing as I suspected it might. After all, he had often indicated to me that he wanted to get involved in real estate, just like myself and his millionaire father-in-law.

He was especially intrigued to learn that at that very moment in the fourth inning, as we were chowing down on spicy peanuts and $4 stadium dogs, I was making $6,500 on a real estate wholesale transaction eight miles away—with absolutely no one there on my behalf except the title agent who was closing the deal.

When I asked him what specific sort of investing he was interested in pursuing, he told me he wanted to buy a few 2 to 4 unit multi-family buildings to generate some monthly rental cash flow. From the story I had just told him, he discovered that I was a property wholesaler... and he did exactly what I'd hoped he would by asking if I had any multi-families available for him to buy.

Since I was focusing only on higher-end single family properties at the time (and still generally do, by the way), I told him I didn't have anything like that at the moment, but that I get new properties in all the time. I then asked him what price range he was qualified to buy in, and how quickly he could close if I found him something he liked. Before he could answer, I also went on to let him know that the faster he could close, and the fewer contingencies he put in his buying contract, the better the deal he could expect to get on something he liked.

He said that he wouldn't need any financing contingencies at all, because he'd already lined up $X in equity line financing, and could close in as little as three or four days. He then went on to tell me that he was really anxious to get a property as soon as possible, so he wasn't really going to be all that picky. In other words, if I could find him something that even remotely resembled what he was looking for, I was only three or four days away from getting a nice, fat, easy paycheck.

It was almost enough to give a guy some wood.

So early the next day, I began putting out feelers in the area that he was interested in, and I quickly found two potential properties for sale that met his basic criteria. One seller was willing to give me a 15 day option, the other told me to kiss his butt, and then went on to suggest that I engage in an activity which would have violated both myself and the physical limits of the human anatomy. Sweet guy.

No matter. When I showed Troy the one property I had under option, he couldn't wait to buy it, and eleven days later (he decided to have it inspected), we were sitting at a closing table where I was collecting a $10,000 check for the difference between my option price with the seller and Troy's purchase price from me.

In fact, to keep things really smooth and simple, I had my title agent deliver just one deed—straight from my seller to my buyer—and cut me a check for the $10,000 difference in exchange for releasing my memorandum of contract. Of course, this memorandum hadn't been recorded yet, or even drafted for that matter. But it would never need to appear in public records if the check from my title company cleared as expected.

Fortunately, it did.

As it turns out, handling the closing this way not only kept me off public record and out of the chain of title (eliminating all of the incidental liabilities that come with that), but it also kept my net profit at the full $10,000. Why? Because I was able to extract myself from the typical "deed-in, deed-out" double closing process, which allowed me to avoid both sets of closing costs that come with it—one set as the buyer, and another as the seller.

LEASE-PURCHASE

LEASE-PURCHASE

A QUICK OVERVIEW

➤ **What they are:** A lease-purchase agreement is one that combines a lease agreement with a purchase contract. It can take the form of a single document, or it can be two separate documents which, when combined, comprise a single instrument.

➤ **What they do:** A lease-purchase gives a buyer the right to both occupy and purchase a piece of real estate for a specific period of time. The seller maintains legal title until the buyer consummates the purchase, if ever.

➤ **How they're done:** Typically, a tenant/buyer pays a landlord/seller an upfront deposit to lease and occupy the property until they can buy it later at an agreed price. If the property is purchased, the deposit is usually applied to the purchase price, often along with some portion of the rental payments. If the property is not purchased within the designated lease period, the agreement expires and the tenant/buyer forfeits their deposit.

➤ **How they can generate revenue:** A lease-purchase has many benefits for sellers: they can generate interest in the property, they can help minimize repair responsibilities, they can command above-market rents, and they can lead to premium selling prices. Some investors "sandwich" lease-purchase agreements, using one to take control of a property, and a separate one to resell it at a higher price with higher monthly payments. This creates three revenue centers: an upfront profit, monthly cash flow, and a back-end payday. Although I like the sandwich concept, in today's market I usually prefer to just assign my agreement to an end buyer.

➤ **Best market cycle:** Lease-purchases work well in up or down cycles, but down cycles are slightly better because there are generally more motivated sellers, making deals easier to find and more lucrative to negotiate. Plus a lease-purchase can help stimulate consumer interest at a time when buyers are more likely to need assistance to buy, as well as more incentives to consider your property above all others.

➤ **Caveats:** Buying on a lease-purchase can create some title seasoning challenges when you're reselling, because you wouldn't appear on title as the owner of record. In fact, whenever you resell a property that you've taken control via a lease-purchase, the process will eventually require a "flip" type double-closing. These are perfectly legal transactions, but unfortunately, many lenders and title agents won't go anywhere near them.

The Basics

In a lease-purchase agreement, a buyer and seller agree on a sale price, a monthly lease payment amount, and the length of time in which the buyer can purchase the property at the agreed price. Typically, the time period will run from two to five years, although there is no standard length. After price and terms are negotiated, the buyer pays an earnest money deposit, and sometimes a rental deposit (although that's something *you* will never do), and then makes monthly payments until either: a) the buyer cashes out the seller at the agreed price—often by getting permanent bank financing or by reselling the property; or b) the lease-purchase term expires. If the property is purchased, the earnest money is applied to the sale price. If it's not purchased, the earnest money is typically forfeited.

Frequently, the buyer will also negotiate for a portion of the monthly payments to be credited towards the purchase price as additional downpayment monies paid in installments. The amount of the monthly credit can vary from as little as $50 to $100 of each payment, all the way up to the entire payment itself. However, if the buyer ends up applying for a bank loan, most lenders will only treat as "downpayment" any portion of the monthly payment that's above fair market rent.

If you're familiar with real estate, this process may sound a lot like a lease-option. That's because they're virtually identical. So why not just use a lease-option? After all, most investors prefer them because a lease-option doesn't obligate them to buy, while a lease-purchase does. And if I'm such a stickler for limiting risk, why would I advocate using a lease-purchase when a lease-option sounds safer?

Well, first of all, being obligated to buy a property doesn't necessarily create any additional risks for you. Remember, we learned earlier in the section on risk management that as long as we control the document language, we control the default remedies against us. So by simply limiting our liability to the loss of our earnest money, we end up creating a contract that's called a lease-*purchase*, but which for all intents and purposes is essentially a lease-*option*.

But why the big fuss over semantics? Lease-option, lease-purchase…who really cares? Well, as you may also recall from earlier in this book, we learned that psychology can be a very important factor in your success; and a lease-purchase can offer some slight psychological advantages over a lease-option when you're buying *and* when you're selling.

You see, when you're looking to buy a property, sellers are much more comfortable and familiar with the term "purchase" than they are with "option", so we need to consider that. Think about it. The concept of a lease-purchase, which by its very name suggests an intent to buy, feels more acceptable and desirable to a frustrated and perhaps nervous seller than a lease-*option* does—especially since a lease-option, by its very definition, gives the buyer permission to just walk away at any time without making any effort at all to buy the property.

Just imagine if you were the seller. How discomforting it would be to know that your buyer seems to be positioning themselves to split at any moment with no consequences whatsoever? It wouldn't be very encouraging, would it? Of course, this is assuming the seller even knows what an option is, which many of them don't. And anytime you ask someone to sign something they don't fully understand, the answer is almost always "No", because it's the safest response.

So basically, whether a seller knows what an option is or whether they don't, their initial feelings about your proposition will be far less enthusiastic than they *could* be—and that's just not a great way to begin negotiations.

Now, when you're *selling* on terms, your goal is to eventually get cashed out, which means a lease-purchase can again offer some psychological advantages. Tenant/buyers naturally feel more obligated to buy on lease-purchase than they do on lease-option, because the latter reinforces the idea that purchasing is optional.

Using Lease-Purchase in the Real World

Lease-purchase is a very effective and non-threatening way to offer sellers some debt relief on their properties. A very common strategy is to lease properties for a payment equal to the seller's monthly mortgage, with the right to purchase it at an amount that matches their remaining mortgage balance. Sounds simple, right? Well, it is—and I eventually got so good at presenting lease-purchase solutions to sellers that I could have gotten two or three properties per week without breaking a sweat. The only downside was that by the time I got that good, the marketplace had shifted more towards aggressive lending policies that made it too easy for people to just buy properties outright; making lease-purchase deals far less desirable to consumers, and therefore a whole lot less lucrative for me.

Although the market has shifted back around in recent years to conditions that would be favorable once again to buying on lease-purchase, it also brought with it a couple of new issues to overcome. One was that most motivated sellers were upside-down in their properties, owing way more than what they're worth. The second challenge was that banks had developed so many new rules about flipping properties, that it can now be quite difficult, even dangerous, to resell properties you're controlling on a lease-purchase—as you'll find out briefly.

For years, one popular strategy among investors was to do something I alluded to in the Quick Overview called a "sandwich" lease-purchase. The way a sandwich lease-purchase works is that you take control of a property with a small downpayment, small monthly lease payments, and the right to buy it at a slightly below-market price at some future point, often three to five years down the road. Then, you turn around and lease-purchase that same property to an end consumer for a shorter period of time, perhaps for one to three years, with a high downpayment, on higher monthly payments, and with a higher sale price than your lease-purchase. This creates up-front cash, monthly cash flow, and a nice back-end payday when your end buyer gets a bank loan to cash you out.

These types of deals are pretty easy to negotiate, because your seller is not really being asked to take a big risk. You're offering them much needed debt relief in the form of monthly lease payments, and they get to retain the title to their property until you cash them out in full someday—if ever. About the only concession they're making is allowing someone to occupy their property, but that's not much different than renting it out, because if you ever default, the seller can simply terminate your rights as a tenant/buyer with an eviction.

As for structuring payments, I used to always tell sellers that since my lease-purchase program was designed to give them relief from monthly mortgage payments, it was my job to make sure my payments matched whatever they had to pay every month. This worked out quite well, because their payments were always lower than the lease payments I could collect from an end consumer—otherwise I wouldn't do the deal.

However, sometimes my sellers had mortgage payments that were significantly lower than what I could collect from a subsequent tenant/buyer, usually because they had put a lot of money down when they purchased it. In those cases, having framed my offer as a debt-relief program—rather than as a lease-to-own transaction—positioned me for high monthly cash flow.

Here's why: calling my deals "lease-to-own" would have removed the seller's payment amount as a factor, by leading them to expect me to pay fair market rent (or close to it), even if their payments were really low. But presenting my offers as mortgage relief programs instead changed the context of what my deals were designed for, and so I got them all to accept extremely low lease payments that matched their low mortgage payments, without even so much as a raised eyebrow.

Neat, huh?

In fact, of all the offers I presented this way, only one seller ever suggested I should make a higher lease payment to him. But when I said it was company policy only to cover a seller's debt until we cashed them out, he nodded in understanding and relented without a fight; because once again, a simple new shift in perception managed to redefine someone's entire reality. So knowing this works, let's make sure *we're* the ones who're deciding which perceptions our sellers are subscribing to.

Of course, on the opposite side of the coin, sometimes your sellers will have payments that are higher than you can reasonably lease their property for. If so, you have a choice to make. You can walk away, or you could agree to cover as much of their payment as you can, and let them make up the difference. I don't care for the second approach, because I prefer to make my lease payments directly to their bank to make sure my money gets there. Trusting the seller to make up the difference is just a default waiting to happen; a default that would compromise you with your end buyer. Given that potential mess, I'd just as soon walk away.

All of this said, however, I'm not a big fan of buying properties on lease-purchase in today's environment, unless (and this is a *big* unless), I'm planning to either occupy the property myself or assign my contract. The reason being is that in a sandwich lease-purchase deal, my name won't appear on title as the property's owner of record at the courthouse, which means I will eventually find myself in a "flip" type double-closing with my end buyer at some point down the road.

This could create some additional hurdles when I try to get my end buyer financed and closed, just like the issues we covered in the section on wholesaling. For one, HUD financing, which is the most likely source of funding my end buyer will want or need, may or may not be available when the time comes.*

This is because as the seller, I have not been a seasoned title holder, meaning that I've not been the owner of record for at least three to six months prior to closing. And even if I can find a lender who will fund my end buyer, every day there are fewer and fewer title companies who will close double-ended deals anymore, no matter how reasonable or justifiable the end buyer's price may be (can you say "That's just stupid?").

However, there are a couple of ways to get around the flip issues if you feel strongly about buying a particular property on lease-purchase. One way is to record a memorandum of contract. This gives you a recorded interest in the property, so that later on down the road when your end buyer is ready to get a (non-FHA) loan to cash you out, their lender will see your seasoned memorandum as proof that this is not an A to B to C flip deal, even though the closing might actually be treated as such. I'm not really a big fan of this strategy, although some of my good friends who both teach and use sandwich lease-options tell me that it works pretty well for them.

But perhaps the best way to circumvent any potential future flip issues would be to assign your lease-purchase contract, as I had briefly mentioned earlier. This is done by taking control of the property by lease-purchase, and then instead of trying to sell the property, you simply sell the agreement instead. By assigning your agreement, you can create a win-win-win scenario: you get a quick payday, your seller continues to get debt relief, and your buyer gets attractive terms while dealing directly with the seasoned owner of record.

For me, personally, when it comes to buying properties, lease-purchase is the third rung down my ladder of preferred techniques—and that third rung hangs far below the first two. When I approach a potential seller, what I'm really looking for is to get a deed, which we'll cover later in the section on *subject to*. If they aren't motivated enough to just sign over their property, I'll step down a notch and try to buy it on land contract (which we'll cover next). If the seller still isn't motivated enough to give up that much control of their property, I'll usually walk

---

*Remember, HUD's 90 day seasoning rule has been temporarily suspended of this writing... but that may not last.

away unless the deal has extreme profit potential, in which case I might try to sell them on the idea of doing a lease-purchase with me.

So what about terms? How long should a lease-purchase agreement be? Well, that depends on who you are at the time. Terms should be as long as possible when you're buying, and as short as possible when you're selling.

First, let's talk about the buy side. If I'm buying a property on lease-purchase, I'll typically negotiate a term of five to seven years—but not all in one chunk, as that sounds pretty intimidating. The way I might phrase it to the seller is to tell them that I need to lease-purchase their property for thirty-five months, with the right to renew for a couple of additional 12 month periods that I will use only if necessary. This effectively gives me control for five years, but helps the seller feel like I'm shooting to get them cashed out in a much shorter period—which I generally am. Plus, keeping the initial term below a three year threshold helps to avoid triggering the *due on sale* language of most contemporary mortgages, which we'll cover in greater detail in the *subject to* section.

Of course, if a five year contract freaks my seller out, I would certainly consider dropping down to a term as short as three years, or maybe even two. But no less than that. Again, I would use the same structuring as before to make the terms seem even shorter, i.e., one year, with the right to renew for an additional one or two years, if necessary. But I just won't agree to buy on a lease-purchase that gives me control for less than two years. Why? Because I know that I may want to resell that same property on a sandwich lease-purchase, and I need to have control of the property for at least twice as long as I think it will take for me to get an end buyer cashed out with permanent financing. And since my first tenant/buyer may very well flake out on me, I need to make sure I have negotiated enough time in advance to give a second tenant/buyer a shot.

Another important aspect to negotiate into your lease-purchase to buy is the right to sublease the property. Without it, you will have to make payments to the seller without the ability to put an end buyer in the property on higher monthly payments. That could be lethal to your monthly cash flow, unless of course, you are planning to occupy the property yourself. Even then, I always insist on having the right to sublease in case I want to move. If the seller declines, I'll either walk away or switch to optioning the property instead. That way, I'll still have the right to buy it at a good price for an extended period, but I won't have to make monthly payments in the meantime.

For me, as a strategy lease-purchase is really best suited only for selling properties—especially those properties which have already been bought by conventional means, by land contract, or *subject to*. These three methods provide you with a recorded ownership interest, which eliminates any flipping concerns when you're reselling them in the future on lease-purchase.

Using a lease-purchase to sell can get you higher earnest money commitments than you would typically get in a straight sale, because the tenant/buyer will be enjoying the convenience of occupying the property for a time before they're required to close. A lease-purchase can also provide you with higher monthly payments than you would otherwise get from renting a property out, because you can arrange for a portion of the payments to be credited towards the tenant/buyer's purchase price if they buy. This not only enhances your monthly cash flow, it further motivates the tenant/buyer to consummate a sale. And if they don't buy, those rent credits are non-refundable, so you win either way.

Lease-purchase agreements can also help you get a sale price that's slightly above current market rates for two reasons: 1) because you are giving the tenant/buyer added value by letting them close their purchase at a later, more convenient date; and 2) because by the time they close, the property will have likely appreciated in value above where it is today.

Unfortunately, many unscrupulous investors in the late 90's and early 2000's thought that these positive lease-purchase and lease-option attributes gave them a license to gouge tenant/buyers on all three fronts. First, they'd charge them tens of thousands in up-front non-refundable fees, which often crippled the tenant/buyer's finances—leading to default. Then, they'd demand significantly inflated monthly rents, which also further drained the tenant/buyer's financial reserves—often trapping them in properties they no longer wanted, while diminishing their ability to actually buy. And last, but not least, they'd escalate sale prices to outrageous levels, knowing that they were likely be aided and abetted by equally outrageous appraisals conducted on behalf of overly-ambitious mortgage brokers who were hell bent on making every deal close—even if it meant committing fraud.

Not me. When I'm selling a property on lease-purchase, my goal is to get cashed out of the property... legitimately. Given that end, I keep my price and rental fees reasonable, while tapping into the subtle psychological advantages that a lease-purchase offers over a lease-option. I'd rather my potential buyer sign a lease-*purchase* and feel like they're committed to buy, instead of a lease-*option* that gives them permission to walk away—which, in providing such consent, often encourages them to do just that. Plus, if they're signing a lease-*purchase* with me, I can further persuade their cooperation by having lots of recourse against them if they don't. After all, it is a purchase contract—not an option agreement.

However, for some people, the idea of having their lease-to-own buyers default so that they can keep reselling the same property over and over again is quite appealing. For some, it's even preferable. That's because each time a buyer defaults, they get to do it again with another buyer; collecting another non-refundable option fee along with above-market rents—and all the while enjoying very little or no responsibility at all for repairs.

If that appeals to you, then you might prefer using lease-option agreements over lease-purchase. But I just don't care for that approach, because in essence you're intentionally putting someone into a position where they are likely to fail, just so that you can generate more revenue from a property that you're really only pseudo-selling. Not only is this unethical—even if the buyer really wants to do the deal—in the long run, it could be damaging to the entire real estate industry.

Look, tenant/buyers will occasionally default—that's just the nature of the game. But too many intentionally compromised buyers will eventually result in a new media "scandal", which can lead to only one thing: even more regulatory control over our activities. And that is just the absolute last thing we need right now. Our God-given rights to freely pursue legitimate profits have been eroded enough already. Believe me, lawmakers won't hesitate to put on their white hats, hop onto their legislative high horses, and ride off into the prairie sunset to rescue all of the brain-dead consumers who think it's their right to just sign up for anything that turns them on, while intentionally ignoring any potential consequences. Why? Because they've been conditioned to believe the whole point of government is to make sure that they're never held accountable for their own stupid decisions. And unfortunately, the government rarely disappoints them.

So maybe a better choice for us would be to proactively protect some of these would-be (idiot) unqualified lease-purchase buyers from themselves, and focus our efforts instead on people who have at least a ghost of a chance at buying our properties. Just my two cents worth—now excuse me as I dismount my soapbox.

One document... or two?

One question I regularly get is whether to use one document or two when doing a lease-purchase. The answer is: it depends on whether I'm buying or selling.

When I'm buying, I want the lease-purchase agreement to be a single document. Essentially, I use a lease agreement which specifically permits subleasing, and that also contains specific purchase details, such as price, terms, closing cost distributions, tax prorations, etc. I do this because as the buyer, I want to have all of the details of my transaction in one place; not only for convenience, but also for protection.

When I'm selling, however, I want to use two distinct agreements; a stand-alone lease, and a separate purchase agreement. There are several reasons for this. For one, if the tenant/buyer defaults, it's a lot easier for me to evict them, because all I have to show the court is the standard lease which they are in violation of. If the judge would happen to see purchase terms within that lease, he might need to bump it up to a superior court level for adjudication, due to the fact that the agreement gives the tenant/buyer an equitable interest in real estate. The other reason is that if you want to make a tenant/buyer responsible for maintaining the property, you can't put it into the lease and make it a tenant responsibility, but you *can* insert it into the purchase agreement and make it a buyer responsibility, most easily as a condition in exchange for giving the buyer an exceptionally long escrow period to close (6 months to 2 years or so).

However, it's very important that you take some precautions when using separate agreements as a single instrument. It's absolutely imperative that they are clearly linked by making sure at least one of them conspicuously references the other. In this case, we don't want the lease to reference the purchase agreement; otherwise it could complicate an eviction. Therefore, it's vital to reference the lease agreement in the purchase contract, not only to tie them together, but also so that you can specify that the purchase agreement would be voided upon any default of the lease agreement. If you fail to do this, an evicted tenant would continue to have a legally binding right to purchase your property, which could preclude you from selling it to anyone else for years to come. In other words, they'll have you firmly by the short hairs... with both hands... while in a bad mood.

Actual Lease-Purchase Case Study

It was two o'clock in the morning and Kevin just couldn't sleep. The moving truck was scheduled to arrive in a few days, but his pin-perfect, four year-old quad-level home still hadn't received any offers through his Realtor friend. He and his wife, Cheryl, had just finished literally praying together for a last minute solution, and although she'd already gone back to bed, Kevin remained wide awake on his worrisome vigil; unable to enjoy the beauty of the moonlight that stretched across his finely-trimmed front lawn.

The next morning, Kevin was casually listening in on a radio cooking show that on any other Saturday morning he would have quickly tuned away from. But that Saturday he didn't, because it was featuring a recipe that he found mildly interesting. Suddenly, one of my radio commercials ran. It was one of those rotator radio commercials I told you about in the chapter on marketing; the ones that got plugged into unsold commercial slots at random.

Anyway, since he and Cheryl had just prayed for a solution a few hours earlier, he was especially receptive to the ad copy, which was written specifically for people who needed to sell their homes immediately at a fair price. The bizarre coincidence of hearing this ad on a show he normally didn't like made him suspect there was a higher power at work. So rather than order the special report and wait two days for it in the mail, he called the radio station and got my company's name and number right away (remember also in that marketing chapter, when I told you how powerful serendipity is—even if it's only perceived?). By the time I'd finished telling him over the phone that the ad he heard was supposed to run the day before, but had gotten bumped into Saturday at the last minute, he was absolutely certain that this was no mere coincidence, but rather full Divine Intervention at work.

Needless to say, they were completely sold on selling me their house before I even got in my car to go see it. Signing paperwork would now be just a formality.

Two hours later, I was sitting in their living room telling them about my long term purchasing program without ever mentioning the technique by name. That's because instead of telling potential customers what my agreements are *called*, I describe what they can *do* for them—because that's all that matters.

So during those next few critical moments, I showed them how they would not be getting some low, all-cash investor offer from me, but instead they were actually going to be getting a fair price offer that was equal to what they owed on the house, which was financed to 94% of its value at the time. Plus, they discovered how I could even make their monthly payments for them for as long as necessary, until at some point in the future when I would be sending their mortgage company a huge check to pay off their mortgage, using the proceeds received by getting my subsequent buyer financed.

They were literally riveted to their sofa.

Of course, the transaction I was describing could have been a lease-purchase, a land contract, or a *subject to*, as all three of these methods could have accomplished all of the same objectives equally well. In this case, I was intending to do a land contract with them.

Why? Well, a couple of reasons. First, as I mentioned earlier, buying on lease-purchase when I'm immediately reselling the property can be problematic; it doesn't give me enough of an ownership interest to satisfy some lenders when it's time to get my end buyer permanent financing. Many lenders in today's market want to treat my end buyer's permanent loan as being part of a "flip" transaction, and will therefore withdraw their offer to finance my end buyer. This is an especially daunting challenge if my end buyer really needs FHA or VA financing.

The second reason I went with land contract was that the loan balance was so close to the market value, I knew I was going to have to add some value artificially, and I was concerned that a lease-purchase might not add enough. I was also fairly new to the *subject to* concept at the time, and had reservations about the due-on-sale clause. That left me with just land contract (yes, I know this is supposed a lease-purchase case study, but I'm getting to that, so hang in there).

Anyway, we wrote up the land contract on-the-spot for $103,000 at $810 per month, with my first payment beginning in 90 days; or sooner if I found an end buyer to whom I could resell the property or assign my land contract. As for their agency listing, their Realtor was a friend who had volunteered weeks before I came along to let them out of their listing if they decided to seek alternative solutions. For the record, I did not, have not, nor will I ever ask someone to ditch their agent so that we can do a deal. It's unethical, and in some cases illegal—as it constitutes tortious interference by inducing the breach of a valid contract.

About three weeks later, I found a tenant/buyer who was willing to buy the property for $114,500 on lease-purchase, with $4,500 down and monthly payments of $995 per month. That gave me a $4,490 upfront profit (after deducting the $10 downpayment I gave Kevin and Cheryl), and a net monthly cash flow of $185 per month. This went on for exactly 12 months, and then suddenly my tenant/buyer stopped sending me any payments.

A few days later, when the buyer's phone was disconnected, I called him at his work number and found out that he'd already moved out of the house, and (surprisingly) had even cleaned it up for me. It seems his wife had left him, and since he was unable to qualify for a loan on his own, he saw no point in continuing the lease-purchase, which was up for renewal that month. Apparently, he also thought it was pointless to clue me in on all of this.

So with no tenant/buyer to subsidize my $810 payment, I simply (but grudgingly) took it out of the cash reserve I had set aside with his $4,500 downpayment. You see, I had anticipated problems from day one, and did something to insulate myself by holding back most of his lease-purchase downpayment just in case. Of course, most other investors failed to consider this possibility, and chose instead to live it up by blowing their entire downpayment wads on boats, cars, motorcycles and big screen home theater systems. Of course, today, I'm one of the few left standing, so we can all see where *that* strategy got them.

I then ran another ad and within three more weeks found another tenant/buyer to buy the property on lease-purchase for $117,900, but this time with $9,900 cash down and $995 per month. This new buyer wasn't even going to need financing, as they were merely awaiting the receipt of a $200,000 cash settlement that had already been awarded to them in a vehicular liability case.

By now, I had generated $15,800 in profits on a house that only had about $7,000 in equity, simply by using lease-purchase. I had received $9,900 and $4,500 in cash downpayments, $2,220 in monthly cash flow profits ($995 less $810 for 12 months), and I'd only paid out $810 for one mortgage payment and $10 as an initial downpayment. Not too shabby.

But I wasn't done yet.

The new buyer leased the house for exactly eight months, got their settlement check, and then went right out and bought another house for full price at $185,000 with all cash. That's not only dumber than dumb (to pay full price when you're paying all cash), but it was also a breach of our agreement. And since I knew they had plenty of money left, as well as where they were keeping it (in their easily-attachable bank account), I simply called and reminded them that they had not yet been released from our agreement of $995 per month.

"You understand," I told her, "that you've forfeited your entire $9,900 earnest money deposit, right?"

Her simple reply was, "That's okay, we have lots of money!"

So I pushed the envelope a little, and went on to say, "Well, since your breach is also creating extra advertising costs for me to run an ad for a new buyer that I wouldn't have otherwise had to run, then it's your responsibility to reimburse me for the cost of those ads as well."

To which she replied again, "That's okay, we have plenty of money!"

So I decided to swing for the fences, and added, "I'm also going to need to make some new signs to direct these prospective buyers to the house." Although I wasn't convinced I was really entitled to the signs, I figured, *"What the heck?"*

To which she replied, "Well, we have plenty of money, how many signs do you think you'll need?"

Frankly, I was so astounded that this strategy was working, that I actually had to think a moment before finally stammering out, "Uhhh, I think maybe four signs ought to do the trick (after all, I didn't want to seem greedy, especially since I knew I was going to design them to be *very* nice and *very* re-usable).

She said, "That's fine, just send us the bill. We have plenty of money." And wouldn't you know, those four signs turned out to be the nicest *For Sale* signs I've ever owned in my life—even to this day.

About six weeks later, I got a call from a Realtor who wanted to know if I would consider selling my lease-purchase property outright for a quick $117,000 cash. She had a buyer who was trying to purchase an identical property just one street away. They had already been approved for their financing, and were just days away from closing when an updated title examination revealed a defect that was going to take weeks to fix. Her buyer didn't have weeks to wait. So they wanted to buy my house for cash and close within 5 to 7 days. All I had to do was agree to pay her 3% co-op commission and a few standard closing costs.

Of course, I was all over that deal, but not before first trying unsuccessfully to bump them up to $118,500 (hey, a guy's gotta try, right?). Twelve days later, I was walking away from a conventional closing table having sent a big check to pay off Kevin and Cheryl's mortgage, while stuffing about $12,500 cash into my own pocket.

When you add that $12,500 to the $15,800 I had already made, and then factored in the additional $1,850 in positive cash flow that I'd made over the last ten months, my grand take was $30,150 on a nice property in perfect condition that originally had maybe $6,000 or $7,000 in equity… if that!

And I couldn't have done it as quickly or as profitably without the lease-purchase technique. Using land contracts with my two defaulted buyers would have given me ulcers, and likely drained my financial reserves just in attorney's fees and court costs.

Plus, each time one of those tenant/buyers walked away, the property would have been tied up in legal processes so long that I would have lost out on getting my subsequent tenant/buyer and my end conventional buyer—both of which were highly profitable and quickly obtainable, due to the fast and easy turnaround times that lease-purchase afforded me.

Story Epilogue— In case you were curious about how many houses I was able to sell with those really nice custom signs that I had "guilted" my seller into paying for, let's just say that my joy with them was short-lived; because within three days of putting them out, somebody stole all of them just for the nice frames.

Oh well, I guess the world truly is round indeed.

SELLER FINANCING

SELLER FINANCING

A QUICK OVERVIEW

> **What it is:** Seller financing usually takes one of two forms:
> **1) Seller Carry Back,** in which the seller deeds the property to the buyer, and holds a note and mortgage for all or part of the purchase price; or
> **2) Land Contract** (*a.k.a.* land installment contract, contract for deed, agreement for deed, etc.) where the seller also finances the buyer's purchase, but retains title to the property until the agreement is paid in full.

> **What it does:** For sellers, it allows them to offer attractive terms that can generate lots of interest in their property. For buyers, it allows them to buy properties more much easily, often requiring less cash (if any) and little or no credit. It also provides the buyer with tax benefits of ownership.

> **How it's done:** After a price has been agreed upon, the buyer gives the seller a downpayment and the balance is financed (usually with interest), just like a bank loan. Payments are often amortized over 360 months, although most deals will also have a lump sum balloon payment due (often in five to seven years), when the remaining balance must be paid in full.

> **How it can generate revenue:** When you're selling, financing the sale lets you sell quickly at above market prices because you've eliminated the hassles of bank qualifying for the buyer, plus there are little to no closing costs. When you're buying, seller financing offers you several exit alternatives. For example, you can choose to occupy it today and resell it later for a profit, or you can opt to profit today by assigning your contract, or by reselling the property either conventionally or on subsequent terms—like a sandwich land contract (not recommended) or lease-purchase.

> **Best market cycle:** Seller financing tends to work much better during down cycles because there are usually more motivated sellers to choose from, making deals easier to find and much more lucrative to negotiate. It can also stimulate greater interest in a particular property at a time when buyers will usually need more assistance *and* incentives to buy.

> **Caveats:** Seller financing often requires continued cooperation of the seller to keep the deed clear. In those cases it's best to minimize your repair or improvement costs, and be sure all promises you make to a buyer are contingent upon your seller's cooperation. **Also there are many severe new restrictions you <u>MUST</u> be aware of under recent state and federal laws (Dodd/Frank, SAFE Act) if you are selling properties to homeowners.**

The Basics

Seller financing is essentially an installment sale of real estate. It comes in two basic forms; either as a seller carryback deal—where the seller deeds the property to the buyer and then holds a note (secured by a mortgage against the property) for some or all of the purchase price, or as a land contract transaction (a.k.a. *land installment contracts, contracts for deed, agreements for deed,* etc.)—wherein the seller provides financing for the purchase, but retains legal title to the property until the contract balance is paid in full, or the balance has been paid down to a certain point as provided by law in some states. For simplicity's sake in our discussion, we'll just use the term *land contract.*

The way seller financing works is that the buyer and seller agree on a price, the buyer gives the seller a downpayment, and then the seller finances the balance-- usually with interest—on either a note secured by a mortgage against the property, or on a land contract agreement. As payments are made, they are applied towards principal and interest, just like a typical bank loan. Even though the seller retains title on a land contract, the buyer receives an equitable interest in the property's title. Unlike legal title, which is a tangible thing (an actual deed), equitable title is an abstract concept. It's like the difference between being a spouse and an in-law. When you marry someone, they become your legal spouse, complete with a physical marriage certificate. But when your sibling marries, you become an in-law; which is an abstract concept because the legal documentation (the marriage certificate) only provides indirect evidence of your relationship.

Seller financing interest rates are generally a little higher than prevailing bank rates, and payments are usually amortized over an extended period, like 30, 40 or even 50 years for two reasons: 1) longer payback rates create lower monthly payments for the buyer; and 2) longer payback rates generate higher profits for the seller, due to slower principal paydown (principal is the amount financed).

For example, a $200,000 land contract at 8% interest will have a monthly payment of $1,911.30 if it is amortized over 180 months (15 years), but the payment drops to only $1,390.62 if it is amortized over 480 months (40 years) instead. Both the buyer and the seller would likely be more attracted to the 40 year amortization rate, but for different reasons. A buyer would like 40 year rate because their payment would be about $520 lower per month. But the seller benefits too, because when the buyer refinances or sells the property to pay off the balloon payment, say, seven years later, the payoff will still be about $193,500, thanks to the slow principal paydown of a 40 year rate. By contrast, if the agreement had a 15 year amortization instead, the payoff at seven years would only be about $135,000.

However, if you're selling, I generally recommend sticking with a 30 year ammortization, because if you ever need to generate cash by selling your note on the secondary market, this will help to maximize the cash resale value of your note.

Using Seller Financing in the Real World

In the late 70's and early 80's, very few people were in a hurry to borrow money to buy real estate, because mortgage interest rates had risen to ridiculous levels of 15% to 20%+. On top of that, sellers were expected to pay upwards of 10 mortgage points on behalf of the buyers to close those deals, so not too many people were jazzed about being sellers when institutional loans were involved.

So what was left? Seller financing. And it was hot. However, once mortgage rates dropped back down to 10% or less, and held steady throughout the late 80's and well into the 90's, most seller carryback financing (where the seller deeds the property to the buyer and holds a note and mortgage) began to fade away. Land contracts (where the seller holds the financing, but also retains title until the contract is paid off) became less popular, but still held their own because they provided sellers with a less risky way to offer attractive seller financing to buyers.

But by the early 2000's, interest rates began falling to record lows, so nearly everyone preferred to get a mortgage of their own; and with the introduction of aggressive sub-prime lending programs, almost anybody could. Because of this, land contracts became far less popular among buyers, because they didn't really like the added risk created by the seller retaining title. And seller carrybacks virtually disappeared altogether, since sellers just didn't need them anymore.

In fact, when this portion of the manuscript was first drafted back in 2005, seller carryback financing was left out entirely because it was so infrequent; accounting for only about 1 in every 400 real estate transactions—and most of those were done by professional investors. Land contracts were waning also, but were still being used often enough to warrant inclusion in the original book block.

But today is a whole new ballgame. The recent credit crisis, caused by the collapse of the real estate bubble in 2008, suddenly made it difficult for many people to borrow money again. In fact, it's estimated today that nearly 50% of the people who can reasonably afford a property can't qualify for a loan to buy it.

This creates yet again a huge need for seller financing, because contrary to popular belief, Realtors, price, and location don't sell real estate—financing does. That's because real estate is a big ticket item that most people just can't simply write a check to buy. So if there isn't any financing available for them, the best Realtor, location, or price in the world won't make a bit of difference.

As for the best use of seller financing as an investor, I've always liked using it to take control of very nice properties in good areas, and then either assigning my seller financing agreements for a fee (my absolute favorite!), or sandwiching the properties back out on a subsequent term deal like a lease-purchase (you can also sandwich them back out on land contracts, but I no longer recommend doing so).

The reason I prefer higher-end properties is that it's difficult to negotiate big discounts when you're also asking the seller to hold financing. So by dealing in more expensive properties, I can greatly increase my profit spread with just a small price concession. For example, a pretty reasonable 7% price discount on a $400,000 property generates a $28,000 profit spread, while that same 7% discount on a $30,000 junker only creates a $2,100 spread. See what I mean?

The other benefit to working with higher-end properties is that when you're reselling, it's easier to manufacture some extra equity for your profit. This is done by selling the property at a slightly above-market price in exchange for offering seller assistance (more on this later), which can tack another 3% to 5% onto your profit spread. On a $400,000 property, that's an additional $12,000 to $20,000. Good luck trying to fudge that much extra into a $30,000 deal.

So why don't I recommend reselling properties on sandwich land contracts anymore, even though I can get twice as much cash down from a buyer than I can on a lease-purchase? Well, two reasons. The first is that I'd reached a point in 2002 where nearly all my buyers were defaulting on their payments, even when they'd paid me large cash downpayments of $10,000 to $15,000. The old rule used to be the more money a buyer had at risk, the less likely they were to default. But that just wasn't ringing true anymore, so I stopped reselling by sandwich land contract altogether. This is despite the fact that I could remove a defaulted buyer in less than 90 days (I'm in Ohio, where a long and costly foreclosure isn't required on a land contact like it is in most states). For me, it wasn't just about getting them out, but rather the ethics of taking large downpayments from people I knew were very likely to default soon. I also felt that it was unprofessional for me to continue teaching this resale strategy to people in foreclosure states, because the time and cost of removing defaulted buyers turned everyone into a loser.

Now even though the quality of land contract buyers is much higher today than it was back then, another reason I don't like to resell properties on land contract is because of hassles created by the SAFE Act that went into effect back in July of 2010. It requires me to be a licensed loan originator on all seller financed deals—which would include land contracts—if the buyer is an end consumer (which they usually are), and the property is not my personal residence (which it usually isn't).

Negotiating Price and Payments

My basic premise for negotiating price and payments when buying with seller financing has usually been to frame my offer as a debt relief solution, rather than as an offer to buy. Ordinarily, I will seek to match my monthly payment with their monthly mortgage obligation, and set my purchase price to equal their remaining mortgage balance. By presenting my offers this way (as a debt relief program), I've been able to put together some very profitable deals without negotiating at all. I've gotten sellers to just automatically agree to monthly payments and purchase prices that were much lower than if I'd have tried to negotiate them from scratch.

Of course, this is assuming that the seller already has some equity in the property. If not, then you'll need to switch into *subject to* mode to take over control of the property, and then into short sale mode to create the equity you need.

This is also assuming that the seller doesn't have a great deal of equity either; otherwise framing your offer as a debt relief solution could end up looking ridiculous. So when I run into a seller with lots of equity or a free and clear property, I'll typically use some of the low downpayment strategies found on page 144 to keep my initial cash outlay as low as possible, and then some of the context-shifting strategies found on page 187 in the next section to try and get the lowest price possible by negotiating net equity instead of price.

When you're reselling with any kind of seller financing—which I generally don't recommend—the upside is that you can get top selling prices during a down market cycle, and above-retail prices during a stable or growing market. Seller financing can be used to buy any kind of property you want (including low-priced long-term rentals), but sticking to pretty houses in desirable neighborhoods can help you turn your properties over very quickly, and create very attractive spreads, as I had alluded to earlier. Let's look at some reasons why it's easy to artificially create a little extra equity to enhance your profits by offering seller financing.

First of all, what do I mean by creating equity artificially? Well, if you're in the business of buying and reselling real estate, your profit has to come from the equity in the property. Some people define equity as the difference between a property's current market value, and what is owed against it. This is not entirely true. Equity is the difference between what is owed against a piece of property and what a willing consumer will *pay* you for it.

So... how can you convince someone to pay you more than retail price for a property without using a gun and a ski mask? You can create some additional value in a property by adding a few benefits for the consumer that a conventional sale wouldn't provide (remember the Law of Income?). In other words, you can instantly add value to a property without actually doing any work to it, simply by improving the financing instead. When you create an opportunity for consumers to buy a particular property with built-in financing that is convenient and easy, you immediately enhance that property's desirability in the marketplace; and in doing so, increase its market value in a matter of seconds rather than months or years.

For example, let's imagine you're a consumer looking to buy a house. You've found 10 identical houses, all with the same number of bedrooms and baths, with similar amenities, and all in the exact same condition (I know that's logistically impossible, but this is an imaginary scenario, after all). Let's say that 9 of those 10 houses are listed for sale conventionally at $150,000, and one is available with quick and easy seller financing at $154,900. Which one will likely interest you?

Well, the first 9 properties must be purchased with institutional funding, which will require you to put down 3.5% in cash ($5,250), endure 30 to 45 days of bank scrutiny, and then pay another 2% in closing costs and pre-paids ($3,000), just for the right to sign personally on a high loan-to-value mortgage that will hold you prisoner for the next seven years until you've paid it down enough to afford a Realtor commission when you resell it. On top of that, these 9 sellers will need 30 days after closing to move out. Sounds like a sucky way to buy properties, doesn't it? Well, if you ask me, it is—even though that's how most people do it.

So, in frustration, you take a moment to look at the 10th property, and find out that even though the price is $4,900 higher, it has a lot more appeal to you because all you have to do is put down $5,000 (which is less than the bank's required downpayment) and you can move into it later this afternoon—not two months from now—on an affordable lease-purchase or land contract. And this 10th seller is even willing to let you try out living in the house for a few years before you'll be required to get a loan; and if you do buy it, he'll go so far as to help you with your downpayment and closing costs by giving you a credit of $250 from each payment you made, as though he'd created an automatic savings account just for you. Nice.

And what if you were a safety-minded, cautious buyer who was worried about what would happen if you possibly lost your job, got transferred, divorced, or just felt that maybe you might not still like the house in a year or two? Would you want to be forced into foreclosure, or perhaps have to fork over $9,000 out-of-pocket to hire a Realtor to sell it for you (which is what would happen if you were to buy one of the other 9 conventional properties)? Or would you rather be able to just walk away anytime you want, as this 10th property would allow you to do?

Better still, if you ever wanted to move out early, this 10th seller might even be willing to share with you a percentage of the new buyer's downpayment as a reward for keeping your payments current and taking care of the house; as well as showing it in a positive light to these prospective new buyers.

Does any of this sound interesting? Would having all of those convenience and safety features make a slightly inflated price worth considering? The two most common answers from consumers to those questions are "Yes" and "*Hell*, YES!" In fact, most buyers would jump at the chance to pay a little extra for that type of safe, consumer-friendly financing—even during tough economic times.

But that's not the only choice the 10th seller can offer you. In fact, if you're willing to put a little more down, say $10,000 to $15,000, the seller might just be willing to assign you the note and deed or the land contract they bought the property with. This would tie you directly with the current owner of record, and provide you with seven years of seller financing instead of only two to five (remember, you're the end consumer in this imaginary scenario, not the trained investor). Either way, you would now have the benefit of deductible interest every year on your taxes. Plus, the financing isn't a mortgage loan held by an institutional lender, which means the $150,000 debt won't show up on your credit report where it can drag down your FICO score (higher total debt = lower scores).

Okay, now...after having placed yourself in the shoes of a marketplace consumer for the last few minutes (you are now back to being the trained real estate investor once again), you can easily see all of the very attractive benefits that seller financing can offer someone who might want to buy a property.

But as you can also see, you (as the investor) will have to be willing to operate on relatively slim percentage margins in order to keep your prices appealing to these same consumers, i.e., you can't charge 20% to 30% over market value and expect people to get excited about it.

That means you need to be able to make a nice profit spread out of a modest 5% to 7% value increase; which is exactly why I like higher priced properties when I'm using seller financing. A 5% to 7% markup on a $300,000 property equals $15,000 to $21,000 in cash, which is not a bad little spread to start with. And it's pretty easily justified if you're offering good terms to end buyers.

Again... juxtapose this with a $40,000 property. At a 5% to 7% markup, you're only looking at $2,000 to $2,800. Even a 20% markup would only net you about half as much cash as the $300,000 deal; and not only would a markup that high on a $40,000 deal be unreasonable to expect, it would also be unethical and predatory. So the higher the sales price, the easier it is to legitimately make more money.

But that's not all. The higher the property's value, the more likely the seller is to have a little equity already. And although they may have thousands of dollars in equity, it's often still not enough to cover their costs to hire a Realtor and pay all of their closing costs. When that's the case, their equity may not do them any good, but it can definitely do you some good by increasing your overall profit beyond just your modest 5% to 7% price mark-up.

Here's what I mean: let's say on your $300,000 deal the seller had a loan balance of about $286,000. That's $14,000 in equity, but it might as well be $0—because that isn't even enough to cover the cost of a discount 5% Realtor, let alone their closing costs, transfer fees, or prorated taxes. Therefore, this little chunk of equity won't help them at all, but it'll bump up your profit margin by $14,000, which will net you about $12,000 more in cash (after deducting closing costs).

Now I know that in today's economic climate, you probably can't imagine anyone having any equity at all, let alone $10,000 to $15,000 or much more. It seems like everyone with a property for sale right now owes more than what it's worth. This is, of course, not true.

However what's ironic is that many of the sellers in today's marketplace who actually have some equity also happen to be the very same sellers who may need to seriously consider offering some kind of selling financing in order to preserve it. But, of course, most of them haven't figured that out yet.

That's where you come in.

The Unique Qualities of a Land Contract

Land contracts are relatively unique animals in the real estate world. They are hybrid transactions that hover somewhere between being a long-term control method and an actual sale.

Here's why: just like a traditional sale or a seller-carryback deal, they are recognized by the IRS as an actual sale of real estate. Because of this classification, the buyer is permitted to deduct the interest portion of their monthly payments, and the seller must claim the same as income on their taxes. This classification also means the seller may need to be a licensed loan originator under new Dodd/Frank and SAFE Act regulations, unless the transaction meets certain exemptions.

However, since the deed does not change hands from the seller to the buyer until the land contract balance is paid in full (or paid down to a certain percentage, as provided in some states), these particular types of sales fall under the category of executory contracts, similar lease-options or lease-purchases. An executory contract is one that has not yet been fully executed (completed), but rather remains open and legally binding as long as the contract's terms continue to be met by the parties involved. If either party fails to meet their obligations, the other can terminate—even void—the sale and seek damages as provided in the agreement.

In other words, even though a land contract is viewed as an actual sale, complete with the tax benefits of ownership, the validity of the sale must essentially be renewed every month as the two parties continue to fulfill their promises to one another. The buyer promises to make the payments and keep the property clean, repaired and insured against catastrophic loss; and the seller promises to deliver the deed in the future, and keep the title clear in the meantime. The seller does this by making sure the taxes are paid, and ensuring that the total of all liens and mortgages are lower than the contract payoff balance at all times. Only when the land contract balance is paid off in the future—if ever—and the deed is delivered as agreed, will the sale actually be considered fully executed.

Land contracts, just like any seller financed deal, usually work best as a buying strategy in a value-driven (buyer's) market—so long as you're not in the middle of widespread massive market depreciation, like the one America recently experienced in 2008. Whenever property values are declining, especially at rates of 20% to 50% or more per year, it's usually best to leave your land contract and carryback documents in your briefcase until things stabilize again.

Of course, the good news is that if values do happen to decline after you've committed to buying a property with seller financing, you can always engage your skills at short-selling (which we'll cover later) to negotiate with the lienholders to create the equity you need, or you can simply walk away and wash your hands of the whole deal—but only if you were careful not to offer any personal guarantees of repayment. You see, personal guarantees are a big no-no in our world.

Four Common Mistakes when Buying with Seller Financing

Speaking of no-no's, there are four other really big ones you need to know about if you ever plan on buying properties with seller financing. The first is giving the seller a big downpayment, which often comes from falling in love with a property or feeling some other kind of desperation to do the deal. Big downpayments aren't good. In addition to increasing your risk of loss, they also reduce or even remove one of your most profitable resale revenue sources: your initial cash margin.

Here's what I mean: when you buy a property with seller financing, your first payday comes when you either assign your agreement or collect a downpayment from your end buyer. If you make a large downpayment just to get the deal, you'll be sacrificing your fastest and most lucrative profit opportunity. Of course, there are always going to be some unique exceptions; but in general, it's recommended to keep your downpayments very low—especially when it's so easy to do by simply engaging the same low downpayment strategy that we discussed in the previous chapter on options.

The second no-no is spending lots of money to repair or improve a property that you've purchased on a deferred deed agreement like a land contract. This is not a good idea, because the property literally belongs to someone else until you eventually get that deed; and on a land contract there's no guarantee you ever will, since seller default is a very real possibility. Although it's pretty rare for a land contract seller to default on you maliciously, it does happen. Sometimes they decide not to cooperate after a nasty divorce, or occasionally they just feel as though they're suddenly entitled to more money, etc. But what you really have to guard yourself against is the *unintentional* default that's much more common and likely to occur. Most often it's caused by sellers losing lawsuits or getting hit with state or federal tax liens. The resulting judgments from these actions can attach to your land contract property, and easily over-encumber it. Other problems can occur when sellers lose touch after moving away to locations unknown, or die unexpectedly—leaving you potentially unable to get your deed when it's time.

The third big blunder is making unconditional promises to subsequent buyers when you can't be 100% sure you can fulfill them. For instance, when you buy a property on a land contract, and then resell it on a subsequent lease-purchase or sandwich land contract, you're promising your buyer that you will deliver a deed to them at some point in the future, when you don't even know for sure that you can—due to reasons we've just explored, and many others we didn't have time for.

Therefore, your resale agreement needs to contain a disclosure which states that your obligation to deliver a deed is contingent upon the cooperation of the current owner of record. But you can't stop there. You also have to identify a remedy in the event you are unable to deliver, and it's a good idea to make sure that this remedy is something that's easily executable… at least for you.

For example, let's say your seller screws up and gets a $50,000 judgment against himself that attaches to the house you're buying on land contract. This will destroy any chance you ever had of getting a clear deed for your buyer in the future. Let's also say that you resold the property on a lease-purchase, and your end buyer gave you a $5,000 downpayment and $200 extra per month for 10 months. That's a total investment of $7,000 they've paid you towards getting a deed, which you now realize you can't possibly deliver. What do you do? Well, that depends on how well you've prepared yourself for such a situation.

An ideal strategy would be to limit their maximum damages to a refund of the money they've paid you to-date, which in this case would be $7,000. This prevents them from getting a judgment against you for the equity they have in the property, which is a highly subjective calculation that could easily reach disastrous proportions. Then, to make things even easier for you, you can go on to spell out that their only means of collecting their $7,000 refund would be through living in the property free of charge until they've received the equivalent of all their money back. At $1,200 per month, that would only take 6 months, and you could easily hold off a foreclosure that long—even in most non-judicial foreclosure states.

The fourth really big no-no is sending your payments directly to your seller when they have underlying mortgages, and then trusting them to use the money to pay it. I just won't do it. In fact, if a seller has an existing loan, I won't agree to buy the property on seller financing of any kind unless they agree to let me pay their mortgage company directly, or pay a third-party servicing agent who will.

Why? Because my payments are almost always going to be exactly the same amount as their monthly mortgage obligation, so if all of the money is supposed to end up at the bank anyway, there's no reason for me to route it there by way of the seller. Not only would this delay the lender's receipt of my money, but it would also create a temptation for the seller to divert the funds for other purposes they deem more important at the moment: such as automobile repairs, past-due credit card bills, or—more trivially—just for some overdue fun and frolic.

Their motivations are generally innocent at first: *"I'll only do it this one time, and I'll make it up when I get paid on Friday,"* or, *"If I don't fix my car today I'll lose my job, so I don't really have a choice,"* etc. But regardless of why they end up hijacking your money, the end result is always the same: they will eventually fail to make up some of the money they've "borrowed" temporarily, and so the mortgage will end up going into arrears. This creates a daisy chain of events that puts your seller in default to both their lender *and* you, and by extension puts you in default to your end buyer. This also puts at risk all of the profits you've worked so hard to create and capture. The good news is that if you've handled your default remedies right, you probably won't lose any money. However the bad news is you might not make any, either. And in case you haven't figured it out, working for free because of someone else's mistake sucks. Big time.

Actual Land Contract Case Study

Robert and his estranged wife, Laurie, decided to reconcile and move to Wisconsin to manage a popular pizza franchise together. They both owned houses, and when they put them up for sale, Laurie's sold quickly but Robert's sat vacant for months.

I stumbled upon Robert's house while aimlessly driving through some subdivisions near my home one morning. When I called him, I found out he'd bought it just a few weeks before deciding to move north. In fact, he had never actually gotten to move into it. I also learned his real estate listing had just expired without an offer after about nine months on the market, so by now he was really motivated to do something creative in order to get a reprieve from his monthly payments.

I told him that he was in luck, because my company had a program that was designed to give sellers debt relief from their mortgage payments. Now, this was early in my career, and for some unknown reason I had just decided on the spur of that moment to start framing my land contract program as a debt relief solution, rather than launching into some long-winded explanation as to why I needed to use lengthy terms to buy his house. And my timing couldn't have been better.

First of all, Robert (like any other seller) couldn't have given a rat's ass what was in the deal for me, so why try to explain my needs just because every other real estate investor does that? Instead, I described the technique's benefits without even telling him what it was called. That gave me his attention *and* a slight first advantage.

Secondly, as it turns out, Robert had put down $40,000 when he bought the house, so his mortgage payments were well below what the property would support in terms of monthly payments. And since I'd begun our discussion by establishing that my general intent was only to cover his monthly debt service, I ended up with land contract payments that were far below what they could or should have been—without even negotiating! Robert had just followed my lead without hesitation.

So I got some details from him: He wouldn't take less than $195,000 (which was $5,500 less than he'd paid) and he wanted a minimum of $1,000 down, which was extremely reasonable. So instead of negotiating him for a lower downpayment, I decided to just make it easier for me to pay it to him. I agreed to give him $100 upon execution of the agreement, and the $900 balance upon my receipt of a clear title report, which, as I told him, could take a few weeks depending on how busy my title company was. Of course, what I was doing was buying time so that I could use part of my subsequent buyer's downpayment for the $900 balance. This was not because I didn't have the, but simply because I just won't put any more of my own money into a deal than is absolutely necessary.

And that's just being smart if you think about it, especially when you're dealing directly with a private owner. After all, many of them don't know (or won't tell you) that the title to their property is a mess. And once you find that out, just try to get your $500 or $1,000 or $5,000 earnest money deposit back. It ain't gonna happen.

Anyway, back to the agreement. I plugged in the $195,000 price and the $1,000 downpayment, which left a balance to finance of $194,000. As for the payment, I put in the $1,210 he needed to cover his monthly mortgage. Based on those two "known" numbers (the balance and the payment), I had my financial calculator figure out what the interest rate would be. I was pretty excited when it spit out 6.375%, especially since banks were charging "A" credit borrowers 7.25% to 8% at the time.

Based on this, a reasonable fair market land contract rate would have been in the 8.5% to 10% range or higher, so had we been negotiating a land contract instead of a debt relief program, my payment would have likely been anywhere from $1,492 (at 8.5%) to just over $1,700 (at 10%). Therefore, not only was I looking at generating lots of equity if I resold the property on a subsequent long-term agreement, I was also looking at some nice monthly cash flow to boot.

As soon as he mailed back the signed agreement and a key, I created a flyer and put a dozen of them in a box on a sign in the front yard that said, "Seller Financing— No Banks Needed!" It took two flyers and three days to find a buyer.

The price and terms of my selling transaction were $209,900 with $14,900 down, and the remaining $195,000 financed on a subsequent land contract (i.e., I bought it with one land contract, and then sold it on a separate land contract) at 8.75% with payments of $1,534 per month. Since I was putting down $1,000 on my buying land contract with Robert, and collecting $14,900 on my selling land contract, I was looking at an upfront profit of $13,900. On top of that, I was going to enjoy cash flow of $325 per month ($1,534 – $1,209), for the next five years without the hassle of "tenant-n-toilet" troubles or any landlord responsibilities.

But just as soon as I was sure the deal was in the bag, the buyers threw me an unexpected curve ball. They had taken their land contact to an attorney to look it over, and he had initially not had any problems with it. However, the very next day, just two hours before I was scheduled to meet them at their attorney's office to sign the agreement (and collect my cashier's for $14,900), I got a phone call from their attorney who suddenly had an issue with the deal.

Seems he had just pulled title and discovered that I was not the actual owner of record. I told him that I had purchased the property on a land contract just a few days earlier, and hadn't had a chance to record it yet. He said that despite this, he still felt uncomfortable allowing his clients to hand over about $15,000 to someone who didn't have full legal title, as opposed to the equitable title rights I had at the time. He basically felt that too many things could go wrong over the next five years, and that his client could potentially lose everything they'd invested in the property to date— which I had to admit (to myself, anyway) was a legitimate concern.

My first reaction was to go on the defensive and try to convince him that our deal was perfectly legal. But suddenly I realized he had no issue with the *legality* of it, but rather with the safety of his client's investment. So instead, I decided to change course, which also came to me instantaneously and without any forethought (from where, I can only imagine).

I openly conceded the attorney's point, which took him aback as I'm sure he was expecting an argument. I then told him, "Okay, then, maybe we should look at having me simply assign over to them my original land contract with the actual owner of record. This would eliminate your concerns by getting me out of the way. Plus, an assignment would save your clients $325 per month, as well as $1,000 on their remaining balance, because their contract shows $195,000 and mine is only $194,000. On top of all that, if they took over my contract it would extend their terms to seven years instead of only five. So given all of these benefits, how much more would your clients be willing to pay me over the original $14,900 for an assignment?" And then I shut up and listened.

He immediately responded, without even checking with his clients, "I'm thinking they'll go as high as $16,000 for an assignment."

I replied back with, "Well, that's only $1,100 more than they were going to pay, and for that I'm expected to give up almost $20,000 in cash flow ($325 per month for 5 years)? Maybe you should check with your client first to see if they can make it more worthwhile for me to give up all that cash flow."

Now, the truth was, I would have been willing to let them have the whole ball of wax for that same $14,900, because it was fast money, and also because it meant I wouldn't have to bother collecting from a land contract buyer who might turn out to be a deadbeat. In all honesty, I wasn't really looking forward to collecting from somebody who might stop paying me someday, and who might also tear up the property in anger while I'm forking over a bundle to remove them. But he didn't need to know that. I'd already established the perception that I wanted—and was entitled to—more money. The reality was irrelevant.

He called me back in ten minutes and told me his clients would go to $18,500 but no higher since that's all the cash they'd have left after paying the $900 downpayment balance on my contract to the seller. I found this interesting, because I hadn't even *asked* them to pay the $900 balance (I'd planned on paying it myself out of their assignment fee). And it didn't matter to me whether or not they were *really* out of money; all I cared about was that I'd saved the transaction by playing to their concerns rather than fighting back... oh, and also that I got to walk away with $4,500 more than I would have otherwise—$3,600 more for the upfront fee, plus I didn't have to cough up the $900 downpayment balance to Robert, since they paid it for me.

The overall result? The seller was happy, because he got full debt relief until the buyer refinanced five years later and cashed him out. The buyer was happy, because they got extended terms and a below-market monthly payment that was mainly tax deductible interest. And I was thrilled because I made an $18,400 net profit (don't forget, I'd paid the seller a $100 downpayment deposit) in only four days, spending less than seven hours doing actual work.

SUBJECT TO

SUBJECT TO

A QUICK OVERVIEW

➤ **What they are:** A *subject to* deal is one where the seller deeds the property to the buyer, without paying off any of the liens of record (mortgages, taxes, and other encumbrances). The name "*subject to*" is an abbreviated term describing a transaction wherein the title is transferred to the buyer while it is still subject to all of the liens and mortgages of record.

➤ **What they do:** A *subject to* transaction instantly gives the buyer full legal title to the property, allowing the buyer to do anything they want with it; occupy it, re-sell it, or rent it out.

➤ **How they're done:** All it takes to execute a *subject to* deal is for the seller to sign over a deed to the buyer. And although it's not a requirement to have a purchase agreement between the two parties, nor to have an attorney close the transaction, both are very highly recommended.

➤ **How they can generate revenue:** A *subject to* deal can be used to generate money any way you wish, because you would be the full legal owner of the property. That means you can move into the property, lease it out, or resell it—either conventionally or on terms. When reselling *subject to* deals on lease-purchase, you no longer have to worry about flip or seasoning issues, because you would be the actual owner of record.

➤ **Best market cycle:** *Subject to*'s can work well in up or down cycles. Up cycles help make *subject to* deals profitable by providing quicker and easier resale opportunities at better prices. But down cycles have the slight edge as the better environment, not just because there are generally many more motivated sellers to choose from, but because foreclosure rates are often higher in downward moving cycles, and *subject to*'s can be a very useful component in certain creative short sale applications.

➤ **Caveats:** In some areas, and under certain circumstances, *subject to* transactions may be either illegal or highly regulated (consult an attorney in your area). Otherwise, about the only significant risk that *subject to* deal can create for you is the potential for the lender to foreclose because of the violation of the due on sale clause. As unlikely as this is, if you intend to lease out the property, or resell it a on long term installment sale, you must be sure to include a clause that limits (and easily liquidates) any liability you'd have to a tenant or end buyer in the event of a foreclosure.

The Basics

In a *subject to* deal, the seller deeds the property to the buyer. End of story.

This is in stark contrast to a typical real estate closing involving the standard conveyance of a deed, because at the closing, the seller is expected to pay off all of the liens, judgments, and mortgages, on the property, as well as all real estate taxes that have accrued up to the date of closing. These are called encumbrances, and they must be paid off in order for the seller to convey a free and clear deed. If the encumbrances are not cleared when the deed changes hand, they remain in full force against the property, which would compromise the buyer's new lender, since they wouldn't have a valid first position lien.

Here's why: In most states, liens are given an order of superiority based not on their function, nor their date of execution, but rather on the date and time they are recorded against the property—on a first-come, first-served basis. So, if any of the seller's existing encumbrances are not paid off at the closing, then the new mortgage from the buyer's lender would fall into place behind the liens that remain, which means it wouldn't be a "first and best" lien.

Being first and best is very important, because when the property is sold or foreclosed upon, the first and best loan gets paid... well... *first.* And since no lender will fund a buyer's purchase of real estate unless they are assured that their mortgage will be in first position, a deed that is not clear means no new mortgage—and that means no conventional sale.

Even if there's no lender involved and the buyer is paying all cash, the seller is still expected to use the buyer's funds to pay off all of the encumbrances against the property, otherwise the buyer would still be obligated to pay them, and would, in effect, have to pay for the house twice.

Making sure that all liens and accrued taxes are paid at closing is one of the primary functions of a title company, escrow agent, or closing attorney. It's their responsibility to collect the purchase proceeds from the buyer, disperse what's necessary to pay off all the lien holders, and then give whatever is left to the seller. But of course, this is how a *typical* closing is done, and as you've probably already guessed, we're not looking to create typical transactions.

In a *subject to* transaction, the seller isn't required to pay off the liens and mortgages with the money you bring to closing, because if you bring any money at all, which you usually won't, it'll only be to pay the seller for their equity and/or closing costs. All they're being asked to do is convey the property to you just as it is, including all of the liens and mortgages that the title is currently "subject to". Then, as the new owner, it will be up to you to take care of paying all the liens and mortgages on the property. Many beginning investors sweat bullets when they think of taking on all of that new responsibility. But the reality is you wouldn't really *have* any new responsibilities, if you actually stop to think about it.

You see, when you buy a property on a *subject to* transaction, you own the property, but all of the liens and mortgages remain in the seller's name, and are therefore still the seller's responsibility. That means you would not be legally obligated to any of the lenders or lienholders (including judgment lienholders), which means that neither your credit nor your assets will be at risk at any time.

So really, about the only risk you face is not being able to find a suitable buyer or tenant to provide you with the cash flow you need to make the seller's payments, in which case the lender would foreclose on the seller—not you. And although you or your entity (if you're using a trust, LLC. or corporation) would be named as a defendant in the actual lawsuit, that does not make you liable for the debt. The lender is required to serve you notice as the owner of record in order to legally extinguish your interests in the property. However, the lender will not be able to come after you or your entity for deficiencies, because you never had a legal obligation to them for satisfying any of the debt. The same goes for unpaid taxes or assessments. The county might eventually force the sale of the property in a tax foreclosure, but you would not incur any losses or liabilities, because property taxes are levied against the property itself, never the owner.

One caution: although your paperwork may legally let you just walk away from any deal at any time you want without risk, that doesn't give you the right to start running around collecting deeds willy-nilly, even if your favorite guru proudly says they do it all the time. It's just not ethical for you to have a standard exit plan of simply bolting whenever things don't go the way you want, leaving your sellers hanging—unless, of course, the seller was already in default. When it comes to solvent sellers who were not in danger of default when you negotiated for them to deed you their property, you had better do everything within your power to protect their property, their equity (if they have any), and their good credit, even if it means bunking with Matt Foley in a van down by the river for a few months.

Why? Well, first of all, it's the right thing to do for someone who had trusted you implicitly to take care of their valuable assets. Second, if you end up creating serious and unnecessary financial hardships for someone who wouldn't have otherwise likely endured them, simply because you were flippant about your responsibilities, negligent in your actions, or grossly incapable of making good on any of the promises you sold them with (regarding doing a *subject to* deal), a judge could theoretically toss out your agreement, along with all of its advantageous default remedies. And if your actions were unconscionable enough, he could even pierce your corporate veil and hold you personally liable for the seller's damages.

Of course, if you're dealing with a seller who is already in default or foreclosure, or who is certain to be there soon, all bets are off. The most you owe someone like that is your best efforts at solving their problem; nothing more. Because if a property ends up in foreclosure when it was already there (or clearly headed there) before you came along, the seller is no worse off for letting you give it a go.

Subject To in the Real World

Most of your prime candidates for *subject to* transactions in the real world will fall into two basic categories: 1) solvent sellers with about 10% to 25% equity who are financially stable, but still highly motivated to sell; and 2) sellers who are in default or foreclosure, and generally ready to just walk away because they have no equity, or are over-financed—often to a significant degree. So let's take a quick look at both types of prospects individually.

Solvent, motivated sellers with 10% to 25% equity—Don't get the wrong idea; just because I've identified sellers in the 10% to 25% equity range, that doesn't mean you can't do deals with sellers who have more equity, nor does it mean you shouldn't do deals with sellers who have less if the situation warrants. That just happens to be the ideal range, and not just because the majority of sellers fall into that category in an average, stable marketplace.

There are two real reasons that an equity range of about 10% to 25% makes these sellers such prime candidates: 1) When sellers have more than 25% equity, they have lots more choices for getting their properties liquidated, and more choice tends to equal less motivation in any marketplace; and 2) When sellers have less than 10% equity, it can sometimes be difficult for you to create enough of a profit margin to make the deal worthwhile.

For instance, sellers with lots of equity can afford to offer premium commissions as a motivator to real estate agents. They also they have more latitude to discount their selling price, plus they can tap their equity with a bridge loan or a second mortgage to hold themselves over for awhile, if necessary. Therefore, even though they may be highly motivated to sell, their large equity spread makes them far less dependent upon someone like yourself to create a solution for them. As a result, you're less likely to strike a profitable deal with them.

On the other hand, if a seller has much less than 10% equity, then you might have some trouble making a worthwhile profit. Why? Because what little equity the seller has can easily get eaten up in just closing costs alone, leaving you little or nothing to collect as profit. And as for turning it into an investment property for rental cash flow, the fact that the property is so deeply mortgaged means it will likely have monthly payments that are higher than what you could reasonably expect to collect from a tenant.

That means if your seller has less than 10% equity, you'll probably be limited to only one exit strategy: reselling it on a long-term agreement, such as a lease-purchase or land contract. Selling this way allows you to create some additional equity, because you can increase your selling price slightly over the current market value by pitching benefits such as convenience and future appreciation (as we had discussed earlier in the sections covering those techniques). But even then, you're only going to be able to increase your resale price by a modest 5% to 10% above the current market value, which may not be as lucrative as it first appears once you factor in some additional costs.

What additional costs? Well, the property isn't going to find a buyer on its own, so you'll have marketing costs. Then, even if the property is in really nice shape (and they usually are), you're still going to have some costs in minor spruce-up, utilities, and yard maintenance if nothing else, until you find a buyer. Plus, when you actually close the sale of the property later on down the road, you'll have to absorb closing costs and conveyance fees as well. So as you can see, even if you have a nice property in a nice area and everything goes well, you can still rack up enough of those nickel and dime costs to significantly impact your overall profitability— especially when you're dealing with meager spreads of only 6% to 12%, most of which came from the 5% to 10% equity you created artificially.

Of course, this is all assuming you don't run into any problems. If, on the other hand, you're unlucky enough to end up with a dead-beat, damage-happy tenant/buyer—or worse, a land contract buyer who defaults on you—then you can figure on kissing goodbye what little profit you were expecting to make over the next two to five years, as you open your wallet and continue the headache of protecting the solvent, low equity, seller you should have avoided from day one.

Sellers in default and/or foreclosure—The other class of sellers that represent your best candidates for *subject to* deals are the ones who are in default or foreclosure, and have little or no equity, or are (more likely), upside down on their mortgages. This means they owe more than what their property is worth— sometimes to a considerable extent, which happens to be pretty common in the marketplace as of the time of this writing.

By now, you may be wondering why sellers with a little bit of equity are considered bad candidates for a *subject to* deal (as we just discussed above) and yet sellers with *no* equity—or even *negative* equity—are excellent prospects. How can this be, if equity is a critical factor in your potential profit?

It's very simple: when you're dealing with sellers in default or foreclosure, you can *create* all the equity you need by negotiating with the seller's lender for a short sale, which is the technique we'll be looking at next.

Another reason sellers like this are such prime candidates for a *subject to* deal is because they are generally ready to just walk away, which makes getting a deed from them pretty easy. And if these sellers have very little equity, or none at all, then they often have very little at risk. That makes getting a deed from them not just easy for you, but pretty safe as well—because the seller's low risk position translates into a much lower assumption of responsibility for you. In other words, if the seller is entrusting you with very little or nothing at all, then there is an equally proportionate reduction in the level of protection that you will owe them; at least from a moral perspective.

Subject To Paperwork

A common question I get asked is: "What paperwork is needed to do a *subject to* deal, and who prepares it?" The only paperwork that is truly required to execute a *subject to* transaction is a deed from the seller to the buyer, which is often prepared by the buyer right on-the-spot. But it's a really, *really* good idea to have a few other documents to support the transaction, and perhaps even a better idea to re-consider having the buyer (i.e., you, as the investor) prepare the deed in the field.

First, let's cover the supporting documents. Foremost among them is an executed purchase and sale agreement, signed and dated by both parties, which clearly demonstrates a full acceptance to the terms of the *subject to* transaction. This is really important, not only so that nothing is left to interpretation, but also so that you can prove later that the seller freely agreed to do the deal with you.

If you don't get this in writing right up front, the seller could go running to a judge later on, crying that you tricked him into unknowingly deeding away his home. When the judge asks for you to produce written evidence that proves the seller was a willing participant, all you'll be able to show him are empty pockets, rapidly spreading sweat stains, and a painful look of hopeless desperation that hasn't been seen since Ben Stiller in *Meet the Parents*.

Another really important document is an Authorization Letter, signed by the borrower, allowing the lender to discuss the seller's loan with you. Without it, it's illegal for the lender to share any details of the loan with you—regardless of how much you plead, and despite whose name appears on the property securing the loan.

You should also have a Loan Operating Agreement, which is essentially a statement given by the seller allowing you to operate the loan on their behalf, e.g., making payments on the loan, changing the official mailing address to your place of business, etc. Many investors wisely blend the Authorization Letter and Operating Agreement into one document for ease and simplicity.

Up until now, all of the documents we've covered have been basic enough that you could, and actually should, just prepare them yourself as a principal member of the transaction. That leaves us with the deed. *Who* should prepare it, *when* should they prepare it, and *why* should they be the ones to prepare it? There are two schools of thought on this issue, both of which are equally compelling.

The first line of reasoning is that you should prepare the deed. That way, you can write it up on-the-spot before your highly motivated seller can change his or her mind. This can be a critical benefit for you, as you may remember from our earlier discussions, when we examined how seller perceptions and motivations are highly fluid. That means sellers can, and do, change their minds frequently—a fact to which I can attest personally.

It never ceases to amaze me how a seller can be ready to just walk away from a property one minute, but then ninety seconds later be determined to do whatever it takes to find a conventional buyer at full retail price. So if you can draft a deed and get them to sign it in front of a notary while they're still in full walking mode, they won't be able to stop the deal later if they develop seller's remorse.

Now, don't get the wrong idea. I am not suggesting that you do this in order to trap sellers while they happen to be in a frantic state of mind. If your seller freaks out a few days later and wants out of the deal, and you haven't yet committed the property to a subsequent buyer, do the right thing and let them out. Of course, make sure you find out what their issue is first, because it may be something you can help them overcome without giving the property back. But if they really want it back, just give it to them, because you're probably going to need their cooperation again later anyway—and if they don't like you when you come back to them for some help, you're going to discover just how hard it is to push a rope.

The good news about potential seller's remorse is that if you've been able to make your seller feel good enough about you—and the deal you've created—they're not likely to change their mind. That's because if they feel the whole "property thing" has been well taken care of, they will develop a mental sense of closure. This will allow them to put it behind them and get on with their lives.

There are some caveats to preparing the deed yourself, though. One is that if you are not personally the grantee (the seller is the grantor, the buyer is the grantee), you are practicing law without a license. The only people who can legally prepare a deed, other than an attorney, are the principal members of the transaction; the grantor or the grantee.

So technically, if the grantee is your corporation or LLC, then it's a gray area as to whether you can legally prepare the deed personally. However, it may be legal and acceptable for you to prepare the deed as an officer of your corporation, or as an authorized member of your LLC—but you need to check with your attorney first before doing anything like that. What many of my investor colleagues do when it comes to identifying the preparer is to simply write the word "Grantee", followed by their entity's mailing address.

Another caveat to preparing the deed yourself is that it would be your responsibility to correct the deed later on if it contains any errors. For example, let's say you filled out a deed in December of 2007, and three years later, your end buyer is ready to refinance the property to cash you out, but the title company who's closing the deal finds a defect in the title you prepared. The entire cost and burden of correcting that deed will fall to you. This may not be a big deal, and may be correctable with a simple affidavit or something similar. But it could just as easily be a serious defect that would require a new deed and the cooperation of your seller from three years ago, who may now be uncooperative, or living in the rain forests of South America, or perhaps even dead. *Then* what?

The last downside to preparing the deed yourself is that your seller may perceive this as a lack of professionalism. While this is a possibility, that doesn't mean preparing the deed on-the-spot will automatically make you look like a rookie. On the contrary, if you build a good one-on-one rapport with the seller, then preparing the deed together can actually become a bonding experience. This can make them feel as though the two of you are on the same team—both resolved to finding a solution for them; and that can be a very strong alliance indeed.

The other school of thought on deed preparation is to execute the *subject to* purchase and sale agreement on-the-spot, but then have the deed prepared by a professional title agent or attorney a few days later. Under that scenario, you and your seller would meet at the attorney or title company's office, where they would sign a "real" deed at a "real" closing table, complete with a simple, but "real", HUD-1 closing statement that memorializes the deal. This enhances the seller's perception that both you, and the deal, are fully legitimate—which can greatly ease the seller's mind and reduce the likelihood of seller's remorse.

Another benefit to having a professional prepare your deed is that if there are any defects with the deed, your attorney or title company will be responsible for clearing everything up for you at their own expense, or at the expense of a claim on their errors and omissions insurance policy, if the mistake is serious enough.

But won't there be some costs if you close your *subject to* deals this way? Certainly, but they will usually be pretty small, and your seller can pay them, or at the very least split them with you. After all, most people are expecting to pay *something* to close the sale of their property.

What do you do if your seller doesn't have any money at all? Don't panic, because you can turn it into an opportunity to become an instant hero. How? Well, if you step up and offer to pay their closing costs, it's an inexpensive way to ensure their cooperation, as well as get a great testimonial you can use later.

Of course, that means your transaction wouldn't be a "no money down" deal, but maybe that would be a good time for you to practice loosening up a little. Here's a news flash for you: The sooner you stop being so cheap, the sooner you'll discover how much easier it is to make money by not squeezing the cash you have so tightly. Think I'm kidding? Just look in the wallet of any real estate investor (if you can figure out a way to get one to open it for you), and you'll find that most of the presidents are grimacing in pain.

Naturally, there is an obvious and unfortunate downside to having the deed professionally prepared at a later date, as it gives your sellers some time to change their minds. But you know what? If a seller is going to change their mind at all, it's usually going to happen within the first couple of days anyway.

So instead of worrying about it, think of this as a hassle-free way for you to weed out any goofball sellers in advance, before they even get the chance to screw up your life. Trust me, you don't want people like that involved in your business dealings at all, let alone having them around to drag down your soul for the next three to five years. It's like stepping in a steaming pile on a daily basis.

Negotiate Net Equity Instead of Price

Perhaps the best approach for selling highly-motivated (but otherwise solvent) property owners on the idea of doing a *subject to* transaction is to focus on offering them debt relief, as well as a reasonable cash-out price that would be equivalent to having listed and sold their property with a Realtor.

A great way to make this concept attractive is to immediately switch the context of the negotiations from price over to net equity—assuming the seller actually *has* some equity. If so, then this can be an extremely effective approach for two reasons, both of which are more psychological than anything else.

So, what is net equity? It's the amount of actual cash that the seller will walk away from the closing table with, after deducting all the costs and fees of the sale.

Why it works

The first reason that negotiating net equity can work so well is because it moves the discussion away from the potentially emotional aspect of price. You see, most buyers assume that sellers view price as a logical concept—which they *should*, since it can be physically expressed on paper. However, price is an emotional element for many sellers because it represents the value of something that has great meaning to them. This can actually create an irrational need for them to defend their asking price, even to unreasonable lengths. Perhaps you've experienced this.

The best way to nip this in the bud is shift our sellers away from the emotional minefield of price, and over to the logical reality of net equity. Although this violates one of the first rules of effective marketing—always sell to emotions, never to logic—we need to get the powerful influence of emotions out of the way when it comes to negotiating price. The fastest and easiest way to do this is by introducing the seller to a little math. What possible role can mathematics have in improving your real estate negotiations? Bear with me, and I'll show you.

In their best-selling book, *Made to Stick: Why Some Ideas Survive and Others Die*, authors Chip and Dan Heath cite a 2004 Carnegie Mellon research study that was designed to see if—and to what extent—a person's state of mind (analytical vs. emotional) could influence their decision-making. The results were astounding.

The study revealed that people who were asked to solve a couple of easy mathematical equations prior to donating money tended to donate considerably less (roughly half as much, on average) to the exact same charity as those who were first asked to describe their "feelings" about warm and fuzzy topics, like babies.

The reason for the disparity in generosity is simple: the mere act of calculating solutions to math problems forced the study subjects to abandon emotional attitudes, and switch over into logical thinking mode. The study results further suggested that these two distinct states of mind—emotional and analytical—appear to be mutually exclusive of one another, even if only temporarily.

In other words, when people engage in deductive reasoning activities, they typically morph into a more logical state of mind—at least for awhile. This makes them far more likely to consider a transaction based solely on its actual merits, rather than allowing their decisions to be gut-driven by feelings or emotions. The reverse proved true as well. The more emotional a person can be made to feel, the less likely they are to exercise prudence in their decision-making—which is why selling is designed to exploit feelings, rather than to encourage thoughtful analysis.

Now, pay close attention... because here is why all of this seemingly irrelevant information matters to you: Unlike price, net equity is a figure that has to be calculated mathematically. So as you walk your seller through the calculations, the logical math functions will subconsciously detach them from their emotional ties, and move them straight into full analytical mode. That means when you finally *do* establish a net equity figure, the seller—being in an actively logical state of mind— is very likely to view the amount as just a number; a non-emotional answer to an equation, rather than an attempt to discount the value of their property.

This leads into the second reason why switching context to net equity is such a powerful negotiating tactic: Removing price as the basis of your negotiations will allow you to short-circuit the "zero-sum" mindset—a mentality to which nearly all sellers (and way too many investors) adamantly subscribe.

What is the zero-sum mindset? It is the popular belief that the only way for someone to make a transaction more profitable for themselves is to make it *less* profitable for the other side by the exact same amount. The reason this makes sense to most people is because they view price negotiations as a sequence of credits and debits which must remain balanced at all times, i.e., every extra dollar the buyer wants to make in additional profit must come from negotiating the seller into accepting an equivalent reduction in selling price. But this is actually a myth.

You see, although maintaining a net difference of zero may be common in things like board games and algebraic equations, it's not a universal principal everywhere. How can this be? Well, if you look back to our discussions on term transactions, you'll see we can easily increase the profitability of our deals without reducing our buying price accordingly, simply by tweaking the terms instead— such as arranging for longer paybacks, lower interest rates, lower payments, equity deferments, etc. This allows us to make our additional profits on the resale side, while still allowing our sellers to get the prices they want on our buying side.

In fact, many highly successful real estate investors intentionally avoid "price only" negotiations whenever they can, opting instead to create a variety of offers consisting of simultaneous adjustments to both price *and* terms. Why do they adjust both variables in each offer? Well, in addition to giving sellers the attractive element of choice, this strategy also eliminates the seller's ability to directly compare the various offers on an apples-to-apples basis, which makes it virtually impossible for them to fall into the trap of debating from a zero-sum point of view.

THE COMPLEMENTARY TECHNIQUES

How to negotiate net equity

Now that we know *why* negotiating net equity is a good idea, let's look at a sample illustration of how it's done. Way back on page 62, we saw a brief example of a *subject to* deal that demonstrated a shift from price to net equity. So in the interest of keeping things simple, let's just revisit that deal and expand on a few details.

As you may recall, the seller in that example had a property worth about $190,000 to $195,000, with a remaining mortgage balance of about $150,000. Most sellers in this situation will simply see the $40,000+ gross equity spread, and already have plans on how they're going to spend it. But equity doesn't matter; only *net* equity. In fact, equity isn't even tangible—it's just an abstract concept. Want proof? Take $40,000 worth of equity to a garage sale and see what it'll get you. You wouldn't even score a scratched and dusty *Muskrat Love* 45 (for you youngsters, that's a cheesy Captain & Tennille record from 1976—not a large caliber handgun).

So if you're really stoked about doing *subject to* deals, you'll have to learn how to enlighten your sellers to the reality of net equity; and the fastest way to do that is to grab a piece of paper and calculate it with them right there on-the-spot.

The mathematical aspect of this alone will switch them into full analytical mode (which we just learned is ideal), but the best part is that as the two of you go down the sheet together, addressing each cost individually, the obvious reasoning behind each figure will help to solidify the entire point of your exercise in the seller's mind. And if you were heads-up enough to have the seller use his or her own calculator to arrive at these figures, it would be virtually impossible for them to dispute the end result. After all, they would be arguing against themselves.

Here's what you might say...	*And here's what you could write...*
"You estimate your property's worth in the low to mid $190's, so let's start this with an initial asking price of $199K. OK?"	Initial Asking Price: $199,000 $199,000 x .963 = $191,637 Round up to $192,000
"Our local MLS shows average sale is 96.3% of list price."	Final Sale Price @ 96.3% : $192,000
"You can probably find a good Realtor at a 5% commission."	Less Commission @ 5 % : $9,600
"Your closing and conveyance costs will be about 2%, and buyers usually want sellers to pay 3% of their closing costs."	Less closing costs @ 5 %: $9,600
"A few minor repairs and pest treatments are very common after inspections, so it's reasonable to allow for some."	Less repairs/pest treatments: $1,000
"Lastly is your mortgage payoff, which will be about $900 higher than just the principal balance, due to daily interest."	Less mortgage payoff: $150,900
"Subtracting all of these costs and fees gives us your likely *'walk away from the closing table'* net equity of $20,900, which we'll just round up to $21,000."	Approximate Net Equity: $20,900 Round up to $21,000

One thing you can usually count on after filling out a sheet like this is a slight jerking back of the seller's head in response to the shock of actually seeing their bottom line net equity for the first time. Even the most hardened, analytically-minded sellers can be blown away by how much of their equity will likely be devoured in the process of selling their property to convert it into cash.

More often than not, your seller is going to have one of the following two standard reactions to this: 1) they'll resign themselves to the obvious truth of what they've just helped calculate, in which case it would be time for you to move on to the step of negotiating how you'll pay their net equity; or 2) more likely, they'll shake their heads in disbelief and go down the list again, item-by-item, looking for costs that don't apply, or which they feel may have been exaggerated.

If they fall into the latter category, give them another moment or two (not too long, though) to let the reality take a foothold in their mind, and then take control of moving things forward by saying something like, "So, given all of this, are you ready to move ahead with our negotiations on the basis that our net equity figure of $21,000 is a reasonable assumption?" If they agree, then move on to the next aspect of negotiations. If not, it might be time to just move on to another seller.

As soon as you and the seller are on the same page with regards to the net equity calculation, your next objective will be to negotiate an easy and profitable way for you to pay it to them. Once again, I highly recommend using the multiple-offer format, to help keep the context focused on the net equity rather than the actual selling price. So let's see how this could be done.

A really smart idea would be to have a form already prepared in advance that has your net equity calculation formula on the front side, and a multiple-offer worksheet on the back. Then, all you'd have to do is flip the page over and handwrite a few numbers into three very basic offers marked Offer #1, Offer #2, and Offer #3, each with its own details already sketched out in advance, like this:

Net Equity = $ 21,000

Offer #1: Purchase your net equity for $ 21,000, as follows:
$ 2,000 at closing, we take over payments, $ 19,000 balance secured by a note payable upon our future resale of the property.

Offer#2: Purchase your net equity for $ 15,000, as follows:
$ 5,000 at closing, we take over payments, $ 10,000 balance secured by a note payable upon our future resale of the property.

Offer #3: Purchase your net equity for $ 10,000, as follows:
All $ 10,000 paid in cash at closing, we take over payments.

Then, as you turn the page around to face the seller, you could go down the list of offers with them one by one, and explain the reason for the different amounts. One of the softest and easiest ways to do this is to introduce them to the concept of the *time value of money*. Even though they may have heard of this term before, and have a pretty good idea what it means, you need to take a moment to share with them how it would apply to your deal.

For example, you could say something like, "So as you can see, the more flexible you can be about waiting for your net equity, the more of it I can pay you overall. This is due to a principle called the *time value of money*. You may already be familiar with this concept, but what it means in our particular case is that the more of your equity you need today, the more I will have to tap into my high-interest reserve funding to give it to you. And the more of that high-interest money I have to use, the higher my costs will be, which leaves less cash for me to give to you. Fortunately, the reverse is also true: the less money you need today, the less of that high-interest funding I'll need, which will leave more cash for your pocket. You see, ultimately, I have to pay that money to *someone*; so the question is, would you rather it be you, or the investment lender who'll fund our deal?"

Notice that so far there has been no mention at all of price. This is by design, because the actual amounts of your three offers would have ranged from $160,000 to $171,000 for a property worth nearly $200,000. Seeing such an apparent disparity (and I say *apparent* disparity because the gap would at first seem unreasonable to any seller who's not yet been enlightened on the true costs of liquidation) would instantly trigger a negative emotional gut response from the seller, resulting in either a deal-killing immediate parting of ways, or a barrage of counter-offers based solely on zero-sum thinking—neither of which would be good for you.

Notice also in that discussion that you didn't wait for the seller to tell you if he actually knows what the time value of money principle is. Instead, you go right ahead and explain to him exactly how it would apply to your particular deal. That was also by design, because it works to your advantage a couple of ways.

Here's what I mean: If your seller *doesn't* know what the time value of money is, you'll make him feel ignorant by leaving him hanging without an explanation—and trust me, sellers don't like to be made to feel stupid. But by appearing to give him the benefit of the doubt (that he knows what it means) because you didn't stop to describe it before going on to explain its implications, you will have essentially demonstrated confidence in his intelligence—which will make him feel good. Conversely, if your seller actually *does* know what the time value of money principle is, then stopping to explain it to him like he's a child before showing him how it would apply to your deal will make you appear to be talking down to him—and sellers don't like that kind of stuff, either.

Due On Sale Clause

If you know enough about real estate, you've already figured out that a *subject to* transaction is a full-on violation of the due-on-sale clause. If you don't know what the due-on-sale clause is or how it applies to creative transactions, I'll take the next few minutes to explain it to you. But buckle up first, because it's a bit of a roller coaster ride... even if it eventually ends up going nowhere.

The due-on-sale clause is a provision in a mortgage or deed of trust that states if the property is sold, or if some or all of the ownership interests in the property are transferred from the original borrower to anyone (or anything) else, then the loan is fully due and payable. If the ownership interests change hands and the loan is not paid off, the lender would reserve the right to accelerate the note and foreclose on the mortgage or deed of trust. There are only three exceptions to this:

1. When the lender agrees to the transfer in advance by approving the buyer as the new borrower. This is called a qualifying assumption, and it usually releases the seller as the old borrower. They are extremely rare.

2. When the lender is simply unaware that a sale or transfer has occurred; or

3. When the lender *is* aware that a sale or transfer has occurred, but just doesn't care. After all, they're in the business of generating revenue by collecting payments, not by foreclosing and owning distressed properties.

So the reality is this: if someone deeds you their property, the chances are pretty small that the lender would foreclose on you simply because of the transfer itself—especially if you're volunteering to send them some money to reinstate a defaulted loan, or planning to make improvements to the property that's securing their loan.

About the only time a lender would be likely to call a loan due in response to a *subject to* transfer is if the loan was already in default anyway. Of course, if interest rates were to suddenly rise dramatically, some lenders might consider foreclosing at a loss just so they can lend the money back out at much higher rates. But this is a pretty unlikely scenario. In fact, you'd be more likely to see the DEA put Charlie Sheen in charge of securing their evidence room before that would ever happen.

But aren't there some gurus running around out there who actually believe that it's literally *illegal* for lenders to enforce their due-on-sale clause? Sure, and they seem to have one thing in common; they all tend to hinge the entire substance of their mistaken argument on the same two liberal decisions that were handed down by (no surprise) California's Supreme Court, way back in the 1970's, when bell-bottoms ruled and disco was still king. Specifically, they like to cite *Tucker v. Lassen Savings & Loan Association* (12 Cal. 3d 629, 1974) and *Wellenkamp v. Bank of America*, (21 Cal 3d 943, 8/25/78).

In both of these decisions, the judges essentially ruled that a lender must be able to prove that a transaction would somehow impair their security and put them at greater risk. If they couldn't prove that, it was the court's opinion that enforcing the due-on-sale clause would create an unnecessary restraint on alienation. In common everyday language, this meant that if a lender was unable to provide some evidence that a *subject to* deal somehow compromised their rights or remedies as a lienholder (which they don't), then the lender had no valid reason for restricting or interfering with the borrower's legal right to deed their property to *whomever* they wanted, *whenever* they wanted, and *however* they wanted. Over the next few years, several other courts found themselves in agreement with California, and subsequently followed suit by rendering similar decisions.

Now, this would be great for us if it was the end of the story, as some gurus will tell you it is… but it's not. A few years later, under pressure from struggling Savings & Loans, the feds passed the Garn-St. Germain Depository Institutions Act of 1982. Among other things, this new law identified more precisely when a lender could and could not enforce their due-on-sale clause. Essentially, this new bill voided all of those favorable past liberal rulings, but that little fact hasn't stopped many of today's gurus from continuing to argue unenforceability based on those same old vintage, tie-died, and—oh yeah—*no longer valid* court rulings.

Today, many of the provisions of that bill have led to most contemporary mortgages featuring a much broader range of activities which can now legally "trigger" the lender's right to accelerate the loan. Among these trigger events are:

1) Whenever the property owner deeds their property without paying off the loan (this one has obviously not changed).

2) Whenever the property owner transfers all or some of their ownership or interests in the property to another person or entity.

3) Whenever a property owner enters into a lease that has an initial term exceeding three years, or a lease of any length which contains an option to purchase.

4) Whenever the property owner enters into any agreement of any kind and of any term length, which sole purpose is to secure the transfer of ownership at some point in the future.

In response to these tighter restrictions, many gurus now teach that you can avoid triggering the due-on-sale clause by getting your sellers to deed their properties into a land trust (instead of directly to you), and then having them transfer (by assignment) all control of that land trust over to you.

What is the purpose of using land trusts to take over title to properties? Well, under Garn-St. Germain, if an owner deeds their property into a land trust, it's illegal for the lender to trigger the due-on-sale clause—at least as long as the owner remains the beneficiary who controls the trust. Of course, the minute the owner assigns their beneficial interests over to you, they're in violation of the due-on-sale clause. But that's not usually a problem, since you and your seller are the only two people on earth who even knows this happened. As long as the lender doesn't know a transfer went down, they won't accelerate the loan.

This is a pretty cool way to get around the due-on-sale challenge, but it's not as bullet-proof as many gurus teach. That's because most sellers will continue to have some contact with their lenders, and they've been known to occasionally develop fatal cases of the dreaded *Help! I'm talking and I can't shut up* disease. And once they've spilled the beans to their lender, the pooch is basically screwed. So if the lender threatens to file foreclosure, about the only thing you can do is call their bluff and hope that's all it is—a bluff.

Long story short, Garn-St. Germain effectively renders every investment technique in this book (and any other book, course, or seminar on creative real estate investing) a violation of the due-on-sale clause in some way. In fact, if you really think about it, even a standard purchase and sale agreement technically violates it. And although simply violating the due-on-sale clause is neither illegal nor immoral, if you entice a seller into doing so without fully explaining to them the risk of acceleration and foreclosure, it could be viewed as being both illegal *and* immoral—because you'd be intentionally compromising them without their full knowledge and understanding.

The good news is that a due-on-sale enforcement is very unlikely to ever rear its ugly head in your investment endeavors. But regardless of this fact, you must always be aware of—and prepared to handle—its potential consequences. And no matter what your favorite guru says, you must never assume that you are completely free of any risk of acceleration and foreclosure while engaging any creative technique to invest in real estate... because the risk is always there.

Actual Subject To Case Study

When Ed and Dorothy found my postcard in their mailbox, they had already been living in their two bedroom rented condo for quite some time, having moved from their nice four bedroom two-story home across town over six months earlier.

The idea behind their move was to eliminate all of the maintenance and repair responsibilities for Ed, whose health had been declining recently. Unfortunately, the trade-off had been a great deal of additional stress brought on by the fact that their house hadn't sold after nearly nine months on the market, which by this time had put them nearly $6,000 behind on their mortgage.

Dorothy was thrilled when she read my postcard, and although I'd like to say it was due to my brilliant copywriting, it was really more a matter of her seeing the right message at just the right time. When you couple this with the fact that my postcard was the *only* marketing piece she had received from *anyone* regarding her house, Dorothy was under the impression that I was the only person in the entire world who had a possible solution for her. Was this true? Of course not! But, once again, perception trumps reality—because there were literally a hundred other investors in town who were capable of helping her with the exact same strategies I was planning to try. However, since my postcard was the only one she'd received, her perception was that I was the only player in town who could help her (check out the Direct Mail section on page 79 in the chapter on marketing to see how this happened).

When Dorothy shared her situation with me over the phone, I told her our best bet would be for her to just deed the house over to me, and I'd do whatever I could on my end to try and stop the foreclosure. But also I made it clear that I wasn't making any promises, especially since her mortgage was already so far behind. I even went so far as to make them both sign a simple statement saying that they understood I was not making any guarantees, and that their extreme arrearages at this late stage meant a foreclosure was likely, despite my upcoming best efforts to help. This was my way of making sure they couldn't come back later and claim that I was somehow the cause of their foreclosure.

When we met, Ed and Dorothy showed me a payment coupon with an unpaid principal balance of about $100,000 and an estimated payoff amount of about $107,000 including late fees and accrued interest (due to the missed payments). So essentially, my purchase price was $107, 000—give or take a few bucks.

After they signed the *subject to* agreement, I went to look at the house I'd just bought. Why didn't I look at the house first? Well, there was really no need to. After all, if I'd taken the time to look at the house first, and then they changed their mind about working with me, I would've wasted an afternoon. But conversely, if I had later discovered that the house was junk after signing the paperwork, I would've had a choice to either do a short sale with their lender, or just walk away and let them keep my lousy $10 earnest money.

Anyway, the house was pretty nice, even though it had a few minor deferred maintenance issues. These were mostly due to the long vacancy, and Ed's inability to keep the place in tip-top shape while they were still living there. There was a torn window screen, some tall grass, lots of overgrown landscaping, and two or three rooms which really needed a fresh coat of paint. Other than that, the house simply needed a thorough top to bottom cleaning. These were all things that an energetic young couple with a few friends and a desire to own a house could easily knock out on a long Saturday afternoon, just before heading out for pizza and beer.

In excellent shape, my Realtor estimated that the house would be worth about $125,000 on a conventional sale. So to make the property attractive, I offered it on seller financing for the same $125,000. In this case, the seller financing didn't add any additional market value, but instead served to make up for the lost value caused by the ugly deferred maintenance.

Three days later (which I'll admit is considerably faster than the norm), I had a couple sitting in my office who were interested in buying it that afternoon. They had decent credit and $12,000 cash. At first, I offered the property to them on a lease-purchase, until I found out that they weren't willing to part with any more than $3,000 as a downpayment to buy it that way. They were, however, willing to put all $12,000 down on a land contract. Since I only needed $6,000 to reinstate the loan, I somehow found myself suddenly able to get them qualified for our company's land contract buying program.

We wrote up the agreement at $125,000 with $12,000 down, and the remaining $113,000 financed on a land contract at 9% interest. That made their full payment (including taxes and insurance) nearly $150 per month higher than the payment I had to make to Ed and Dorothy's lender.

As soon as I got the $12,000 cash in my hands, what do you think I did first? No, I didn't buy a Corvette. I called Ocwen (Ed and Dorothy's lender) about reinstating the loan. Now, did I call them to ask where to send the entire $6,000 arrearage? Of course not! I called them to ask what's the least they'd be willing to accept to reinstate the loan. They told me if I sent them $2,000 and a recent financial statement from Ed and Dorothy, they would not only reinstate the loan, they would also (get this) lower the monthly payment as well—and I didn't even *ask* for a lower monthly payment (where the heck was my head, anyway?)!

So I sent them $2,000 of the $12,000 downpayment, and kept the remaining $10,000 as my upfront profit. Then, thanks to the unexpected loan modification, I got to enjoy a monthly cash flow of about $275 per month, instead of the $150 per month I was expecting.

My new buyers moved into the house, cleaned it up nicely, and 22 months later decided to refinance it with a lender of their own. It appraised for $135,000. Of course, the title company who was closing their refinance called me to get the payoff figure for the land contract, and even though I already knew exactly how much their payoff was, I still asked the title company to give me a day or two to put together an official figure. Why the delay? Because in order to deliver a clear deed to my buyer, I was going to have to pay off Ed and Dorothy's lender; so I needed some time to get an official payoff letter from them.

According to their lender, the remaining payoff was at roughly $102,500 ($106,000 less the $2,000 reinstatement fee, less about $1,500 in principal reduction over the last 22 months). This meant that my back–end payday was going to be around $10,000, because my buyer still owed me about $112,500 on their land contract payoff (if you're curious as to why their payoff was still $112,500 when they had only financed $113,000 to begin with, it's because I had amortized their land contract over a 40 year period, which gave them a slightly lower monthly payment, but an excruciatingly slow paydown as well).

So, getting back to Ocwen, did I ask them to send me a payoff letter for the full $102,500? I think you know better than that by now. Instead, I told them I was trying to put together enough cash to pay off this loan, so I was wondering if there was any way they could work with me on the $102,500 payoff in order to get this problematic debt off their books within the next few days.

They called me back two days later, and said—almost apologetically—that the least they could discount the payoff to was an even $98,000 cash. Now, I realize that negotiating a $4,500 discount may not get me my own Nightingale-Conant late night infomercial (*Yes, you, too, could be making up to $4,500 more on your next real estate deal! Learn how for just 3 easy payments of $49.99!*), but it still meant an additional $4,500 was going into my pocket just because I took five minutes to ask for it. You have to admit, it's pretty hard to beat that kind of return on such a small investment of time.

When all was said and done, my total take on this deal was about $30,550, which consisted of the $10,000 net downpayment (after sending the lender $2,000 to reinstate the loan), another $6,050 for positive cash flow ($275 per month for 22 months with absolutely *no* repair responsibilities), plus an additional $14,500 on the back end. Not too bad, considering the property only had about $1,000 in *real* equity when I first bought it with only $10 down.

*   *   *   *   *

As you can see, the trick to successful investing in creative real estate is learning how to apply knowledge to an existing situation. It allows you to create transactions out of thin air which would have otherwise never materialized, and positions you to legitimately generate revenue without exploiting or defrauding the people involved.

Remember, it's absolutely necessary to take advantage of each and every situation you can in this business, but it's never acceptable to take advantage of the people who happen to *be* in those situations—and there's a big distinction between those two agendas.

One will land you in *a* big house, the other will land you in *the* Big House.

SHORT SALE

SHORT SALE

A QUICK OVERVIEW

➢ **What they are:** A short sale is when a bank or lender agrees to take a discounted payoff so that a property can sell for less than what is owed against it. The terms "lender" and "bank" includes other lienholders, such as lines of credit, seller carry-back mortgages, judgment holders, etc.

➢ **What they do:** A short sale allows a property owner to sell at a price that is acceptable to the buyer, when they would have otherwise been unable to do so because of the total debt owed against the property.

➢ **How they're done:** Usually, short payoffs are only considered by lenders if one or more of the loans against the property are in default or foreclosure. Lenders will also normally require a written request for a short payoff, along with information about the property's value, and details of the seller/borrower's finances to determine if a short sale is necessary and/or in the lender's best interests.

➢ **How they can generate revenue:** Short sales can be used to instantly and artificially generate equity in properties that previously had none. For investors, the most popular use of a short sale is to negotiate a large enough discount from the lender to create a wholesale transaction on a property that was fully financed, or even *over*-financed.

➢ **Best market cycle:** Short sales can work well in either up or down real estate market cycles. Up cycles help make reselling the deals fast and more lucrative due to the higher demand for properties. But once again, down cycles have the slight advantage as the better environment, not just because there are generally many more properties in default and/or foreclosure to choose from, but also because higher foreclosure rates often motivate lenders and junior lienholders to take more aggressive discounts.

➢ **Caveats:** If they're done right, short sales actually pose little, if any, risk to you as the investor engineering the deal. However, the two most common complaints are frequently long lender processing times (often taking one to three months or longer), and the extensive documentation that many lenders require. Even then, it's not unusual for lenders to refuse approval of the requested short sale at the offered price—which means the entire process often results in nothing more than wasted time and effort for everyone involved—you included.

The Basics

A short sale is when a lender and/or lienholder agrees to take a discounted or deferred payoff in order to permit the borrower to sell their property for less than what is owed against it (and BTW, for simplicity's sake, I'll be referring to all lenders, lienholders and judgment holders as just "lenders" or "banks" from this point forward. It makes for much cleaner prose).

So, why would any lender agree to take a discounted payoff when they're entitled to more money? Usually, they will only consider a short payoff if their loan, or a superior lien, is in default or foreclosure.* A default situation places their loan in jeopardy, not only because they'll likely lose some of their investment (or perhaps all of it, if they happen to be a 2nd or 3rd position lienholder), but also because foreclosures can be expensive and time-consuming—which increases their exposure to risk and loss. These additional costs can become substantial if the property goes all the way through the foreclosure process and the auction fails to result in a third–party sale (which is pretty common). Because whenever a lender gets a property back, it creates liabilities as well as ongoing costs for property preservation, maintenance, taxes, insurance, and eventually Realtor commissions.

This is a scenario most lenders would prefer to avoid, if at all possible. Therefore, a short sale can sometimes prove to be in the lender's best interests as a means for liquidating the property quickly, because it not only minimizes their immediate losses, it removes any risk of future losses and liabilities.

In order to process a short sale request, most lenders usually require a fully executed purchase agreement, as well as a documentation package that helps give the lender an idea of the borrower's financial situation. This documentation usually includes a financial statement of the seller's assets and liabilities, copies of tax returns and bank statements, a hardship letter that explains why the seller went into foreclosure and needs a short payoff, and a copy of the agency agreement, if the property is listed for sale with a Realtor. All of this helps the lender decide if a short sale would be in their best interests, and to what extent they need to short.

It's not usually necessary to provide the lender with a professional estimate or appraisal of the property's value in its current condition, as they usually prefer to order one on their own. This will ensure that the professional estimator (usually a Realtor) or appraiser will have accountability to the lender for the accuracy of the valuation. Once all of the required information is received, the lender will take anywhere from 3 weeks to 5 months on average to make a final decision on how much they will be willing to discount, if they'll agree to discount at all. This extended processing period can be extremely problematic, as many buyers are not willing to wait that long. Unfortunately for the sellers, when buyers bolt, they have

---

*Starting in 2010, some lenders began taking short payoffs on loans which were not in default. At the same time, temporary new federal programs began providing some incentives to lenders and home sellers alike to engage in short sales as a means to boost sagging real estate sales—regardless of whether or not any loans were in default.

to begin looking for another buyer with whom to start the process all over again—which creates an even deeper debt for them with every day that passes, as they helplessly fall even further behind on payments.

On the upside, when a lender *does* approve a short sale, the seller (borrower) is often released from liability for the shortage—although this is not always the case. Occasionally, lenders will sometimes release their interests in the property so that it can be sold at a discount, but only if the seller signs a legally-binding unsecured promissory note agreeing to pay back some, or all, of the shortage. This varies based on a variety of factors, such as the borrower's financial ability to pay, and the lender's policies for forgiving debt. But the idea that the unsecured promissory note is not a big deal simply because it is "unsecured" is not accurate at all. In fact, the term itself is a bit of a misnomer, as anyone who signs an unsecured note is actually putting *everything* they own at risk.

You see, when a note is unsecured, it merely means that nothing specific has been identified as collateral for the loan. But that does not release the borrower from a legal obligation to pay, and if the borrower has made the commitment in their own name, then everything they own in their name—such as real estate, automobiles, boats, bank accounts, etc.—can be confiscated, attached and/or auctioned off in the event of a default. Probably the only good thing about an unsecured note is that it can be more easily extinguished in a Chapter 7 bankruptcy, assuming the borrower is legally qualified to file one.

Short Sales in the Real World

Short sales are a great way to invest in real estate with no money down, which is ironic when you consider that the lenders will expect you to pay them all cash (and quickly) in exchange for agreeing to a short payoff. Of course, that just means a short sale is really nothing more than another form of buying properties wholesale; except in this case the equity didn't exist until you created it through your negotiations with the lender (or lenders).

Essentially, as soon as you successfully negotiate a short payoff, it's simply a matter of closing the deal just like you would any other wholesale deal, using your buyer's money, transactional funding, or a privately-funded mortgage loan.

Common short sale misconceptions

Before we explore how short sales are done in the real world, I want to get a few common misconceptions out of the way first. This is a great place to start, because whenever I meet with investors who are having difficulties getting some short sale deals done, it's usually because they don't understand the true point of a short sale, or they've developed a blinding faith in one or more of the following misconceptions that are being perpetuated by many of today's gurus.

Misconception #1: *Banks are TERRIFIED of getting properties back in a fore-closure, and will do anything they can to prevent it from happening.*

First of all, suggesting that inanimate objects like large financial institutions are capable of experiencing human emotions (called *anthropomorphism*) is ridiculous, and I get so irritated when I see a guru do this. Of course, their objective is to exploit your subconscious fear structure by painting a desperate mental image that you can relate to personally—that of a panicked bank executive wringing his hands and losing sleep. Emotional manipulation like this can make you more vulnerable to ad copy for overpriced courses; most of which teach little more than to make a gazillion absurdly low offers in the hopes that maybe a couple of them may get accepted.

The real truth is that most lenders are large institutions with deep pockets and apathetic decision-makers who have no personal stake in the matter. Banks are perfectly capable of absorbing properties in a foreclosure—especially if doing so will net them a lot more than the obscenely low offers you're being taught to make.

Misconception #2: *There's a "secret trick" or "magic phrase" that gurus can teach you to get banks to accept huge discounts.*

It just burns me up every time I see a guru spew ridiculous hype in their marketing materials like: *"You'll learn the dirty INSIDER secrets that banks don't want you to know!"* (you mean like who *really* shot JFK??) or, *"Discover the magic phrase that forces banks to bend over and grab their ankles as they cough up HUGE discounts for you!"* (which would explain why bankers avoid public showers and keep their soap on a rope—even at home). Come on…you're smart enough to know that's just a bunch of made-up crap to get you to buy their stuff.

Now, I'm not saying that there *isn't* a technique for getting banks to take huge discounts, because there is. But it's not a secret, and it's not a trick. In fact, here it is right now: Submit short sale offers that appear to be beneficial for the lender, and you'll get some of them (not all of them) to accept significant discounts.

Misconception #3: *Banks are willing to take extremely deep discounts so that you can buy properties for just pennies on the dollar.*

This is a misconception that's actually more of a mis-*direction*, and the reason it's such a believable and persuasive misnomer is because it contains a kernel of truth. There's no question that banks are often willing to take enormous discounts, and will nearly always let properties sell for less than what they're worth—I'm not arguing that. But when experts talk about banks taking deep discounts to pennies on the dollar, this is usually based on the remaining payoff balance of the loan, *not* on the property's current market value—and there's usually a pretty big difference between the two. In fact, let me share a brief illustration of what I mean.

Imagine that you've just come across a really nice house in a beautiful Miami suburb that's currently in foreclosure. Let's further imagine that this same house has a value of about $200,000 in today's market, but the balance of the defaulted mortgage is hovering at around $450,000, because that's what the house was worth back in 2006 when the seller refinanced it.

Most banks wouldn't hesitate to discount their $450,000 payoff way down into the neighborhood of 37 cents or so on the dollar, because that would still net them about $165,000 cash, which is a reasonable 82.5% of the property's current market value. But good luck getting that same bank to discount down to 37 cents on the dollar based on the property's *value* (as some gurus suggest you'll be able to do every day if you'll just buy their course), because that would only net the lender $74,000 in cash. Now... how often do you think banks are accepting $74,000 cash offers for $200,000 assets? If you said about once every *other* blue moon, you'd be right—and even then it often happens only when the bank has been deceived.

Misconception #4: *The only way you can make a profit with a short sale is to steal the property at a really, really cheap price.*

This is a common myth even among seasoned pros, because most gurus mistakenly preach that there's only one way to make money with a short sale—and that is to buy properties dirt cheap so you can either wholesale them to other investors, or fix them up and resell them to end buyers. This is only partially true, because there are other possible exit strategies that can be just as lucrative, which we'll explore a bit later. The truth is that as long as you can get a lender to approve a short sale at a price which is less than what you can resell the property for, you can make a profit; and you can do it with no money down.

BTW, if you want to enhance your odds of stealing properties on short sales, you need to stick to the ugly ones, because the rules of wholesaling apply here too.

Misconception #5: *The bank is the seller in a short sale transaction.*

Like 22" chrome spinners on a Prius, this is just *wrong*. And it blows my mind when I hear people say this. Especially when they're pros who ought to know better; like Realtors, attorneys, or (worse) yay-hoos who think they're real estate investors just because they took one seminar and have an *I Buy Houses* sticker on their car.

Look... the only time that a lender is the seller of a property is if they already own it, and in the case of a pre-foreclosure short sale, they just don't. The owners of record are the ones who own it (please feel free to insert *"Duh!"* here). Of course it's true that the bank will have to approve the price of your short sale transaction, but if you don't have a fully executed contract with the current owner, then there simply *isn't* a short sale transaction for the lender to approve.

Short sale realities

Today's unprecedented rate of mortgage default has certainly created a crazy marketplace loaded with tons of opportunity. But the only way you're going to make any money in it is to get your *perceptions* about the short sale business aligned with the *realities* of the short sale business, and this is how you do it:

Immediately get yourself unsubscribed from the email database of every guru who's pitching anything that looks like the crap we've just debunked. Your time would be better spent reading spam about penis enhancement formulas, because they're more likely to work for you—even if you don't *have* a penis. Then, after you've spent a few more minutes finishing this book, get some further guidance and education from a reputable short sale expert or guru who is still actually doing short sales in the real world today. This is important, because if your guru hasn't worked at least one short sale in the past six months, the changing marketplace has probably already rendered their methods and tactics obsolete. Time to fire 'em.

The Ten Basic Steps to a Short Sale

These are the ten basic steps to executing a typical short sale. Don't worry if the brief descriptions in these steps seem vague or a little confusing at first. We'll be look at all of them in a little more detail on the following pages.

1) Find a property owner who's in default or foreclosure.
2) Get a variable price contract and a *subject to* deed from the owner.
3) Have the seller complete a short sale package.
4) Call the lender(s) to get their loss mitigation department contact info.
5) Calculate and submit your initial short sale offer.
6) Line up a funding source.
7) Meet the bank's BPO agent or appraiser at the property.
8) Accept or negotiate the lender's counter-offer after the BPO.
9) If an agreeable price is reached, arrange for a closing or double-closing.
10) Cash your profit check at your favorite neighborhood bank.

A closer look at each step

1. Find a property owner who's in default or foreclosure.

Notice it says find an *owner*, not a *seller*. This isn't to suggest that active sellers should be excluded from your marketing cross-hairs. Rather, this was meant to reinforce the fact that some of the best marketing targets for short sale deals are the people who are facing foreclosure, but are not yet actively trying to sell their property. We'll talk more about how and where to find them later.

2. Get a variable price contract and a *subject to* deed from the owner.

I know this step sounds odd, and you might have to read through the details a few times before you get it. But it'll be worthwhile, because this can get you the best price possible, and a much smoother short sale negotiation. Here's how it works:

First, get your seller to sign a *subject to* purchase agreement that says you'll be buying the property for $10 cash (or whatever minimum consideration is required in your area), plus an amount equal to the payoff and/or release of all the liens and mortgages. This is a perfectly legitimate way to identify your purchase price, but since it doesn't specify an exact figure, the lender won't be able to process a short sale with it. That means your seller will also have to sign a blank and undated price addendum for you to attach to your contract. This will let you more easily negotiate price with the lender, because you can use a pencil to fill in your initial price on the addendum, or make several copies of it before writing your amount in pen. Then, as you and the lender go back and forth on price, you can easily grab another blank copy to make another offer, or use a pencil eraser to modify your price, without having to track down your seller each time to initial the changes.

Of course, you might think that sellers would balk at signing a blank, undated price addendum, fearing that you will just write in a cheap price that's far below the discount their bank will agree to (which would legally obligate them to bring cash to the closing to make up the difference). But the truth is that I've never had a problem getting a seller to sign one, because my contracts remove that risk by automatically being null and void if my final price creates a need for them to bring any cash to the closing table beyond the amount of their own closing costs.

But why go through all the trouble of using a *subject to* agreement with a blank price addendum, rather than just having them sign a blank all-cash offer? Because the *subject to* agreement also allows you to get a deed from them immediately, which, in most areas, legally transfers ownership of the property to you—even if you don't record it (which you won't right away, because it would kill your short sale with the lender). Having the deed can come in handy on your selling side, because your ownership interests would allow you to list the property with a Realtor if you want, plus your new buyer's lender might need to see your name on a seasoned deed. Being able to produce one has saved several deals for me.

3. Have the seller complete a short sale package.

Our owner is now officially a seller (if they weren't one already), so now it's time to collect some documentation that their lender will need to process a short sale request. The documents most lenders will need from the seller are: a signed authorization that gives the lender permission to speak with you (as a third party) about the loan, a brief financial statement of their debts and assets, a hardship letter explaining what caused them to fall into default, their two most recent bank statements, their past two tax returns, two or three recent paycheck stubs, and any other documentation that would support their need for a short payoff—such as divorce settlement papers, a death certificate, hospital bills, etc.

4. Call the lender(s) to get their loss mitigation department's contact info.

As soon as you have the contract and completed short sale package in your hands, it's time to call the lender or lenders and get all of the contact information for their loss mitigation (a.k.a. *loss mit*) department. This includes a direct number (if they have one—some do not), their main fax line, and a physical mailing address.* Don't bother asking for the name of the individual who will be processing your paperwork. Most lenders don't assign anyone to handle the negotiations until they've actually received a formal offer.

Of course, you may be wondering why you would ask for the physical mailing address of the loss mit department at all, especially since just about every guru out there suggests that you conduct the entire short sale negotiation by phone and fax. While I agree with them that the majority of the deal should be handled by phone and fax, you might want to consider overnighting your short sale package to the lender, instead of faxing it like everyone else does.

Here's why: the short sale negotiation process cannot begin until the lender has received every single page of the short sale package in its entirety, and in fully legible form. This can be a pretty difficult feat to accomplish by fax, since many of these packages can reach 20 to 50 pages in length, and often consist of various-sized pieces of paper which can sometimes be two-sided, wrinkled, folded, or torn (making them difficult to feed through a fax machine), or which can also have critical portions that don't fax well, such as photos or shaded areas of text.

Overnighting your package overcomes all of this by assuring you that all your documentation will arrive in one piece, at one place, at the same time, and all in readable condition. But even more than that, sending your package via overnight service can grant you access to the lender's loss mitigation department through a portal that is far less utilized, and therefore usually less backlogged. This can help your offer get assigned to a negotiator more quickly, because your package will be slipping effortlessly through the lender's back door, while everyone else is busy trying to ram their package through the lender's fax-jammed front door.

This neat little trick of overnighting the short sale package to begin the process seems to have helped me get priority processing on my deals, although I have no way of knowing for sure how much faster my deals were processed—if they were processed faster at all—than if I would have faxed them instead.

Perhaps it's only my perception.

---

*Some lenders, like Bank of America, no longer accept faxed or mailed short sale packages; only online web uploads.

5. Calculate and submit your initial short sale offer.

Calculate your MAO (maximum allowable offer) using the forms and formulas from the earlier section on wholesaling, or by any other method you prefer. Then, pick a figure somewhere below your MAO as an initial offer, and write it onto a *copy* of the blank and undated price addendum. Don't write your offer on the original blank addendum unless you're using pencil, because you will likely be adjusting this figure a few times during your negotiations with the bank.

In addition to your purchase offer (with its price addendum), you will also need to send the bank an estimated net sheet, usually in the form of a standard HUD-1, which shows them roughly how much cash they will come away with after all closing costs and conveyance fees. This sounds complicated, but it can actually be quite easy if you own HUD-1 software, or (even easier) subscribe to an online service like **www.FastHud.com**. FastHud offers a very user-friendly system of generating estimated HUD-1's in a matter of seconds, even if you're a novice. All you have to do is enter some basic information into a few text boxes, press "Submit", and the software automatically formats everything into a professional looking HUD-1 that you can print out for inclusion in your short sale package.

Once you've finished inserting a copy of your initial offer and the estimated HUD-1 into your short sale package with all of the seller's documentation, prepare a brief fax cover (or cover letter, if you're overnighting it) that summarizes your offer, and send it to the lender's loss mit department. If you are overnighting your package, be sure to make a copy of everything first, and then send them the copied version while holding on to all of the originals.

6. Line up a funding source.

While the bank is chewing over your short sale offer, you can start looking for a buyer or a funding partner to provide the money for your purchase. If the property is in really poor shape, and you're attempting to buy it at a price that is below wholesale value, you can locate a cash wholesale buyer to flip the property to using the techniques in our earlier section on wholesaling.

If, on the other hand, you'd rather buy the property than flip it, that's your choice as well. However, if you have very little or none of your own cash to close the deal with, you will have to get the money from somewhere else. Since I wholeheartedly discourage using recourse bank financing at all times, that means you will have to align yourself with a cash investor.

As for how your investor will earn a return on their investment, you actually have a couple of alternatives. The most obvious is that you can offer to partner with them and split the profits, which is usually expected to be 50/50—unless you're experienced enough to understand that good deals are more plentiful than cash, and know how to leverage that information into a better share for yourself.

Another option you have would be to forego the partnership route, and instead offer the investor an opportunity to be your own private "bank". This can be an extremely attractive proposal for them if you frame it right—especially during times when interest rates are at all-time lows, like they are during this writing. As the potential mortgage lender for your deal, you'd be offering the investor a unique place to put their money that is not only safe and secure, but lucrative as well.

The safety and security aspects of your proposal will come from the fact that you would be offering to collateralize their investment with a low loan-to-value first mortgage, courtesy of your wholesale purchase price. This can be a very safe alternative for an investor who happens to have their money currently parked in a volatile stock portfolio, where their investment is secured only by paper stock certificates with the potential to become worth less than the paper they're printed on overnight without notice. The lucrative nature of the investment would come from the premium interest rate you would be willing to pay, which at 8% or 10% would be highly affordable for you, while at the same time being significantly greater than the miniscule 1.25% they're probably getting from their passport savings account, or the ridiculous 2.75% from their five-year CD.

Of course, all of this is assuming that you're able to buy the property at a really low wholesale price. However, if the property is in pretty good shape, and many of them are, you need to understand that you're not likely to get a wholesale offer accepted by the bank. Now, I'm not saying it never happens, because it does; just not as often as your favorite guru has probably led you to believe. And if you can't get the sale approved at a good wholesale price, then you'll have to abandon the cash investor funding approach, because the LTV will be too high for you to offer them a safe investment—and we're not in the business of compromising people.

So what do you do at times like these? That's when you whip out the deed you got from the seller up front as part of your *subject to* deal. Having the deed in your hands would give you some additional exit strategies, such as wholesaling the property directly to end consumers in your own buyer's list, or marketing it to the retail public at large (via signs, the internet, or an MLS listing), or perhaps buying the mortgage from the lender, and then simply recording your deed as though it were a deed in lieu of foreclosure. Don't worry if I've lost or confused you with those different exit strategies; we'll cover all of them in more detail momentarily.

7. Meet the bank's BPO agent or appraiser at the property.

Once the bank has received your paperwork, they will begin processing your offer, so long as they feel it has at least a reasonable chance of being approved by the investor who actually owns the defaulted note.*

---

* Quite often, the banks you'll deal with will not be the actual owners of the loans, but rather servicers for the investors who do; such as Fannie Mae, Freddie Mac, or perhaps a Wall Street investor as part of a stock portfolio.

Most lenders will have already a rough idea of what the property is worth before they've even received your offer, because they will have usually ordered an inexpensive drive-by BPO as soon as the loan fell far enough into default to suggest that a foreclosure was imminent. One of the first things they will need to do in order to process your offer is to get a better idea of what the property is worth by ordering a more comprehensive interior appraisal or BPO. This will tell them a lot more than a simple drive-by, since the interior of the property is typically where most of the repairs or improvements would need to be made.

It's my policy to arrange for myself, or someone from my office, to be listed as the bank's contact for access to the interior for the BPO. This will ensure that I will be there to plead the case for as low a valuation as ethically possible, to give my short sale offer at least a chance of getting accepted. I will usually position myself as a concerned acquaintance of the seller (which I am), who unfortunately couldn't be there to plead for as low a price as possible to help stop their foreclosure. I've found that this often works a lot better than trying to talk the property down as the buyer, because BPO agents are usually more interested in helping the poor seller than they are about lining the pockets of the buyer.

This is my approach, even if the seller is still in residence, because they will be asked not to be there during the BPO so as not to get offended by any candid negative comments about their property. I've also discovered the hard way that sellers are virtually unable to stop bragging about the best features of their property, to the extent that they've been known to talk their lender right out of doing the short sale with me, as well as at any price below their mortgage balance.

8. Accept or negotiate the lender's counter-offer after the BPO.

Once the bank has received the results from their interior BPO, they will do one of three things: 1) Flat-out reject your offer, which happens pretty often; 2) Accept your offer, which means you've probably offered more than they would have taken, or more than what the property's actually worth (don't laugh, I've done that!); or 3) Counter your offer, which is probably the most likely response.

If they reject your offer, you might want to consider moving on because the lender may not be very motivated, or you'll have to re-submit the entire package again, this time with a higher offer and a new estimated HUD-1. If they accept your offer "as is", you might want to take a minute to look again at your numbers to be sure your values are right, then skip to the next step. If they counter your offer, you can either accept their counter-offer, or raise yours to a point somewhere in between, but only up to your MAO (maximum allowable offer). Every time you change your offer price, you'll need to submit a new price addendum—which is why I had you make copies of the blank price addendum first—and a new estimated HUD-1—which is why I recommended a site like **www.FastHud.com**.

9. If an agreeable price is reached, arrange for a closing, or double-closing.

Once you've come to a mutual agreement on a price, the bank will fax you a payoff demand letter that will state how much they've agreed to take, what date their acceptance of the short payoff offer will expire, how they are to receive the funds (wire transfer or overnight mail, etc.), and any other miscellaneous details.

Usually they will also state in their letter that the seller is to receive none of the sale proceeds (unless it is an FHA loan) and that a copy of the signed final HUD-1 must accompany the payoff check. Once you have this letter, fax it to your closing agent, along with your purchase agreement, so that they can prepare a closing for you if you're buying the property, or a double closing if you're flipping it—in which case they'll also need a copy of your contract to sell.

I cannot recommend strongly enough how important it is for you to find a title agency or closing attorney to work with on a regular basis who fully understands and supports exactly what you're doing—especially if you're doing a lot of legitimate flip transactions. I also cannot over-emphasize how much easier your life will be if you'll just put the name of your title company right into the language of all of your buying and selling contracts as the only one authorized to close your deals. You could even make this a non-negotiable condition whenever you're the buyer, or whenever you're the seller on a deal that will require a double-closing.

Trust me, you haven't seen a transaction from hell until you've let your buyer pick their own title company on a double-closing deal. Their title company will pull title two days before the closing, and want to stop the world because they'll assume you're some kind of crook who's trying to pull a fast one over on their client. Only when you're the seller on a standard resale (where no flip is involved) should you even consider conceding on the title company selection.

10. Cash your profit check at your favorite neighborhood bank.

This step is optional, but highly recommended. If you should happen to need any further clarification on this issue, you should immediately return this book for a full refund and move back into your parent's basement before you get hurt.

Dealing with Junior Lienholders

This is actually an interesting time to bring this subject up, because a really good way to boost your odds of putting together a successful and profitable deal—without the burden of having to convince lenders that their mortgaged properties are nothing but worthless mold-infested roach motels—is to focus on properties which have multiple liens against them.

The reason these deals can be so lucrative is because many second and third position lienholders are expecting to get completely wiped out when they discover that a superior lienholder is foreclosing. As a result, they'll frequently jump on just about any offer they can get, often settling for pennies on the dollar. Of course, you and I know it's not universally true that every junior lienholder will get completely wiped out in every foreclosure, but since that is the perception shared by most of them, it's no real surprise that tremendous discounts from subordinate (junior) lienholders have become almost standard.

Before we go much further, let's review what the terms "first mortgage", "second mortgage", "superior lienholder" and "junior lienholder" mean. A *first* mortgage is the recorded lien against a property that will be given first, or priority, treatment over all other liens when it comes to paying off the debts against that particular property. Typically, this lien will be in the form of a security instrument, such as a mortgage, a trust deed, or a deed to secure debt, depending on which state the property is located in. This mortgage or trust deed is considered to be *superior* to other liens and/or mortgages against the property—except for property taxes, which are superior to *all* liens and mortgages in most areas.

A *second* mortgage is a term that refers to any lien that will be given second priority when it comes to paying off the debts on that same property. Not all second mortgages are actually mortgages, sometimes this is a reference to a second position lien such as an equity line or seller carry-back. In most states, the only determining factor as to which position a lien is awarded (i.e., first, second, or third position, etc.), is the order in which they were recorded at the county clerk's office. Issues such as the amount of each debt, the intended purpose of it, or the date on which the instruments were signed, are usually of absolutely no significance. Since liens or mortgages in second and third position are considered inferior to all mortgages ahead of them, they are referred to as *junior* or *subordinate* liens.

To illustrate the hierarchy of this relationship, let's assume that a homeowner goes into default, and the first mortgage holder has decided to foreclose on the note, and force the sale of the property in an attempt to collect on the unpaid balance due. If the foreclosure auction brings an actual buyer, the proceeds of the sale would be distributed first to county taxes, sheriff fees and county foreclosure costs, and then to the first lienholder. If the first lienholder gets paid back in full and there is still some money left over, it would get distributed to the second lienholder. Then, if there is still anything left after all of that, it would go to the third lienholder, and so on.

Knowing this, and understanding that first lienholders rarely collect enough money to pay off their balance in full, you can see what might drive a junior lienholder to accept a deeply discounted payoff on their lien or mortgage, once they've been notified that a superior lienholder has filed for a foreclosure.

However, even though these lenders are likely to be very highly motivated, you have to exercise some caution when approaching them to propose a short payoff. It's best to assume that they are already expecting to be wiped out either partially or completely by the foreclosure. This will help you develop the proper negotiating posture so that neither your initial approach nor your offer would give them any reason to believe otherwise.

To avoid sabotaging or unnecessarily complicating your negotiations with these junior lienholders, ask them up front what specific documents they will need in order to process an offer for a short payoff before you fax anything to them. It's not always a good idea to just start plowing ahead and sending them a pile of documents, even if some of the paperwork would appear to help justify your low offer. Doing so can create opportunities for you to inadvertently open a can or two of deal-killing worms.

Fortunately, most junior lienholders will only want to see a few things, such as an authorization allowing them to release information to you, a signed letter showing the amount of cash you're willing to pay them for a payoff or release of their lien, and a written payoff letter from the superior lienholder showing the full amount they are owed—including all attorney's fees and foreclosure costs.

Occasionally, a junior lienholder will also want to order a BPO to get a feel for the property's value and the LTV ratios, but that's usually about all they'll need to make a decision. This is a welcomed change from most first mortgage holders, who often ask for a mountain of paperwork in order to process a short sale offer.

It's also a good idea whenever you can help it to avoid sending junior lienholders a copy of the Short Sale purchase agreement you have with the borrower. Of course, if they ask for it, you'll need to provide them with one. Just don't volunteer it up front. The reason you want to avoid this is because you should try to isolate your negotiations with these junior lienholders whenever possible, so they won't know what your intentions are with the first mortgage holder. They usually won't ask how, why, or even *if* you're planning to short sale or reinstate the first mortgage. So treat them like the U.S. military would—don't ask, don't tell.

Throughout the entire negotiation process, try to maintain a pleasant but slightly aloof demeanor. If you seem too eager or anxious about getting their lien removed, or if you expose too much of your game plan, you'll sometimes find that your junior lienholder—who should be grateful for whatever you're willing to give them—will suddenly decide that they want to play some hardball. If you start giving off signals that suggest you're about to make a killing on a deal, they can sometimes turn the tables and make it much more difficult or expensive for you to get rid of them.

In other words, a junior lienholder's motivation tends to drop in direct proportion to their perception (there's that word again) of how critical their cooperation seems to matter to you. In fact, if you give them enough of an indication that the deal you're pursuing is highly profitable, they'll sometimes cut off negotiations with you entirely and contact the superior lienholders to work out something on their own. That happens pretty infrequently, though, as most of them are content to just extract more cash (and perspiration) out of you instead.

Always remember that one of the most powerful motivations driving any junior lienholder's decision to deeply discount for cash is their predisposed notion that they don't have any other options—which may or may not be true. As a junior lienholder, there are often several ways to protect their investment. But if they don't know that any alternatives exist beyond your short sale offer, and their loss mitigation employees are unable to come up with any other solution, remember: it's not your job to educate them. Instead, take a moment out of your busy day every so often to thank God for slothful loss mitigation reps, because heaven knows their ignorance and lack of resourcefulness will eventually be a blessing to you—as they have been to me quite frequently.

Can You Short FHA Loans?

Absolutely! As a matter of fact, in a totally bizarre twist that I didn't see coming—like the end of *The Sixth Sense*, when it turned out that Bruce Willis' character had been dead all along—I discovered that doing a short sale on an FHA loan can actually be kind of, well... *easy*.

This was such an unexpected surprise, because it defies all common sense. After all, you'd normally expect a huge government bureaucracy like HUD to take something which is already complex enough—like a short sale—and turn it into a convoluted nightmare so full of confusion and frustration that people would literally fling themselves from tall buildings just to end the madness. Instead, the ordinarily clueless folks at HUD managed to develop a standardized short sale program called *PFS* (for Pre-Foreclosure Sales) which is actually quite sensible, reasonable, and even occasionally appealing. Who knew?

In hindsight, the fact that a PFS short sale is so easy to execute turned out to be a good thing, because many of the loans that were underwritten by this behemoth were destined to end up in default from day one, even before the collapse of both the job and housing markets—courtesy of their laxed lending criteria and exceptionally risky 97% to 100% loan-to-value ratios.

Anyway, here are at least four good reasons why HUD loans are easier to work with than most others when it comes to short sales:

1. HUD's standard process removes subjectivity, while adding accountability.

Since HUD follows a template formula for calculating acceptable short sale payoff amounts, they've effectively removed the variable of subjective human emotions and interpretations. That means you won't have to try to scare or intimidate the loss mitigation rep into giving you the lowest possible price, nor would you have to (at the other end of the spectrum) romance them into developing a personal desire to help you get your deal done. None of that matters with HUD, because they work strictly by the numbers, which is usually a good thing—although I guess it could work against you if you're especially gifted at intimidation or flirtation.

Here's another plus to HUD short sales, and I love this one: If your loss mitigation rep ever gets lazy or becomes difficult to work with, you can go straight over their heads—as well as the heads of their department supervisors (who are often even lazier jerks that couldn't care less)—and make one phone call to the regional HUD office. Just give HUD a few details of what's been going on, along with the name and direct phone number of the loss mit rep who's been yanking your chain, and within a few minutes, your magically-transformed loss mit rep will be calling you back to respectfully offer whatever assistance you need to get your deal done. You just can't do that with most other types of loans, because it's virtually impossible for you to find out who the true note investor is that will actually be taking the hit if the loss mit rep keeps screwing around.

2. HUD's short sale payoff formula is more reasonable than most others.

As of March, 2009, HUD began using a tiered formula for determining acceptable short payoff amounts. First of all, the property must appraise for at least 63% of the outstanding mortgage balance to even qualify for a PFS. If it does, then the bank is permitted to accept a net offer as low as 88% of the appraisal in the first 30 days on the market, dropping to an 86% net for the next 30 days, and finally to a net of only 84% of the appraised value after 60 days on the market.* That means HUD short sales can be approved for as little as 53 cents on the dollar of the outstanding mortgage balance.

For example: let's assume you've run across a property with an expired $200,000 overpriced listing in very good shape that's only worth about $175,000. Let's further assume that it has an outstanding FHA loan balance of around $250,000, and that the HUD appraiser set the fair market value at $160,000 (fortunately, HUD appraisals for PFS deals are often pretty conservative). This property would qualify for a PFS, because the $160,000 appraised value is equal to 64% of the outstanding balance.

Now, since the property has obviously been on the market for more than 60 days, as evidenced by the expired listing (which was unsuccessful due to serious over-pricing by a dead-beat Realtor who was either stupid, or just didn't understand how short sales work), you know that you can potentially pick it up for as little as $134,000 net to the bank. What could you do with that knowledge?

*HUD's parameters are subject to occasional changes, so consult a local professional for their current guidelines.

THE COMPLEMENTARY TECHNIQUES

Well, one option would be to get a deed from the owner (as we learned earlier), list it with your own Realtor for $174,900, and just wait for someone to come along who wants to buy it. When you find a retail buyer, you could simply arrange for a double-closing with *your own* title company (which you will insist upon if you want the deal to ever have a chance of closing), where you'll buy the property and resell it at the same closing table.

Another choice would be to find a cash partner to put up, say, $139,000 for an 8% mortgage, so that you can buy the property outright and market it for a re-sale at $179,900 on lease-purchase. Then, you could use the first $1,020.00 of each one of your buyer's $1,250 lease-purchase payments to make your monthly mortgage payments to your investor. When your buyer gets financed and cashes you out a year or so later, you pocket the majority of the $41,900 spread (between your $179,900 sale price and your $138,000 loan payoff to your investor) as profit.

One thing you need to be aware of, though, is that these percentages only represent the *minimum* prices that HUD will permit for short sales on loans they've underwritten. However, that doesn't mean the particular bank you're working with won't want more, which is their right—regardless of how unreasonable it might be.

3. HUD allows borrowers and subordinate lienholders to get cash at closing.

Typically, sellers are not allowed to receive any proceeds from a short sale of their property, but HUD will allow them to have up to $1,000 at closing. That means you can offer your sellers some cash as an incentive to sell to you, and also as a motive to cooperate throughout the short sale process as necessary.

When it comes to second mortgages or other junior lienholders, most lenders will only allow up to $1,000, if they allow anything at all. HUD permits them to receive up to $1,500 of the sale proceeds, or up to $2,500 total cash if the borrower agrees to contribute their $1,000 allowance to the second lienholder as well—which they will often gladly do if that's what it takes to save the deal.

When I'm making offers to junior lienholders on HUD deals, I use HUD's policy of $1,500 maximum as a way to justify my low $1,500 offers. Since they're probably unaware that the borrower can also contribute their $1,000 to the junior lienholder, I'm not inclined to educate them otherwise. That way, I can play *"Good cop, bad cop"* and let HUD take the blame. Only if the junior lienholder decides to play hardball will I bring up the borrower's contribution. But what if they want even more than the maximum $2,500 that a HUD deal can get them, and will kill the deal if they don't get it? Then you can try buying the loan and collecting the $2,500 yourself at the closing as the new junior lienholder. Otherwise, your hands are pretty much tied—although I do know some investors will occasionally send subordinate lienholders some cash out of their own pocket as a final payment on the loan, and not as part of the payoff. But that can be risky, and perhaps even illegal as well.

4. HUD will usually waive any deficiencies against the borrower.

I have yet to see a HUD deal where the lender pursued the borrower for a deficiency after a short sale. I'm not saying they don't do it; just that I haven't seen it. In fact, sometimes their Pre-Foreclosure Sale Approval letter will literally state that the lender will be accepting the short proceeds as payment in full and that they will note the loan as "satisfied" or "paid as agreed".

Can You Short VA Loans?

Not if you want to make any money. VA's current policy is to accept only full appraised value for short sales, which eliminates your ability to create equity.

Alternative Short Sale Profit Strategies

In case you haven't figured it out yet, things don't always go according to plan. This is especially true in the world of real estate, and even more so in short sales. That's why it's a good idea to develop more than one possible way of capitalizing on every potential short sale opportunity. Having more than one exit strategy means added flexibility, which leads to enhanced odds of success and sometimes additional profits for you. On the following pages are a few examples of lateral thinking which can help make a deal happen where it might not have otherwise.

Alternate Strategy 1: Wholesale directly to retail consumers.

Selling wholesale direct to consumers is a concept that's exploding in many other areas of consumer goods, but not really so much in real estate. In our case, this is not about selling properties to consumers at *actual* wholesale prices, because properties which can be purchased that cheaply (even on short sales) are almost always hideously ugly; and it's a well-known fact that consumers are repulsed by ugliness—except when it comes to hybrid automobiles.

No, this is something altogether different. Wholesaling directly to the retail consumer market is an exciting approach that can be used either as a primary short sale strategy, or merely as a "Plan B" for capitalizing on what would have otherwise been a dead short sale deal. As a primary approach, this technique eliminates guesswork while helping you maximize the profitability of each short sale deal you actually do.

The way it works is that you would list the property in the MLS with your favorite Realtor (using the up-front deed you got with your *subject to* purchase agreement) at a price that would be just low enough to excite consumers, but not so low as to make it difficult for you to negotiate a profitable short sale with the bank.

Then, as soon as you get a solid offer or two from some qualified end consumers, you go to work negotiating a total short sale payoff from your lender that's as far below these prices as possible.

In other words, you would be engineering your short sale to work in reverse, finding your buyer first, and then using that "crystal ball" knowledge to decide how much you'd be willing to pay for the property. This takes away any speculation as to whether or not the properties you're working with actually *have* any market appeal in the first place (which can save you the trouble of negotiating short sales on dud properties), while also exposing exactly how much of a resale price the market will support for them. Having advance knowledge of both of these issues can make negotiating your short sales much easier and less stressful.

Plus, since you won't actually be buying any of the properties until you've already got them under contract to resell, you'll be able to maximize your profitability by eliminating holding costs you would normally incur while looking for your end buyer on a typical short sale deal; such as maintenance and repair costs, hazard insurance, real estate taxes, or monthly interest costs on borrowed money from a private lender.

As for the other use of this technique—as a back-up "Plan B" to revive an otherwise dead short sale deal—this is how it would work: Suppose you're negotiating a short sale to buy a property with a very reasonable lender, and although they're motivated enough to accept a final price that's well below the current market value, it's clear that they're just not going to discount all the way down to meet your really low wholesale offer.

Instead of just walking away from the deal and looking for another property to short sale (like most other gurus would suggest), you can pull out that deed you got on day one, and use it to do exactly what we just covered a moment earlier. Only this time, you would use your advance knowledge of what the lender is willing to accept to set a list price in the MLS (through your favorite Realtor) that would be low enough to cause end consumers to flock to your property, but yet high enough to still net you a decent profit.

Now, when it comes to setting an attractive price, some gurus advise against going in low, as they believe it makes you appear desperate; leading to even lower offers. This may be true sometimes, but when it comes to nice properties in desirable areas, I've found that low pricing often has the exact opposite influence. I call it the *eBay Effect*. The eBay Effect is an emotional element that can come into play whenever a consumer sees an opportunity to get something really nice at a really low price. The excitement of getting a deal can create within them a blinding obsession to acquire that object, as anyone who's been in a last-minute eBay auction can attest. Since consumers make many of their decisions based on gut emotion, not logic, it's not unusual to see them quickly bid the full asking price (it's low, after all), or even engage in a bidding war that drives the price over asking. I've seen this happen.

Alternate Strategy 2: Don't short all of the mortgages.

Just because you're doing a short sale, that doesn't necessarily mean you have to short all of the liens and mortgages against the property. Sometimes, if the first mortgage balance is low enough, it can make a whole lot more sense to just reinstate it, and then do a short payoff on only the junior liens and mortgages.

In today's world, there are lots of properties out there that fit this description, because up until the recent bubble collapse, mortgage brokers and investment advisors were brainwashing property owners into subscribing to the dangerous "dead equity" principle. This premise argues that any equity in real estate is basically nothing but "dead" capital since it isn't earning any returns for the owner. Of course, millions of consumers bought into this hogwash, and used equity lines and second mortgages to cash out whatever equity they had—which they then went out and subsequently lost in the stock market, or simply wasted on boats, bad investments, or just a temporary swim in the rich and famous lifestyle pool.

When you come across a good prospect property for this type of transaction, you'll need to know how to combine two different methods—a short sale and a *subject to*—on the same deal. We've already seen examples of how it can be beneficial to roll these two different techniques into one transaction, because it allows us to get our hands on a deed, if necessary. But in this case, we need more than just a deed—we need to have the right to take over the mortgages, too. Another good reason for using a *subject to* transaction to take title on a short sale deal is that it expands our potential back-end profitability, by providing us with the flexibility to resell the property on long terms if we so choose.

But let's not get ahead of ourselves; let's start at the beginning, because regardless of which exit strategy turns you on the most, the process will always begin the same way, with you taking title to the property subject to all of the liens and mortgages of record.

Once you're holding the deed (which needs to remain unrecorded for the time being), your next step would *not* be to negotiate a short sale with the first mortgage holder (as you would normally do), rather, it would be to negotiate for significant discounts of pennies on the dollar from the second mortgage holder and/or any other junior lienholders. Then, if you're successful with the junior lienholders, you can contact the first mortgage holder and have them send you an official reinstatement letter that identifies how much cash it will take to reinstate their loan. After that, you're free to close your deal and release the short payoff funds to the junior lienholders, as well as the reinstatement money to the first mortgage holder.

I would strongly recommend that you use a professional title attorney, escrow company or title agency to close complex deals like this, due to the amount of cash involved (most of which will probably not be yours), as well as the need to protect yourself from any risk of mistakes in the title work or document preparation.

As you can see, this type of transaction has you leaving the first mortgage in place, and essentially treating it as your purchase money financing. Therefore, the ratio of the first mortgage balance to the overall value of the property is going to be a critical factor in deciding if this strategy would make sense for you. In a nutshell, if the balance of the first mortgage, plus all the cash needed to reinstate the first and short the junior lienholders, adds up to an amount that's far enough below the property value to justify doing the deal, that's the only criteria necessary.

Being able to leverage the existing first mortgage not only positions you to buy nice properties at reasonable prices, it also frees you from having to qualify for any mortgages or raise lots of cash. Usually, all you'll need to close your deal is a few thousand dollars to cure the first mortgage default, and perhaps a couple thousand more to pay off the discounted junior liens and cover your closing costs.

If you don't have any cash to work with at all, that's okay because there are several ways to get whatever money you need. One choice you have is to align yourself with a cash investor to either partner with, or to act as a private mortgage lender who would be willing to provide you with a small amount working capital in exchange for a *new* second mortgage (remember, you'll be getting rid of the old one when you buy the property). This would give you the cash you need to reinstate the first mortgage and extinguish the subordinate liens, as well as complete any necessary repairs or improvements. Then, you could put the repaired property on the market at retail value with your favorite Realtor, and wait for an end consumer to buy it at somewhere near full retail price.

If you're really patient, you could choose to increase your profit and reduce your costs by rolling yet another technique into this one deal (a *subject to*, plus a short sale, plus a lease-purchase) and sell it yourself on extended terms at a higher price without a Realtor. The monthly payments you receive from your tenant/buyer would give you cash flow, plus enough money to service the payments to your first mortgage and your private lender on your new second mortgage (if you have one).

Or, if you don't want to be bothered with repairing or improving the property, or with selling it on longer terms to fully maximize your resale price, you could instead opt to wholesale it directly to consumers, which is a method we're going to explore in a moment. Basically, the way you do this is to price it at a point which is well above wholesale (to discourage cash investors from trying to steal it), but yet far enough below retail value that end consumers would be motivated to buy it quickly, in spite of any repairs or improvements it may need. This can still net you a nice paycheck relatively quickly, because you'll be leap-frogging past the often lethargic repair and improvement process, as well as avoiding a lengthy term sale.

Still yet, another choice for liquidating the property—if the first mortgage balance is low enough—would be to roll the wholesaling strategy into the mix (instead of a lease-purchase), and then flip the property to an investor before you even buy it. All you do is get the investor to pay you a large assignment fee for the right to close the transaction directly with your seller, then the title company or attorney closing the deal would send a portion of the assignment fee to the first mortgage for reinstatement, another portion to the junior lienholders for their releases, and the rest to you for your profit. As for the closing costs, let the investor pay them—after all, they're the buyer—not you. Here is an example of what a reinstatement/short sale deal could look like:

Example: Let's say you find a homeowner in foreclosure with a property worth about $150,000 in repaired condition, and needs about $10,000 in repairs. Let's say there is a defaulted $79,000 first mortgage that needs about $3,500 to reinstate, a $56,000 second that is $3,500 in arrears, and a credit card judgment against the seller for $7,000. That's $149,000 worth of liens against a damaged property.

Now, let's pretend you were successful in negotiating the second mortgage holder down into accepting only $3,500 cash for a payoff, and getting the judgment lienholder to agree to release their lien for only $500. That would make your total purchase price only $88,000, and you could literally close your purchase with as little as $9,000 in cash ($3,500 to bring the first mortgage current + $3,500 to pay off the second + $500 to the judgment holder + $1,500 closing costs). Where would the $9,000 come from, and how would you get paid? That would depend on how you choose to liquidate the property.

If you want to wholesale it directly to consumers via a Realtor, you could borrow the $9,000 from an investor/partner, or on a new second mortgage from a private individual acting as a lender—be it a friend, family member, associate, or whoever. If you prefer to hold out for top dollar, you could borrow an extra $10,000 more from either of the same two sources to repair the property and bring it back to excellent condition, after which you could then sell it at full retail price via your Realtor, or on your own using a lease-purchase for an even higher price.

If, on the other hand, you'd rather just flip it for a quick profit without ever buying it, the low first mortgage balance would permit you to do so. You could simply collect an assignment fee of maybe $15,000 to $18,000 or so from a landlord investor or handy homeowner, who would then close the deal in your place as the buyer, and take title directly from your seller. As part of the closing, the title agent would clear up the title issues by taking the first $7,500 of the assignment fee to: a) reinstate the first mortgage; b) pay off the second mortgage; and c) get a release from the judgment holder. Then, they'd send you the $7,500 to $10,500 (or so) remaining balance as your profit.

Seeing this example may prompt a couple of questions for you. For one: the investor in this deal would have to pay above the wholesale threshold to get the property from you, so why would they do it? And two: What if the first mortgage balance is too high for you to get the property at a wholesale price?

As for the first issue, some investors are willing to pay well above wholesale because they either don't know what in the hell they're doing, or they're simply willing to work on razor-thin margins for too little money—which is really just another way of saying that they also don't know what in the hell they're doing. All of that aside, there are plenty of landlord-type investors who would jump at paying above wholesale if they can get some built-in permanent financing as part of the deal. For them, a wholesale margin isn't all that important if the deal provides reasonable payments that would allow them to create a long-term cash flow profit center. If yours would provide that, they'd be crazy to pass up the opportunity just because the purchase price would happen to fall above the wholesale level.

But what if the mortgage balance is already well above the wholesale value? In other words, what if the remaining first mortgage balance in our example had been, say, $91,000 instead of only $79,000? What then? That would make our total purchase price $100,000 instead of only $88,000—assuming that we'd still need the same $9,000 to close the deal. This amount is clearly way above the wholesale mark; and not only that, the higher $91,000 loan that we'd be passing on to the landlord investor might have payments which are too high for them to create a reasonable positive cash flow. What options would we have then, if any?

About the only exit strategy we would have in a case like that (besides walking away) would be to try wholesaling it directly to a retail consumer using our Realtor (as in our first alternate strategy), because no intelligent investor will want it.

Alternate Strategy 3: Buy the mortgage instead of the property.

Sometimes it can make more sense—and more money—if you buy the *loan* on a piece of property, instead of the actual property itself. If it's done right, this can be a very effective back-door method for acquiring real estate, and fortunately you can exploit some of the same capital resources that you would use to fund your wholesale and short sale deals.

But buying a mortgage is not the same as buying a property, so if you're planning to start buying some loans in order to gain control of real estate, there are going to be some unique issues that you will have to be aware of. Here are five of the most important things to consider:

1. Always get a discount off the loan's full face value when you buy it.
Whenever you're buying a note and mortgage (or deed of trust, depending upon your state), you need to make sure that you're getting a discount off the full face value (payoff amount) of the note. This is a pretty typical requirement if you're buying a junior lien, because 99.99% of the time, the situation will require you to buy them at mere pennies on the dollar.

However, getting a discount is also very important when you're buying a superior first position lien, as well—even if the loan-to-value ratio is very low. Why would you need to discount a low loan-to-value first mortgage, if the large equity spread makes it a safe investment already? Because if you are looking to get the deed, and not become a lender, then there are going to be some additional steps to come—and these steps will require that your investment in the note be for an amount that's less than the note's full face value.

For instance, if you buy the first mortgage at full face value, and the borrower finds a short sale buyer before you can finish the foreclosure, then the most you'll collect on the note is exactly what you paid for it—full face value; which means you won't have a nickel's worth of profit with which to pay the investor who funded your note purchase. Likewise, if the property goes all the way to foreclosure auction and somebody else wins the bidding, then the full face value of the note is the most you can receive from the proceeds disbursement, leaving you again with no profit. Another challenge is that foreclosure auctions in many areas have minimum bid requirements, which means if your payoff is lower than the minimum bid amount, you've got two choices—both of which are problematic.

Your first choice would be to try to win the foreclosure auction to get the deed. However, since the minimum bid is higher than the amount you're owed, your bid would have to be higher than your payoff. Now, as the foreclosing lender, you can bid up to what you're owed without paying anything to the auctioneer, but if you bid higher than your judgment amount, you're responsible for paying the difference in cash. Why? Because if the sale price exceeds the face value of your note (including the foreclosure costs and fees), then the junior lienholders (if there are any) and/or the property owner are entitled to those additional proceeds.

Of course, in light of this you could always choose instead to abstain from bidding at the foreclosure auction, so that you wouldn't get stuck with paying the difference. But that means somebody else could win the bidding, and if so, the maximum amount you would be entitled to collect is what you paid for the loan; again resulting in a profitless transaction for you. If, on the other hand, nobody else bids the price up to the minimum amount, the sale itself would be voided, and you would have to start the foreclosure process (or a large portion of it) all over again—which could take several months or even a year or more just to get yourself right back into the same lose/lose predicament you were already in earlier.

2. Make sure you're actually buying the loan, and not just paying it off.
This may sound so obvious that it defies the need for discussion, but many lenders will misunderstand what you're offering, and may assume that the money you want to send them is for a short payoff, when in fact it is for a discounted purchase of the note and an assignment of the mortgage (or deed of trust).

So whenever you make an offer to a bank to buy their loan, make sure the actual agreement they send you states that you'll be getting an *Assignment of Note and Mortgage* (or *DOT*) and not a *Satisfaction of Mortgage* in exchange for the money you're sending them. An assignment transfers ownership of the note and mortgage to you, while a satisfaction states that the debt has been paid off. If you make that mistake, you won't own the loan because it wouldn't exist anymore. Of course, you'll probably get a really nice birthday card every year for the rest of your life from a very grateful homeowner—so I guess it wouldn't be a *total* loss.

3. Make sure you get a valid deed from the owner before buying the loan.

You have to remember that whenever you buy a loan, you essentially become the lender on the property; not the owner. Since your goal is to eventually own the real estate, it's a great idea to get a deed from the owner to hold in escrow before you even buy the mortgage. That way, as soon as you take possession of the mortgage, you can just record the deed as though it were a *deed-in-lieu* of foreclosure—assuming there aren't any junior lienholders.

If you don't have a deed, and can't get one from the owner, then you can still buy the note and mortgage—but you'd be flying blind, so to speak. Whenever I do that, I always insist on getting an additional discount to insulate myself from property damages and other complications of a potentially non-cooperative owner. Usually, I will only buy loans that are already in default, so that I can be justified in either filing a foreclosure, or completing one that's already in progress.

4. Get written agreements for discounts from all other lienholders.

Before you close the purchase of any note or mortgage, have title work done first to make sure that your lien is in the position you thought it was (first, second, etc.), and that there aren't any other liens and judgments you weren't aware of. If you're buying a junior lien, be sure that you've received a written payoff statement directly from all superior lien holders.

As for determining note balance and payoff figures, you should never rely on your seller's loan statement, because they do not reflect all accrued costs and fees. If you're buying a superior lien, make sure that any and all junior lienholders behind you have already agreed in writing to a discounted payoff or lien release fee that is acceptable to you. If you don't, then the only way you'll be able to get them removed is to foreclose them off. This can be a lengthy and costly process, which leads us into a discussion of our last major concern: foreclosure costs and fees.

5. Remember to factor foreclosure costs into your offer, if necessary.

If you want clear title to the property and you're not getting any cooperation from one or more of the junior lienholders, you will have to foreclose them off. But don't get caught up in revenge. All things considered, it can sometimes be a lot faster and far less expensive to just pay a junior lienholder a little more than you'd like, rather than obliterating them in a foreclosure—as good as that would feel.

I had a junior lienholder once who insisted on a $5,000 short payoff amount for their $20,000 second mortgage, even though the house was only worth about $50,000 and the first mortgage I was buying had a face value of $70,000 (although I only paid $25,000 for it). Clearly, their lien had no real cash value, so they should have been content with the $2,000 I had offered them. But they weren't.

Since it was only two weeks away from the scheduled foreclosure auction, and all of the foreclosure costs had already been paid by the lender that I bought the first mortgage from, I went ahead and just foreclosed them off. It felt great and I even got to save the $2,000 I had originally offered them. However, I had to wait over two more months for the sale to be confirmed and another three months to get the Sheriff's deed. That's a five month delay!

Fortunately, it took me almost that long to repair the house and get a qualified buyer (my second one) to a closing table. If I would have had a buyer who wanted to close any sooner, I'd have been in a real pickle. Next time, I'll probably just pay the junior pissant lienholder a little more cash for the convenience of clearing the way to record my the deed from the seller immediately.

After all, if I still feel a lingering need to extract some revenge, I can always have a tech-savvy friend hack into their mainframe and Rickroll their employees to the point of mutiny. That would be more fun than foreclosing them off anyway.

Alternate Strategy 4: Consider Becoming a Realtor

Yes, I'm fully aware that such a suggestion could be considered somewhat heretical by many real estate investors who would be about as likely to consider becoming a Realtor as the Pope would consider converting to Buddhism. This is unfortunate, because the two professions do not have to be mutually exclusive of one another, as many very successful Realtor/investors have clearly proven over the years. Here are just a couple of really good reasons why being a Realtor could be highly advantageous to your investing career.

For one, being a Realtor would increase your odds of capitalizing on every short sale lead, by positioning you with yet one more potential way of generating revenue from it. As a Realtor, you could always resort to listing the property in the MLS and collecting a commission on any deal that would have otherwise died because you were unable to negotiate a way to buy it or wholesale it.

Both your seller and the lender would appreciate the extent to which you would be able to help them stop a foreclosure, because the offers you would be submitting for short sale consideration would likely be at or near the full retail value of the property.

Another benefit to being a Realtor is that you would have access to the single most valuable database in the real estate world—the MLS. With a resource like that, you would be able to conduct incredible amounts of research, such as immediately generating targeted lists of expired properties looking for motivated sellers, or quickly finding comps for your potential deals before you make a short sale offer to buy, or before setting your list price to resell. As an agent, you would also be entitled to half of the commission when you're buying or selling properties, which can help make your deals a little more profitable on both ends.

Alternate Strategies Stack the Deck

Of course, the whole point of discussing these alternative profit strategies was to boost your potential conversion percentage for those times when you come into contact with a short sale prospect. While most other short sale investors are focusing only on the limited number of properties that can be purchased at dirt-cheap wholesale prices, you'll be capable of cashing in those very same properties plus a wide range of other deals that feature property owners in many other situations and with a broader variety of needs. In short, being several times more flexible than other investors will make you several times more likely to turn your prospective property owners into cash-producing customers.

To demonstrate what I mean, let's assume you were to incorporate all of these ancillary ideas into your agenda. That would allow you to be flexible enough to run each potential deal through a series of options.

You could first try: a) stealing the property at a below-wholesale price; and if that doesn't work, you could try: b) flipping it to a rental investor at a price somewhere above wholesale but below retail; and if that doesn't work, you could try: c) flipping it directly to a retail consumer at an attractive price somewhere below retail; and if none of those work, you could try: d) simply listing it in the MLS and attempt to collect a real estate commission on a full retail sale. Having four different ways to cash in on every potential opportunity instead of only one is called "stacking the deck". And although you're still not guaranteed of making any money, your chances would be four times better than everyone else's.

Unique Short Sale Marketing Considerations*

Obviously, you can use any or all of the marketing methods we looked at in the chapter on marketing to generate short sale leads, but you have to keep one thing in mind: short sale deals, by their very nature, have a relatively narrow marketing window. In this niche, timing is everything.

---

* IMPORTANT NOTICE: Effective January 31, 2011, the new MARS Rule went into effect. As a real estate investor, there are certain disclosures that you may be required to make to every potential short sale seller. To ensure that you remain in full compliance with the MARS Rule at all times, consult your local real estate attorney.

You have to reach these property owners as soon as they become a qualified prospect—not just because that's when they will likely be the most motivated to seek assistance, but also because you have to get your message in front of them before everyone else does.

You see, once their default situation becomes public record upon the filing of a foreclosure suit, a Notice of Default (called NOD's in trust deed states like California), or a lis pendens (which is a public notice of a pending action), all the other investors seeking short sale deals will come screaming out of the woodwork like an army of roaches to begin chasing the very same prospects you are. If that happens, your message had better be one of the first that they receive, and it also needs to be one of the most compelling as well. Otherwise, your letter or other direct mail marketing piece will get buried in a postal avalanche.

To find these prospects in advance of any legal postings, you can always have some type of display or classified ad running which is targeted towards helping people who are in default, or people who are likely headed towards default soon. Finding these people before their situation becomes public knowledge will give you a head start, because if you reach them at a time when no one else is marketing to them, you will also have the advantage of being perceived as the only one in town who has a possible solution for them. After all, if they aren't aware of any other alternatives beyond yours, then no other alternatives exist for them—because this perception will define their reality.

As for a classified ad, it could read as simple as something like:

Facing Bankruptcy or Foreclosure?
We can help you! No Equity? No Problem!
Call now before it's too late **(513) 555-7720**

Notice that the ad isn't specifically targeted toward sellers—people who are already trying to sell their properties. It's aimed at property owners who are in financial trouble, without excluding those particular owners who may also be trying to sell their property right now.

Throwing "bankruptcy" into the headline is designed to capture the attention of people who are likely candidates to be in default on their mortgages, and/or have so many liens and judgments attached to their properties that they may even be upside down—meaning the total of all the liens exceeds the value of the property. You will need to do a little research into how and when you can legally work with owners when they are in bankruptcy in your area, but the general rule is either before they file their bankruptcy petition or after their 341 meeting of the creditors (usually about 45 days after filing). Regardless of the timing requirements where you live, this can be a profitable strategy, especially since bankruptcy tends to promote high levels of motivation for property owners to work with you.

Even if you can't—or don't—reach these property owners before their situation becomes public knowledge, you can still have a great shot at capturing them by making sure your direct mail piece is among the first ones they get, and that it also has at least a couple of different choices for them as to how you can help them stop their foreclosure, i.e., sell it to you, or list it with you.

However, without a doubt being one of the first to reach them is the single most important objective for you, because no matter how compelling your copy is, it won't do you any good if they've already contracted with someone else. That means you—or preferably your assistant—will need to check daily courthouse postings, which can be done online in most areas.

If there is no way to do it online in your area, then you may be tempted to subscribe to one of those services that collect daily foreclosure postings and send them to you in list form once or twice a week. Don't do it, because they're not sending this information only to you, they're probably sending it to just about every other foreclosure investor in town as well—which destroys your objective of being first in the door (or mailbox, in this case).

I hate to say it, but if daily foreclosure postings can't be found online in your area, you really don't have any other choice but to physically go (or better yet, send someone) to your local courthouse to view these filings every single day. That sounds really challenging, I know, but here's the good news: because this is so hard to do, no one else is going to bother doing it—and that is *exactly* what will give you the advantage! In other words, the harder it is to uncover a targeted lead, the less competition you'll have, and the more money you'll likely make.

Last of all, in addition to being first and offering people choices, there is one more important element to marketing for short sale prospects: repetition. You need to create and keep some sort of record or database of each prospect to whom you've sent your first marketing piece. That way you—or your assistant—can easily send at least one follow-up mailing to them about two or three weeks later. After all, if you went through all the time and trouble of digging all these leads up, why not do your best to get your money's worth out of each one?

I've actually gotten some pretty good response rates on my follow-up communications, which I usually do in the form of an oversized postcard. That's because some people are so deluged initially, they don't even open my letter—and if they do, they sometimes get overwhelmed by all the input they're receiving from all fronts. Others are in denial when the process begins, and so they sometimes ignore *everyone's* initial mailings. Over time, some of these people end up changing their minds and are finally ready to hear about the benefits of what I can do for them. Still others just simply resonate better with the message on my postcard versus the copy in my initial letter. In other words, as we learned earlier in our discussion on general marketing, repetition works.

Actual Short Sale Case Study

When Jack (his real nickname, not his real first name) called me about the foreclosure on his three bedroom ranch home in Sayler Park, I thought I stood a good chance of buying it on a short sale. He only owed $68,000, and its wholesale value looked to be about $50,000 or so, which meant his lender wouldn't be asked to take a huge hit.

But after talking with him a little, I discovered that his $68,000 debt was actually spread over two mortgages; about $35,000 on a first to CitiFinancial, and around $33,000 to HFC on a second. I nearly wet myself in light of this new development, because I knew that many second position lienholders will just automatically discount to pennies on the dollar, even when they don't have to—mostly out of sheer knee-jerk stupidity. I was hoping HFC would be one of them.

So I hopped into my car and ran over to get his house under contract, at which time I confirmed that his estimates were pretty accurate: his house really did look like it would be worth about $85,000 to $90,000 in good shape, and probably only needed about $7,000 in repairs to get there (hence the estimated $50,000 wholesale price).

Jack and his wife, Janice, were very nice during my visit, and they were clearly in alignment with their desires to see the foreclosure stopped. But that's where any commonality between the two ended. Jack was a fairly slight and very soft-spoken man well into his 70's, while his wife was a tempestuous firecracker about 30 years his junior, with deadly 2½ inch long raptor-like fingernails and enough bling wedged betwixt her ample cleavage to embarrass Flavor Flav. My only guess as to how these two ended up together was that since he was a retired bar owner, she may have been a regular customer or former employee. But I don't know... and I didn't ask.

Anyway, we signed a contract, he gave me a deed, and then I rushed back to my office to put together a short sale offer; mostly for HFC, because I knew CitiFinancial probably wouldn't budge off their full $35,000. I submitted offers to both lenders anyhow, and (as expected) CitiFinancial wanted full payoff. HFC, on the other hand, was willing to discount, but only down to $25,000. That made my total purchase price $60,000, which was no good since that was $10,000 over the wholesale value. I was disappointed, but rejection is a pretty big part of this business. So I simply moved on to other properties and wrote this deal off. Clearly, it was as dead as a doornail.

Or so I thought.

A few weeks later, Jack called me out of the blue and said he had some bad news about our deal. Now, if we had been a week or so away from closing, I would have been a nervous wreck to hear him say something like that. But since I thought our deal was already long dead, nothing he had to say could have made it any more worthless. In fact, if anything, what he was about to tell me might actually get me off the hook for forgetting to be a professional and call him back to let him know I'd decided to give up and move on. *Whoops.*

Well, as it turns out, it was a really good thing I had forgotten to call him.

"There's been a pretty bad accident involving Janice and one of my Cadillacs", he said. It didn't surprise me that he mentioned his car, because I already knew how much he loved both of his Caddies. But I was obviously concerned for Janice.

"Is she okay?" I asked.

"Oh, Janice? She's fine. So is my car." (*again,* not surprised). "But the house... well, that's where we have a problem."

He went on to tell me that Janice had fallen asleep behind the wheel, and had accidentally crashed into the front of the house. This was a pretty difficult scenario to imagine, seeing as how she had to have been awake in order to make the 90 degree turn into the driveway. This only left her a distance of 25 feet, in which she would have had to suddenly fall asleep, accelerate, and then execute a bold NASCAR maneuver ten feet to the right in order to reach the living room. Severe Narcolepsy? Probably not.

Frankly... I think she was aiming for Jack.

But regardless of who or what her true target was, this sounded like something that could actually work to my advantage, so I raced over to his house see the damage. I'll never forget the shock I felt when I got there and saw this:

Which, a few days later when the brick wall finally collapsed, became this:

I told Jack to call his insurance man and get a repair estimate right away, because most insurance estimates run about twice as high as it really costs to fix something. He said he'd already called them, and then he showed me the $10,000 settlement check the insurance company had already issued. When I asked how he had gotten the check so soon, he sheepishly admitted the accident had occurred several days earlier, and he'd been afraid to call me any sooner.

I gave him a brief stern look of disapproval, but since it looked as if I just might be able to make some kind of deal out of this, I didn't crucify him. So I began getting my ducks in a row. I pulled out the deed he gave me earlier, and had him sign the back of the insurance check and hand it over to me, so that later I could overnight it to his first mortgage company at some point before I had to pay them off. I then sent a copy of the $10,000 damage estimate and some photos of the collapsed wall to both lenders just to see what they would say. As expected, the first mortgage company called right back and said, "So what? We still want $35,000."

But the second mortgage company said, "Okay... we'll take $1,500 now." This, of course, changed everything. After adjusting my wholesale value down by $4,000 to cover the additional repairs to the wall, I thought my deal was going to look like this:

My adjusted wholesale value:	$46,000
Less payoff figure from 1st mortgage:	$35,000
Less payoff figure from 2nd mortgage:	$ 1,500
Equals potential gross wholesaling profit of:	$ 9,500

But I had forgotten something. I didn't factor in the $10,000 check that I still had in my file which was made out to the first mortgage company, CitiFinancial. So after I overnighted the check to them, my numbers actually ended up looking like this:

My adjusted wholesale value:	$46,000
Less new payoff figure from 1st mortgage:	$25,000
Less payoff figure from 2nd mortgage:	$ 1,500
Equals potential gross wholesale profit of:	$19,500

Within fifteen days, I had the property under contract with a HomeVestors guy, whose nickname also coincidentally happened to be Jack, just like my seller (what were the chances of that?). Jack, my buyer, successfully negotiated me down from my original $49,900 asking price, which was okay with me since he could close quickly at the $46,000 price he'd offered (which was the exact wholesale price I'd calculated).

About a week later, as I was on hold with my title agent scheduling my double closing, I was skimming over the two payoff letters when something suddenly struck me: neither of the two lenders had put a requirement in their payoff statements saying they had to approve a copy of the purchase agreement or the HUD-1... or even see a HUD-1, in fact. Both letters simply stated a payoff figure and expiration date.

This made sense for CitiFinancial, because they weren't even taking a short payoff. They couldn't care less who sent them their full $35,000 or why. What surprised me, though, was that the second mortgage holder (HFC) didn't ask to see any document-ation, either. My only guess was that their payoff letter was drafted from a basic template that they used whenever they were shorting behind a defaulted first mortgage, because the first mortgage holder usually ends up calling all the shots anyway.

So, what did all this mean for me? Well, it meant that since I already had the deed, and a *subject to* agreement signed by my seller, I could declare the entire $68,000 total loan balance as my official purchase price. Why would that matter?

Well, think about it: If I had chosen to buy the property for $26,500 cash (the sum of the two lender payoffs), and then flipped it for $46,000 cash, that would have netted me a $19,500 short-term gross profit—which probably would have raised some "illegal flip" flags, right? But instead, if I elected to combine my deed and *subject to* agreement to claim a purchase price of $68,000 (using line 503 on the HUD-1*), then I had an opportunity to create a transaction that could completely redefine my proceeds check.

To see what I mean, let's look at how the deal actually went down: I purchased the property officially for $68,000, and then a few weeks later I resold it to a HomeVestors franchisee for $46,000. After my title agent used $26,500 of that money to cut payoff checks to the two lenders, I still netted the same $19,500 in gross proceeds. But in this case, those proceeds no longer qualified as short term profits anymore, because I had technically sold the property at a $22,000 loss! Do you get it now?

You know, I still remember the shrieking sound of my title attorney's voice when I scheduled my $46,000 closing to sell the property, and asked if he would go ahead and also record the deed I had gotten a couple weeks earlier when I bought it for $68,000.

"I won't be part of some illegal flip," he yelled," where you buy a house for only $46,000 and then flip it 'as is' for $68,000! I'd get shut down by the FBI!"

"What? No!" I replied. "You've got it all reversed. See... I *bought* it for $68,000, and now I'm flipping it 'as is' for only *$46,000*—not the other way around."

"Oh," he said quietly. "Well," he continued a moment later, "I guess *that's* legal. But why would you even want to do that? Are you, like... *stupid* or something?"

"Momma always says," I stammered slowly, "stupid is as stupid does, sir".

After all was said and done, this deal ended up teaching me two really big lessons that I'll never forget as long as I live.

The first lesson I came away with was that being able to roll several types of real estate techniques into one deal can sometimes make the deal a lot easier, and in some cases more profitable too. In fact, there have been many times that my deals would have actually died if I hadn't been capable of engaging more than one technique simultaneously. On this particular deal, I used three different techniques at various times; starting with a *subject to*, switching over to short sale mode, and then finishing off by wholesaling the property. Had I not known how to do every one of these techniques, my results would've been less than they could have been.

The second lesson I learned was that if I've done absolutely everything I can to make a short sale deal work, and nothing I try seems to be working, I've always got one more ace up my sleeve...

---

*Line 503 on the HUD-1 provides for the entry of loan balances that were taken over *subject to* as part of the overall purchase price. In the case of our story, this amount is equal to the entire $68,000 purchase price.

I CAN ALWAYS CALL JANICE!!

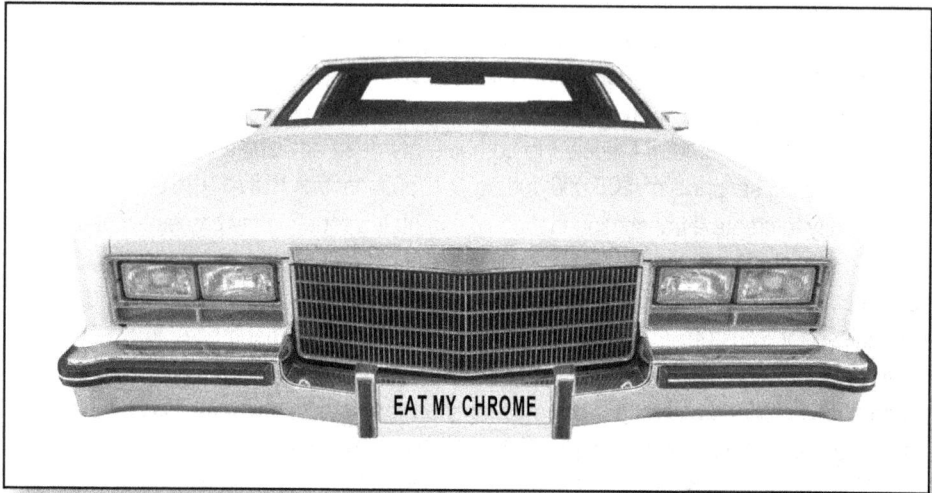

*   *   *   *   *

You know, whenever I'm speaking to a large group at a state or local real estate conference, this particular story never fails to start an interesting debate among the audience as to whether or not you can legally write off a $22,000 loss, while at the same time putting about an $18,000 profit in your pocket. Well... *can* you?

Unfortunately, I'm not going to answer that for you. I'll just let you and your accountant spar over that one. But as you do, here are a couple of things to consider: First of all, your proceeds check often has little to do with your taxable gain. Your proceeds check on any sale simply represents your net equity, which could have been due to a large downpayment. For instance, if you paid $50,000 cash for a property, resold it for $70,000, and then walked out of the closing with a $65,000 proceeds check, that doesn't mean you have a $65,000 taxable gain... right? No way!

And second, if a lienholder on a property that you own decides to take a short payoff for any reason, it doesn't change your initial cost basis (purchase price), nor does it qualify as an event that would adjust your cost basis. A property's basis can only be adjusted up or down by two things: a) by the amount of improvements made to the property itself to increase the property's market value; or b) by the amount of any depreciation that has been taken by the property's owner, which is subject to recapture and taxation.

So as you can see, a short payoff has nothing to do with either of these two factors, because it does absolutely nothing to increase the property's market value, nor is it tax-deductible write-off of depreciation that needs to be recaptured.

8

final ramblings
& recommendations

I n writing this book, it quickly became apparent that I was going to have to include a brief epilogue of sorts. If not, I knew I'd run the risk of leaving you with too little information, while simultaneously managing to piss off everybody I know in the world of real estate—along with many others whom I've not yet met.

In other words… I got some 'splaining to do.

First of all, I want you to understand that my sole reason for writing this book was to help you leverage all of the idiot mistakes that I've made while enrolled in the most expensive learning institution of all. And by that, I mean the school of real life—not Harvard. My main objective was to keep you from having to endure the headaches and heartaches of being a first mouse like I had to… repeatedly. And JSYK, this is difficult to do without coming off a bit like a pompous jerk from time to time. So if you felt I was guilty of that at any point, please accept my apologies because it was unintentional.

Look, I'll be the first to admit I'm not perfect. I make mistakes. And like anyone else I have demons that I secretly wrestle with every day—like my neurotic addiction to hairspray, or my disturbing ability to name all of the *Real Housewives of Orange County*. I mean, how screwed up is *that*, right? So until I'm completely cured of my debilitating obsessions with hair care products and D-list reality stars, I'm certainly in no position to judge anybody.

Okay… so now that we've established you're in a safe place with me no matter who or *what* you are, we're ready to move on to sharing a few of my favorite resources. They can all help you augment the things we've covered in this book, but don't be surprised to find out that most of them are not even real estate related. Why is that? Well, because your success in this business will be due less to the real estate strategies themselves, and more to your abilities to sell people on them.

BTW, before we continue there's just one last thing I wanted to address. You may have felt that earlier in this book I was pointing some pretty big fingers of blame at speakers, gurus, and group leaders for the flaws in today's real estate educational system. But if you read them again, you'll see that my comments were designed only to make you aware of certain elements within the system itself so that you could exercise due caution. They were not intended as blanket indictments against *all* speakers, gurus, and group leaders. After all, *I'm* a part of that mix too!

In fact, there are many real estate associations that I've been fortunate enough to work with—and within—several times over the past twenty-something years. So I can personally vouch for their authentic concerns over the safety and success of their members, despite many lucrative opportunities to just "go for the green".

Most notably in particular are my local group, Cincinnati REIA, of which I am currently a board member and executive officer, the Greater Dayton REIA group (GDREIA) about 50 miles to my north, and Jane Garvey's Chicago Creative Investors Association (CCIA) group in the Windy City, where I've had the pleasure of being a featured speaker and seminar host on several occasions.

Of course there are lots of other good associations and group leaders out there across the country, but I just don't have the time to individually exonerate all of them here. So please don't read anything negative into the conspicuous absence of any mention of your local group, or any other group for that matter. I am not suggesting anything about anyone, except this: caveat emptor. Let the buyer (you) beware.

The same goes for gurus. Please don't assume anything because I didn't exonerate any of them here. I don't have the patience to put together an exhaustive list of who's good, who's bad, who's real, and who's not—especially when the guru pool grows by about one new member every day. That's what God created John T. Reed for.

So here we go:

Real Life Nothing Down (a course manual by yours truly)

Okay, before you get the wrong idea and assume that this resource section is self-serving because it begins with a recommendation of a course that I wrote, please understand my purpose in referring you to *RLND* is that it contains a line-by-line analysis of all the real estate methods we've just discussed.

In fact, right now would be a perfect time for you to get it, because it can take you back through each technique and fill in some of the detail gaps for you with lots of specific information; much the same way that a prequel goes back in time to flesh out some of the background details leading up to the storyline of a book or movie you've already seen.

I'll even give you a break on the price. I've sold hundreds of these manuals for $325 and more all over the U.S.; from Seattle to Miami, and from Maine to San Francisco. But as a purchaser of this book, you can download the full e-Version at **www.FullFrontalRealEstate.com/RLND** for only **$79**, along with a bonus file which contains every form and agreement I'm using today in WORD format. That way you can easily tweak them in just a couple of minutes to make them your very own.

T. Harv Eker: *Success Trainer and Motivator*

Harv doesn't teach anything about real estate investing, but that didn't stop him from becoming one of the three most important and influential mentors in my entire life.

You may remember Harv from earlier in this book, when I told a brief story about how he duplicated his retail fitness store to 10 locations in just 2-1/2 years, and then became an instant millionaire when he sold just half of his holdings for $1.6 million dollars to the H.J. Heinz Corporation. If you're an entrepreneur, you may already be familiar with Harv's story. But what you may *not* know is how it ends.

Just two years after coming into all that money, unbridled spending and a few bad investments put Harv right back to where he started at square one. It was only then that he came to realize that he had some severely flawed perceptions about how wealth works, and what truly dictates the flow of money. And it is the combination of lessons he learned from both his meteoric rise to success, and his equally speedy fall from it, that makes him such a valuable resource for you and me.

I first met Harv in 1995, when he spoke in Gatlinburg Tennessee at a real estate investor's retreat. He was just beginning to gain popularity with the release of one of his first bootcamps, *The Street Smart Business School*, yet at the time he was still accessible enough on a personal level that he would occasionally call me personally to answer my questions.

Harv has come a long way since then, having impacted nearly a million people in more than 80 different countries. But the one thing that hasn't changed is that anyone in any kind of business can reap massive benefits from the core principles that Harv teaches—and I highly recommend that you become one of them.

Chip and Dan Heath: *Writers, professors, researchers, and co-authors*

As soon as I saw the bright orange cover featuring the image of a large strip of crumpled duct tape, I knew instantly that I was going to resonate with the contents of *Made to Stick: Why Some Ideas Survive and Others Die*. Wow, was I ever right.

In fact, it turned out to be one of the best books I've ever read. Why? Because it exposes how several key elements can actually help make a new concept or idea interesting—and even more importantly, memorable—by exploring the way people tend to think and listen. For me, the insights in this book had twice the impact, because not only am I a real estate entrepreneur, I'm also a speaker and author.

After all, our unique profession will often find us faced with the daunting task of marketing and presenting non-traditional offers to very traditional consumers; and quite frankly, if you don't know how they tick, or what you can say to bring them around to your end of the continuum, you're going to miss a lot of deals and leave way too much cheese laying around for your competition to just roll in behind you and gobble it up.

Seth Godin: *Author, speaker, internationally recognized marketing guru*

Much to the chagrin of the people who weren't paying much attention when they really should have been, the world of marketing has forever changed. There are several reasons for the shift, but the two biggest contributors have been expanding technology *for* consumers, and shrinking attention *from* consumers.

In this new age of marketing, all the power has transferred from the marketers to the consumers; and any marketer who ignores this change, or is unwilling or unable to adapt to it, will face certain doom... or at the very least a much smaller paycheck than necessary. This includes you and me.

Seth's books are a refreshing new take on this age-old profession. And because you and I both have such a desperate need to cut through the glut of noise created by the incessant wave of ads competing for the time, attention, and money of every one of our potential future customers, his unique perspectives couldn't be any more timely or relevant for us. I suggest buying everything that has his name on it.

I did.

Charles J. Lewis: *Professional photographer, teacher, mentor*

Ok, granted: Charles isn't going to be much of a real resource for you unless you also happen to be a professional photographer too. But he's in here anyway. Why? Two reasons.

The first is that one of his business strategies was something that proved to be quite helpful for me as a real estate entrepreneur. He called it his P.R. Pack, and as I had mentioned way back on page 78, it was something that I had repurposed for use in our business—and which was then subsequently re-branded again by a big-name guru into a powerful tool called the Credibility Kit. So yes, I was the one who brought credibility kits into our industry...but no, I didn't invent them. Truth be told, Charles didn't either. He borrowed the concept from someone in the insurance industry. So I guess there really *isn't* anything new under the sun.

The second reason he's in here is because he triggered the single most defining point in my life and real estate career at one of his *photography* workshops, of all places. It happened in the final few moments of the day-long event, and the most ironic thing is that I wasn't even supposed to be there in the first place.

You see, by the time he came to town that day, I'd already retired my Hasselblad, and had forever packed away all my strobes, gobos, light stands and modifiers. I was no longer pursuing a career as a professional photographer. But I had promised the year before to help him out if he ever came to Cincinnati, so there I was in the back of the room stacking course manuals at the end of an 8-hour lecture, completely unaware that my life was about to change forever.

Charles was preparing to give his normal closing spiel to sell photography courses. But just as he was starting, his wife walked to the front of the room and handed him a new testimonial. Charles quickly looked the letter over, took a couple of moments to compose himself, and then began reading it to us.

It was a heart-wrenching story from a man who's 3 year-old son had just passed away. The letter thanked Charles for teaching him how to run his photography business in such a way that he no longer had to work 12 to 14 hour days just to make ends meet. This gave him much more time with his family, which turned out to be a huge unexpected blessing because he got to spend so many extra priceless moments with his little boy that he would have otherwise missed.

When Charles finished reading, the silence was deafening. It suddenly seemed as if all of the air had been sucked out of the room, because I literally couldn't draw a breath as I thought about my own newborn son at home.

After the event was over, I rushed home and stood over my son's crib as he quietly slept. I promised myself right then and there that I would go full-time in real estate as soon as humanly possible, so I could be there for him every morning when he woke up, and every night when he went to bed.

And because of my burning desire to keep that promise, I succeeded in quitting my regular job and going full-time in real estate just 24 months later. That meant with the exception of a few overnight trips to speak at various real estate conferences around the country from time to time, I was able to be there for him every day and every night for the next 15 wonderful years of our lives.

Of course, by then he'd become a 17 year-old teenager, at which point my wife and I began looking for every chance we could…

…to get away from him.

Well, that's about all I've got for you... so I guess this is the end.

If you're still reading at this point, it means you've probably enjoyed the book—in which case I'd like to extend to you my sincere thanks. It could also mean that you're one of those obsessive types who sits in the theater long after the movie is over, reading the credits all the way to the end of the reel—in which case I'd like to extend to you the number of a good OCD therapist.

Either way, I've gotta run. It's Friday night, which means a hot homemade pizza is coming out of the oven, brand new episodes of *Breaking Bad* and *30 Rock* are cued up in the DVR, and Joel McHale will soon be skewering all of my favorite reality show freaks on *The Soup*.

Life is good.

About the Author
(If you absolutely *must* know...)

Nicholas Modarelli is a real estate entrepreneur, speaker, author, mentor, coach, former syndicated radio host, and occasional nut-job. Over the past 28 years he has bought and sold hundreds of properties worth tens of millions of dollars in eight different states. He also specializes in buying and selling defaulted mortgage notes. Nicholas is perhaps best known for his unconventional marketing and negotiating strategies, as well as his unique and often humorous teaching style. He lives in Ohio with his wife and business partner, Arlene, their son Cameron, and their hilarious miniature dachshund, Murray.

Contact Info:

Email: **nick@FullFrontalRealEstate.com**
Website: **www.FullFrontalRealEstate.com**

www.ingramcontent.com/pod-product-compliance
Lightning Source LLC
Chambersburg PA
CBHW051208200326
41519CB00025B/7049